I'LL BE WATCHING YOU

"Phelps has an unrelenting sense for detail that affirms his place, book by book, as one of our most engaging crime journalists."

   —Katherine Ramsland

IF LOOKS COULD KILL

"M. William Phelps, one of America's finest true-crime writers, has written a compelling and gripping book about an intriguing murder mystery. Readers of this genre will thoroughly enjoy this book."

   —Vincent Bugliosi

"Starts quickly and doesn't slow down. . . . Phelps consistently ratchets up the dramatic tension, hooking readers. His thorough research and interviews give the book complexity, richness of character, and urgency."

   —Stephen Singular

MURDER IN THE HEARTLAND

"Drawing on interviews with law officers and relatives, the author has done significant research. His facile writing pulls the reader along."

   —*St. Louis Post-Dispatch*

"Phelps expertly reminds us that when the darkest form of evil invades the quiet and safe outposts of rural America, the tragedy is greatly magnified. Get ready for some sleepless nights."

   —Carlton Stowers

"This is the most disturbing and moving look at murder in rural America since Capote's *In Cold Blood*."

   —Gregg Olsen

SLEEP IN HEAVENLY PEACE

"An exceptional book by an exceptional true crime writer. Phelps exposes long-hidden secrets and reveals disquieting truths."

   —Kathryn Casey

EVERY MOVE YOU MAKE

"An insightful and fast-paced examination of the inner workings of a good cop and his bad informant, culminating in an unforgettable truth-is-stranger-than-fiction climax."
—Michael M. Baden, M.D.

"M. William Phelps is the rising star of the nonfiction crime genre, and his true tales of murder are scary-as-hell thrill rides into the dark heart of the inhuman condition."
—Douglas Clegg

LETHAL GUARDIAN

"An intense roller-coaster of a crime story . . . complex, with twists and turns worthy of any great detective mystery . . . reads more like a novel than your standard non-fiction crime book."
—Steve Jackson

PERFECT POISON

"True crime at its best—compelling, gripping, an edge-of-the-seat thriller. Phelps packs wallops of delight with his skillful ability to narrate a suspenseful story."
—Harvey Rachlin

"A compelling account of terror . . . the author dedicates himself to unmasking the psychopath with facts, insight and the other proven methods of journalistic leg work."
—Lowell Cauffiel

Also By M. William Phelps*

Perfect Poison

Lethal Guardian

Every Move You Make

Sleep in Heavenly Peace

Murder in the Heartland

Because You Loved Me

If Looks Could Kill

I'll Be Watching You

Deadly Secrets

Cruel Death

Death Trap

Kill For Me

Love Her to Death

Too Young to Kill

Never See Them Again

Kiss of the She-Devil

Bad Girls

Obsessed

The Killing Kind

She Survived: Melissa (e-book)

She Survived: Jane (e-book)

I'd Kill For You

To Love and to Kill

One Breath Away

*Available from Kensington Publishing Corp.

IF YOU ONLY KNEW

M. WILLIAM PHELPS

PINNACLE BOOKS
Kensington Publishing Corp.
http://www.kensingtonbooks.com

PINNACLE BOOKS are published by

Kensington Publishing Corp.
119 West 40th Street
New York, NY 10018

All Kensington Titles, Imprints, and Distributed Lines are available at special quantity discounts for bulk purchases for sales promotions, premiums, fund-raising, and educational or institutional use. Special book excerpts or customized printings can also be created to fit specific needs. For details, write or phone the office of the Kensington special sales manager: Kensington Publishing Corp., 119 West 40th Street, New York, NY 10018, attn: Special Sales Department, Phone: 1-800-221-2647.

Pinnacle and the P logo Reg. U.S. Pat. & TM Off.

ISBN-13: 978-0-7860-3724-7
ISBN-10: 0-7860-3724-5
First Kensington Mass Market Edition: August 2016

eISBN-13: 978-0-7860-3725-4
eISBN-10: 0-7860-3725-3
Kensington Electronic Edition: August 2016

10 9 8 7 6 5 4 3 2 1

Printed in the United States of America

For Cherry . . . I miss you.

January 26, 2004–December 13, 2014

PART 1

She would defend herself, saying that love, no matter what else it might be, was a natural talent. She would say: You are either born knowing how, or you never know.

Gabriel García Márquez,
Love in the Time of Cholera

CHAPTER 1

SOME THINGS IN LIFE are not what they appear to be at first glance. Take, for example, the quiet stillness of the night inside her patrol car, interrupted only by the crackling static of a police scanner every so often. It was that sound, rolling over her relaxed breathing and the occasional shuffle and leathery crunch of her well-oiled duty belt, that had misled Patrol Officer Lynn Giorgi into thinking it just might be a slow night, devoid of any major public evils.

Officer Giorgi had worked for the City of Grand Rapids, Michigan, before becoming a police officer in Troy, about a 150-mile drive east, two years prior. Troy is sandwiched between slices of Lake Michigan, Lake Huron, Lake St. Clair and Lake Erie. Troy is, essentially, part of the metro Detroit region, within Oakland County. A family-oriented city, one of the largest in the state, Troy bills itself as the "most dynamic and livable" metropolitan area in the Wolverine State. It's the schools, everyone says, that attract the yuppies and hipsters to settle down with their snobby kids and live the good life in suburbia.

As Officer Giorgi patrolled through downtown during the early-morning hours of August 12, 2000, near the halfway point of her midnight to 8:00 A.M. shift, the otherwise quiet radio in her cruiser buzzed with a voice. It was dispatch: "Man down . . . not breathing. . . ."

A second request then came in for an ambulance.

CPR run, Giorgi thought.

Some poor bastard probably had a heart attack, was fighting for his life.

Up until then, it had been an inconsequential night in Troy. Generally was.

As Giorgi hit the lights on her patrol car and took off toward 2090 Grenadier Drive, a rather swanky end of town, she expected to arrive at the scene and find a man she needed to perform first aid on. In two years with the Troy Police Department (TPD), Giorgi had answered maybe ten of these same calls.

As Giorgi pulled into the driveway at 4:25 A.M., colleague, friend and fellow officer Pete Dungjen pulled in right behind her. The single-family home, with four bedrooms and three and a half baths at about three thousand square feet, was spacious and well-kept. The area had a reputation for plotting half-million-dollar homes. Not necessarily the ultrarich, but most of the people in this neighborhood did not have to worry about money.

Giorgi went directly into her trunk and took out the first aid CPR kit and ran toward the front door.

When she reached the stoop, the door opened. There were two females, Giorgi later said, standing in the foyer, waiting on the TPD to arrive. Both women seemed "calm," but also in great need of someone to help the victim inside the house.

One of the women, whom Giorgi would later come to

know as Billie Jean Rogers, said, "He's in there—in the kitchen." Billie Jean pointed the cop in the right direction.

Billie Jean was the man's wife.

Inside the kitchen, Giorgi's training kicked into action. On the floor was a man "in his fifties," she later guessed (he was much older), lying on his back, on the floor. There was a chair turned over on its side next to him. Without any other information, she surmised that the man had grabbed for the backrest of the chair on his way down to the floor, flipping the thing over as he hit the ground.

Donald Rogers was seventy-four years old. Billie Jean's husband was a local business owner, who had made quite a bit of money manufacturing a line of automotive assembly tools. In the "car capital of the world," Don Rogers and his business partner, Don Kather, had started the business together back in 1977. Kather actually bought Rogers out in 1990, but Rogers had still invested in the company and went into the office every day, helping to keep it afloat after the car industry boom left only ashes in its wake. Kather had gotten together with Rogers on August 11, as they did daily, to meet for lunch. Rogers looked and sounded good, Kather later said. Rogers was "very frugal" with his spending habits, Kather explained. He had plenty of money, but he never went on vacations or bought luxurious items or drove glamorous cars. Same as when he went out to eat, Don Rogers chose middle-of-the-road restaurants, always forgoing the four-star hot spots. He lived life simply. And yet, there was one thing Don never skimped on—something he spared no expense at and did every day: drink.

Billie Jean was quite the polar opposite when it came to spending money—most of which was her husband's.

"Well, if she saw something she liked," her daughter

later said, "she would just buy it." Billie Jean had no real "concept of money," the daughter added. "She saw money as fun . . . that was what it was for, in her mind." More than that, Billie Jean was a "very poor money manager."

Billie Jean had lived both sides of the coin: In Tennessee, where she grew up with seven siblings, she was "dirt poor." There was not even running water in the house; she literally lived hand to mouth; hand-me-downs and handouts were a way of life.

As Officer Giorgi prepared to work on Don Rogers, Billie Jean Rogers, Don's wife for a second time—they had married once, divorced and then remarried—stood over her, explaining what she thought had happened.

"He's been drinking—he has a problem with alcohol," Billie Jean said. "He's a chronic alcoholic." Then, oddly enough, Billie Jean added, "He suffers from rectal bleeds."

Apparently, the drinking had gotten so out of hand, she was saying, Don often bled from his rectum, all over the place.

Giorgi noticed that Don Rogers had very slight bruising on his face and one small abrasion on his upper lip. But one would expect some mild scuffs and scrapes on a guy who had supposedly passed out drunk and fallen on the floor. Suffice it to say, he probably fell into that chair, which was on its side lying next to him, and had probably made a habit of falling down and into things if, in fact, he drank as much as his wife claimed.

Giorgi had to move the chair so she could kneel next to Don and begin to work on him.

Acclimating himself to the situation, trying to figure out the best way to help Don Rogers, Officer Pete Dungjen walked up and knelt on one knee next to Giorgi. By now, Billie Jean was a bit antsier, but not at all frantic or exceedingly concerned, both officers noticed.

From the way she acted, this fall seemed to be perhaps a common thing around the house: Don tying one on and passing out on the floor.

Dungjen touched Don Rogers.

"He's cold," Dungjen said to Giorgi. "Rigidity has set in."

Giorgi didn't have to check for a pulse. She knew.

Don Rogers wasn't passed out this time.

He was dead.

CHAPTER 2

THE OTHER FEMALE STANDING next to Billie Jean Rogers as law enforcement backup was called in to determine what happened to Don Rogers, and if the scene warranted further investigation, was Vonlee Nicole Titlow. Born in Maryville, Tennessee, a Deep South town at the foothills of the Smoky Mountains, Vonlee had lived in Nashville and in Denver. Vonlee even had a penthouse in Chicago at one time. Vonlee's aunt Billie Jean, her mother's sister, had invited Vonlee to stay with her and Don in Troy, and Vonlee had been living at the house for the past few months. While the age difference spanned decades, Billie Jean and Vonlee shared a common love of going out and partying at the local casinos in Detroit. Whereas Billie Jean was more focused on gambling, Vonlee was a nightlife gal, dancing and drinking, working the rooms. She'd been an exotic dancer and had run an escort service in Denver and Chicago, making upward of—Vonlee later claimed—twenty thousand dollars a week. Back then, Vonlee added, she was dating a few different men at the same time.

"I took care of them," she claimed. Meaning, she paid for their lifestyle and living accommodations. "It was kind of like a power thing. Kind of fun . . . you know, I loved those guys."

Moving to Chicago from Denver in 1999, Vonlee was effectively running from the escort lifestyle in Denver, while still dabbling in it to make some money in Chicago. But she wanted the simple life now. From the early 1990s until that move to Chicago, Vonlee had been running from herself, essentially. She'd gotten caught up in a life of booze, men, clubs, cars, clothes. Material things. By the time she made it to Chicago, Vonlee had a life waiting for her, if she wanted it. A man she had been dating signed over the deed to a house she could live in, rent-free. All she had to do was be there for him when he needed her. The man wanted to take care of Vonlee. "A lot of men did this throughout the years," Vonlee told me later. However, as Vonlee thought about it, she was nobody's possession—nobody's "thing" to have when he wanted. Whereas it might have been something she went for during her younger years, not anymore. Vonlee was now in her thirties. She needed to focus on herself and what *she* wanted.

"It's on the counter," she said one night when that man came home.

"What?"

"The deed. I signed it back over to you—I'm going home to Tennessee."

By now, Vonlee had been to rehab, a familiar face in Alcoholics Anonymous (AA) meetings around Chicago. She wanted out of the big city, away from that fast-paced nightlife she had taken part in through much of her twenties. Back in Tennessee, she took a job at the local Waffle House and went back to living with her grandmother Annis Lee, the woman who had raised her.

"I was giving her twenty or thirty dollars a day for rent," Vonlee said.

Life was simple. She was around family. The smell of that Tennessee air. There was nothing like it. The down-home, simple folks she interacted with every day. The sheer snail's pace of life itself. She'd take her nephews fishing. Go for drives in the country to see friends. Attend barbeques the relatives spent all day preparing. Enjoy Sunday dinners after church services.

"I was extremely happy," Vonlee recalled.

But then something happened.

"Aunt Billie Jean shows up. . . ."

Vonlee was actually working when Billie Jean walked into the restaurant, sat down and called her over. Vonlee hadn't seen her in over a decade. She'd spoken to her, but that was it. Now Billie Jean sat in front of her during the spring, early summer of 2000, surprising Vonlee with the visit, making a proposition Vonlee had a hard time turning her back on.

As Vonlee approached the table, shocked to see her aunt there all the way from Troy, Vonlee noticed she was laughing.

"A waitress," her aunt said in a mocking tone, talking down to Vonlee. "You're a waitress in this dive? I cannot *believe* you took to waiting on tables, Vonlee."

Vonlee wanted to curl up in a ball right there. She felt belittled and a total failure.

"Sit down," Billie Jean said. It sounded as though she had an offer to make.

"What are you doing here?" Vonlee asked. She was looking back toward the kitchen and register. She didn't want her boss to see her sitting in a booth with a customer.

"Look, honey, you don't have any drinking problem. What are you running from?" Vonlee and Billie Jean, living somewhat close to each other in the upper Midwest, had communicated, and Billie Jean knew about

Vonlee's journey into recovery. In some ways, there was a bit of envy on her part. She valued Vonlee's no-holds-bar attitude, not giving two shakes about what people said or thought about her. The older woman wanted to be her own person, same as Vonlee. She knew the more she hung around Vonlee, the more of a free spirit she would become.

As for Vonlee, she certainly had the pizazz, flare and fortitude, along with the clichéd sassy Southern charm, of a luxurious, expensive call girl. She looked the part with her long, muscular, yet feminine, legs, bleached-blond hair, down to her shoulders, and curvaceous, feminine figure. And if you asked Vonlee, she had no trouble taking on clients when her girls couldn't handle the influx of calls or the specialized requests from such a high-powered clientele.

But that was another time, another life. She was back home now in Tennessee and pretty content living a simple life.

During those preceding months leading up to the early morning Don Rogers was found dead inside the kitchen of his home, however, Vonlee was determined to spend her free time seeing old friends and spending time with her rather large family. Chicago and the escort business were rather old and worn. And Billie Jean, who claimed she was back to visit family, insisted that Vonlee come back to Michigan at once with her and live inside the home she shared with Don. The aunt told Vonlee that a restaurant, waiting tables, was not the place she wanted to see her niece. It was degrading.

Vonlee considered the question: *Should I go back? It isn't Chicago; it's Troy, Michigan. What kind of trouble is in Troy?*

"You don't have no dranking problem, Vonlee," Billie Jean said. She was leaning over the table, almost whispering. "You just need to buy bigger bottles and drank it slow all day long." The aunt laughed.

Vonlee considered the idea: *Maybe I don't.*

"Let's you and me get out of here," Billie Jean said. "I got money."

"Where?"

Harrah's, she suggested.

July Fourth weekend was a day away.

"In North Carolina?" Vonlee asked.

"Yes."

Vonlee took off her apron, tossed it into the kitchen and headed out the door. She would pack something while Billie Jean waited in the car and, like Thelma and Louise, she and Billie Jean would head out to Harrah's Cherokee Casino Resort in Cherokee, North Carolina, to party it up for the weekend. Any sobriety Vonlee had earned, she had just given away.

It was a spur-of-the-moment decision that would change Vonlee's life forever.

CHAPTER 3

OFFICER LYNN GIORGI GATHERED Vonlee and
Billie Jean in the den of the house and began to assess
Don's medical history, trying to figure out what might
have happened. With no outward signs of trauma, no
injuries that Officers Giorgi or Dungjen could see, the
"alcoholism" bell Billie Jean had rung when the officers
showed up now seemed most plausible. Giorgi wondered
if this was the root cause of Don's demise. Hell, in just
the short time she'd been a patrol officer, Giorgi had seen
death come to people in the most unimaginable ways.

Billie Jean was not at all surprised by Don's death. Or,
rather, she didn't come across that way to Giorgi and
Dungjen. She then went through all of the ailments Don
suffered from, beyond being what she described as a
chronic drinker who guzzled goblets full of vodka as
though it was water.

"He'd take one of those mason jars and fill it up,"
Vonlee explained. "Then down it. I had seen him do it
more than once."

Dungjen and Giorgi got together and decided their
next move.

"We should probably call for the detective on duty and an ME," Giorgi offered.

It was a formality, both cops considered, a not-so-routine part of their day, but an obligation, nonetheless. They did not suspect foul play, but that was, of course, not their call to make. First responders show up, evaluate the scene, do what they can to help, ask some questions and then call in the investigators if they believe a case warrants their time.

Giorgi covered Don with a yellow blanket and then sat with Vonlee and Billie Jean in the den. She wanted to ask a few more questions and hopefully help to figure out what happened. The mood in the house was subdued; despite however anxious Vonlee, who later admitted to being totally inebriated during this time, seemed. Billie Jean appeared composed, with a handle on things.

"Understanding," one of the first responders called it later, referring to Billie Jean's demeanor.

Although, perhaps, alarmed that her husband was on the floor of their kitchen, dead, the wife's behavior, at least initially, seemed appropriate to the circumstances.

Vonlee, on the other hand, was acting "surprised and out of place, considering the situation," that same first responder recalled. She was "resisting" questions posed by both officers.

"Vonlee and I went to the casino," Billie Jean told Giorgi. "We were gone for a few hours—Donald did not want to go."

In a statement Billie Jean later gave that night, she wrote about leaving for the casino at *9:30–10:30 . . . [and] came home at 4:15,* at which time she and Vonlee then called 911.

Billie Jean was "pretty calm" and "very quiet," Giorgi observed. "Didn't really speak unless I asked her questions."

Billie Jean also paced at times and chain-smoked cigarettes.

Probably nerves. Her husband was dead.

Giorgi walked back over to Don Rogers and thought about the scene a bit more, trying to picture what might have happened. Don lay directly next to the kitchen table. He was on his back, his legs crossed at the ankles, his arms outstretched in kind of a Jesus-on-the-Cross position. This didn't raise any red flags, specifically; but the more they looked at it, the way in which Don's body was lying seemed almost staged. Feeling this, the intuitive officer considered that she ought to look even closer. They had to wait for the detective and medical examiner (ME), anyway. What would it hurt?

His legs are crossed at his ankles? Giorgi kept going back to it. This fact seemed odd, taking into account that Don might have fallen from the chair. How many people fall out of a chair and wind up on the ground, faceup, their legs crossed?

"It looked kind of unusual," Giorgi later explained. "It appeared that he had fallen out of his chair . . . It just seemed unlikely that you could fall from somewhere and end up with your legs perfectly crossed at the ankles."

Maybe it happened as one of the women tried reviving him? Maybe they had done this inadvertently?

Both said no.

Giorgi walked over to Billie Jean and asked several more questions. The officer was more direct and accusatory in her tone this time around. Maybe she didn't mean to be, but that was how it came out.

Vonlee stood by and appeared agitated with the officer. She viewed the situation as the officer attacking Billie Jean.

"You all just need to leave her alone right now," Vonlee snapped at one point. Vonlee didn't think Billie Jean needed to be treated in this way—at least not right after her husband had died. "Why do you have to ask her all of these questions *now*?"

With her sassy Southern attitude and noticeable accent, Vonlee was "very excitable and very loud . . . and very protective of [Billie Jean]," Giorgi noted later.

"Why are you being so rude?" Vonlee then asked the officer. "You must be a cold person to be asking all of these questions."

Giorgi and Dungjen tried to explain that they were just doing their jobs, but Vonlee wasn't having any of it. She didn't want her aunt subjected to such harsh treatment while her uncle was lying dead on the floor in the kitchen. It could all wait, Vonlee seemed to be suggesting.

"Look, this is a process," Giorgi explained, trying to put out a Southern brush fire now gathering fuel, "and we've called in a detective and the medical examiner. . . . These are necessary questions we need answers to. I need to write a report."

Giorgi asked Billie Jean and Vonlee if they could sit, calm down and perhaps write out for her what happened that night, what they did, what they came home to. Details would be important. Would they mind writing a statement?

Neither indicated any interest in doing this.

Giorgi changed her tactic, as she often did in situations when people became stressed. She, instead, asked questions that did not pertain to the situation. Questions with answers they did not need to think about. How old are you? Where'd you grow up? Where do you work? Things of that nature.

That tactic did not work, either. Vonlee hemmed and hawed about how the cops were being unsympathetic to Billie Jean and the notion that Don was dead.

Giorgi continued to insist that both females needed

to sit down and write out a statement she could include in her report.

"Oh, well, okay, then . . . ," Vonlee said.

She began writing. But as she did, Vonlee quickly put the pen down and stated, "You know what, I am not doing this right now!" She was angry.

"Miss Titlow, these are things we need to know," Giorgi said again, more pleasantly than she had been previously in her tone.

Vonlee refused.

Billie Jean walked over and Giorgi asked about Don having any prior medical conditions—if either woman could shed any light on that.

"One time he passed out in the bathroom upstairs and hit his head on the tub," Billie Jean said. "He was bleeding and I wanted to call 911, but he told me not to."

The officers decided to check out the rest of the house. It was possible, since Vonlee and Billie Jean said they had just walked in and found him, that someone else had come by. But the only unlocked door into the entire house was the pedestrian door from the kitchen into the garage.

"That's how we came in," Billie Jean said when one of the cops pointed it out. "We used the garage door opener to open the garage and then came in through that door."

None of the windows or any of the other doors in the house were unlocked or seemed broken into. Even in the basement, Giorgi noticed when she went downstairs to look around, those windows seemed to be fine. No glass broken. Nothing out of place. All of them locked.

Giorgi went into the family room, which had a fully stocked bar. She noticed not one bottle was open or even out. Everything appeared to be in its place on the shelves. But when she walked over to the pantry area of the house, just beyond the kitchen, not far from Don's body, there were several large bottles—"gallon sizes"—of vodka. But upon a careful examination of those, they saw none of them had been opened, either.

Giorgi found Billie Jean. "Listen," she asked, "you said he once blacked out and hit his head."

"Yes," she answered.

"Let's take a walk upstairs to check and see if anything like that might have happened again."

They went upstairs and walked through all of the bedrooms and the bathrooms.

Nothing seemed out of place.

When they got back downstairs, she showed Giorgi one of the living-room chairs with blood on it. The blood was crusty and dried up.

"That's from Don's rectal bleeding."

It was the only spot in the entire house where they could locate any blood.

Giorgi was stumped. And yet, with all the talk going on inside the house, including the questions Vonlee and Billie Jean had asked, the one inquiry neither had made was rather telling in and of itself: *What might have happened to Don?* Neither Billie Jean nor Vonlee seemed to be interested in the opinions of the two officers.

"Can't we do this tomorrow?" Vonlee asked one of the officers. She was tired of all the questions. Accusations, as Vonlee saw them. She was mainly worried about her aunt, Vonlee said, not herself.

"She was just sitting, at one point, smoking cigarettes and staring," Vonlee later said of her aunt.

What the hell? Vonlee wondered.

"I thought she was maybe ready to snap. I had never seen that look on her face before—it was eerie."

CHAPTER 4

BILLIE JEAN ROGERS RENTED a hotel room at the casino in North Carolina for her and Vonlee back in July 2000. As they partied throughout that weekend, Vonlee was, at best, lukewarm about the prospect of heading back into the party lifestyle and starting up all over again. It was as if that time in her life had come and gone, and although the drinking and gambling and dancing and doing drugs had been fun, it wasn't who she was anymore. Vonlee wanted to go back to the Waffle House, show some humility, then beg for her shitty job back.

The pull of her addiction, however, as she later described it, was too much. Vonlee was back on the bottle now—and the alcohol, her one vice, had just taken back control of her life and was telling her what to do once again.

As they were walking into the parking lot to get into Billie Jean's Chrysler LeBaron, the aunt said, "Didn't I park the car there?"

"What?" Vonlee asked.

"My car, Vonlee, where is my car?"

Billie Jean had issues with drinking herself, Vonlee

claimed, the court record later backing this up through testimony. "She was addicted to gambling and she was an alcoholic, too," Vonlee had once said. So it was hard to consider what she was saying after a night of losing at the casino—which she did on this night—and having a few too many pops.

They searched for the car. It was nowhere to be found.

Billie Jean filed a police report. She rented a car and asked Vonlee to drive her back to Michigan.

"Look, drive me back, if they ever find my car here, you can have it."

Vonlee agreed.

They set out on the road back to Troy.

"That's how I ended up back in the upper Midwest," Vonlee said.

The car was eventually located and Billie Jean kept her promise. They had been back for a day or so and the North Carolina authorities called to say they had located it, but that it would take about two to three weeks to process.

"You stay here with us at the house," Billie Jean said. "Don won't mind. When they call for the car, you go back and take it."

What the hell, Vonlee considered. *A free car.*

Vonlee soon found out that life inside the Rogers household, that suburban existence behind closed doors, was anything but hospitable and pleasant. Billie Jean and Don fought like two people that hated each other, Vonlee soon learned. And Don, Vonlee said, drank himself into oblivion almost daily. He'd fill large mason jars with vodka and down them in front of her and Billie Jean and then pass out.

"It was clear to me that this marriage was for convenience," Vonlee explained later. "There was no love between them."

One of the major issues Don had with Billie Jean was her incredible spending, not only on gambling, but her enormous shopping sprees, too. She spent a lot of time at the Detroit area casinos, and most of that money came from Don's savings and investments, filtered through credit cards Don had given to his wife. This was the cause of much conflict between them, as Vonlee stood on the sidelines listening and watching so many of their fights.

As chaos reigned supreme inside the household during the latter part of July 2000, Billie Jean took a call one night that sent her into a terrible spell of dread and worry. Her son from a previous relationship had been involved in a car crash in California, where he lived, in which several others involved had been killed. He was fighting for his life, in critical condition.

"I have to go out there," she told Vonlee and Don. "I have to get him and bring him here." She left.

Don and Vonlee were alone in the house.

CHAPTER 5

LYNN GIORGI LEFT THE scene about 7:30 A.M. as Officer Pete Dungjen hung around, waiting for the investigative team to arrive. As he stood in the living room, Dungjen thought back to how Billie Jean had failed to show any "real emotion, to speak of" throughout the entire time he and Giorgi had been there. This seemed odd to the officer, who had been at so many of these scenes he'd lost count. Most people were distraught and crying, but with Billie Jean, everything seemed so matter-of-fact.

Don's over there. . . . He probably fell. . . . Take him away.

Another factor Dungjen observed was that Don had been cold and lividity had set in. This meant he had been dead for a long time; it wasn't as though he'd fallen, passed out and died within an hour or two.

When the paramedics arrived, Dungjen explained what he and Giorgi had come upon. One of the emergency medical technicians (EMTs) lifted Don's shirt, put a heart monitor on his chest and determined, if only following procedure, that there was no heartbeat. Donald Rogers was dead.

"You notice those feet crossed like that?" Dungjen

said to the paramedic as he removed the chest tabs from Don and put away his equipment.

"I do."

"That's odd, huh?"

The guy shrugged. What could he say? Every death felt a bit different. No one died in the same manner, under the same set of circumstances. Death was unpredictable.

Fast.

Slow.

Loud.

Quiet.

Don's death appeared to be a heart attack brought on by years of excessive drinking.

As Dungjen went back and talked to Billie Jean, trying to get any details he could from her, she kept going back to Don's alcoholism.

"One or two gallons of vodka a day," she said.

That was a lot of booze. No two ways about it.

Dungjen had noticed a half-full glass of clear liquid on a den table, with a pair of shoes on the floor next to it. He asked her about this. It felt like someone had been sitting in the chair, drinking a glass of what had been confirmed to be water.

Both Vonlee and Billie Jean spoke at the same time. Billie Jean said the shoes were hers, as Vonlee yelled in the background about the cops and what in the name of God were they doing busting on Billie Jean at such a volatile, sad time in her life.

"How did those shoes get there?" Dungjen asked, ignoring Vonlee's crude, drunken rant.

"We came home," Billie Jean explained, "came in through the garage door and in through the laundry room and I got a glass of water, went into the family room, sat down, took off my shoes and started sipping on the water."

This felt strange to Dungjen as he thought about it: *How could Billie Jean sit in this chair and sip a glass of water and not notice her husband on the floor in the kitchen?* If what she said was true, she would have come in, gotten a glass of water and walked around or over her husband's body on the floor before sitting down. The officer put himself in her position. Sitting in the chair sipping the water, she would have had a clear view of her husband on the floor in the kitchen. But that was not what she had told him.

Dungjen had called Detective Don Tullock, a twenty-five-year veteran of the TPD, the last fourteen with the Detective Bureau (DB), and explained that they had an "unexpected death" at the residence. Tullock was the investigator on duty. Tullock, of course, could sense that Dungjen's instinct told him something was off. Maybe he was overreacting to the situation, but the cop's gut was speaking to him and it was always, Dungjen knew, better to err on the side of caution when a potential murder was at stake.

Dungjen met Tullock outside in the driveway. "Her demeanor," he told the detective. "I'm concerned about her demeanor . . . her lack of concern." He was speaking of Billie Jean.

Tullock was told about Don's drinking.

"She's been living with the situation for so long," the detective said, "and as a result, she might have become desensitized toward him."

Tullock thanked the officer and told him he'd take it from here.

As Tullock met with the paramedic on scene, it was clear that Don had been dead for some time before the call had been made. Lividity took twenty minutes to begin and Don had "severe lividity and rigor mortis" clearly already set in. The lividity, especially, was obvious. Lividity is the pooling of blood, which is heavier than tissue. As gravity works its magic, the blood in the body is drawn downward. Don had dark red "splotches" on the bottom of his face closest to the floor, and also on his back. Blood, after death, finds the lowest point on the body and settles. Don also had what is called "cyanosis," the bluing of the lips. Blood drains from a dead person's lips and they subsequently turn blue.

"Perfect," the paramedic told Tullock. "He looks to be laid out perfect, like he himself laid down on the ground."

"And . . ."

"It's unusual."

The paramedic explained that he had been to "hun-dreds" of death scenes throughout his years of being a medic and he had not ever run into someone in this position with their legs crossed, lying on the floor almost as if placed there.

On top of that was the lack of any trauma to Don's body. Generally speaking, when an unexpected death oc-curred, the person fell and hurt himself as he fell down. There should have been some bruising or abrasion, at least on the elbows or hands as instinct took over and Don's body tried to break the fall. But not a scuffed knee or an obvious bruise was on him.

"Especially with a person this old—they're more brittle."

Apparently, a seventy-four-year-old, one-to-two-gallon-a-day vodka drinker had fallen on a hard surface inside his kitchen and had not suffered one bump or scrape.

An investigator for the office of the Oakland County Medical Examiner (OCME) arrived next. Robert Alleg-rina was responsible for making the decision whether to bring the body in for further examination, or to release it to the family for burial. The OCME's protocol here was simple: "As a general rule," Allegrina said later, "we observe the scene, photograph the body, document the evidence, talk to the family and witnesses and make a determination. . . ."

When Allegrina spoke to Billie Jean, she said her husband had not been to a doctor for as long as she could recall. He was one of those manly men who didn't think he needed a doctor. He'd rather not know what was wrong with him.

"Look over there," Billie Jean said. She pointed to the carpet. They were upstairs in Don's bedroom. Vonlee was there by her aunt's side, ready to lash out at the detective if he became too aggressive.

There were "spots on the carpeting that appeared to be fecal matter, could have been dried blood."

Allegrina wrote it down, documenting everything he saw.

"Are you opposed to an autopsy," Allegrina asked, "under any religious reasons?" The doctor later explained he often asked that question because there were a lot of Jewish families in the area and he wanted to be mindful of their beliefs.

Billie Jean said no.

Allegrina's job was to report what he found at the scene to the medical examiner—and so that's what he did. And as long as the family wasn't opposed, an autopsy was probably warranted here. It was important for the state to understand how and why this man had died. There was plenty of evidence indicating he likely perished because of natural causes—rectal bleeding from ulcers in his stomach or colon cancer, severe alcoholism and maybe a host of other medical issues associated with those conditions or other medical issues that no one knew about. Yet both TPD officers and the detective on call had questions. With any luck, the medical examiner could clear them up and sign off on Don's death as natural causes.

After law enforcement cleared out of the house and

Don's body was taken away, Billie Jean and Vonlee sat in the living room.

"What's wrong?" Billie Jean asked Vonlee. Vonlee was crying, shaking and had a hard time getting a handle on herself. Vonlee wanted a drink.

"What's wrong? I cannot believe he's dead, Billie!"

"Get over it," Billie Jean snapped.

"Get over it? What do you mean?"

Billie Jean walked over and sat down next to Vonlee. She put her arm around her shoulder. "Just pretend like it didn't happen, Vonlee."

CHAPTER 6

WITH BILLIE JEAN ROGERS traveling to California to fetch her son after he endured a life-threatening car accident, Vonlee Titlow and Don Rogers were alone inside Don's expansive house. Vonlee did not work. Don went into the office, but came home at all hours of the day. So they were home together, alone, a lot. Vonlee now waited to hear from Billie Jean about how her son was making out.

"What do you say we go out and celebrate your birth-day?" Don asked Vonlee.

It was July 12, 2000. Vonlee had been at the house now since that July Fourth weekend she spent with her aunt in North Carolina. Vonlee had just turned thirty-three. She was thinking about heading back to North Carolina. The Chrysler had been repaired after it had been stolen and impounded for investigative purposes. Vonlee was told she could pick it up anytime now.

"Sure," she told Don. What a nice gesture, Vonlee con-sidered. The guy had a big heart, she realized since moving into the house. He meant well. It was the bottle holding him down. Billie Jean had him all wrong.

Don made reservations for the two of them at Bloomfield Hills Country Club, an exclusive, eighteen-hole golf course with one hell of a four-star restaurant attached, about a fifteen-minute drive from the house. Vonlee liked to be treated like a lady. She'd dated some wealthy men in her life and knew what luxury living felt and tasted like. Her aunt did not want her to leave for North Carolina until—the earliest—she returned with her son. Keeping Don busy and reaping the benefits of that were favors Vonlee felt obligated to do while her aunt was away. Billie Jean made it clear to Vonlee before she left for California that she had plans for the two of them, her and Vonlee. The accident her son had been in might have derailed those plans somewhat, but it did not cancel them out.

"Stay," Billie Jean had said over the phone.

"I will," Vonlee responded.

Everyone at the club knew Don well. Here he was with this beautiful woman on his arm, walking in and sitting down to a nice, elegant birthday celebration. For Vonlee, going out to dinner with an older gentleman was not such a stretch; she'd run that escort service and doing this exact thing had been part of that world for her and her employees—along with all things sexual, of course.

It was clear from the moment they arrived that this night would not be anything but a routine night in Don's life. He'd drank all day long. And by the time they got around to ordering dinner, "He was so blitzed! I had to get the manager of the club, who—thank God!—knew Don well, to help me carry him out into the car," Vonlee later recalled.

They hadn't even eaten dinner.

Vonlee had no clue how to get back to the Rogers house and got lost for an hour or more until she finally found her way. When they arrived, Vonlee managed to wake Don up enough to get him to stagger with one arm over her shoulder up the stairs and into bed.

Damn, she told herself walking down the stairs. Billie Jean wasn't lying about the way Don drank. He never had a few pops and got a good buzz on; Don went all out, every day. Passing out was part of his routine.

At some point during the night, Vonlee awoke to Don, in bed next to her, grabbing at her, she later said. In fact, Don had woken her up by placing his hands on her large breasts. He was fondling her violently, perhaps in a drunken stupor or even a blackout.

"Come on, baby . . . come on . . . ," Don mumbled.

"Don . . . Don . . . what are you *doing*?" Vonlee screamed, waking up.

Don continued, "Come on . . . Vonlee . . . come on."

"No, no, no, Don," Vonlee said. "Stop that!" She jumped out of bed.

Vonlee decided to go downstairs and sleep on the couch. She told Don to stay put and don't follow her (not that he could manage, anyway). Nothing was going to happen between them. Not tonight, not ever. There was no way Vonlee was sleeping with her aunt's husband, who, by lineage, was her uncle! Vonlee loved Billie Jean. She understood from what Billie Jean had told her that she and Don had more of a partnership than a marriage and had not touched each other in years, but still.

Vonlee woke the next morning and thought, *What the hell.* She couldn't believe what had happened. As mad as she was at Don, however, she wasn't going to say anything to Don or Billie Jean about it. Don was blasted. He probably wouldn't even recall the incident, anyway. Why make a bad night worse?

"I've been drunk before," Vonlee recalled, "and done some stupid things. It was no big deal."

Vonlee walked upstairs into her bedroom. Don was

awake. His arms, she could not help but to notice, were all bloody. There was blood everywhere, in fact: from the bathroom, down the white carpeting in the hallway, into Don's room and her room.

"Don, what the heck?"

"I fell," he said.

"Fell?"

There was way too much blood to believe it was from a fall.

"Look, Vonlee, you have to help me clean up all this blood. If Billie comes home and sees it, she's going to go crazy."

Vonlee went down the hall and into the bathroom and saw that Don had ripped the door off the hinges. He must have cut himself, she deduced, in the process of doing that. But also, when she looked in his bedroom, there was blood all over his bed. Don had been bleeding from his rectum again.

The other problem Vonlee now had was that if one followed the blood trail, it went from Don's room into her room and into her bed. Although the bleeding had started after she went downstairs to sleep on the couch, her aunt still might think they shacked up together, if she followed the bloody trail.

So Vonlee got a bucket, some bleach, got on her knees and went to work.

"I didn't want to tell her," Vonlee explained. "Nothing happened. But I liked Don and I didn't want to see them have a conflict. He was nice guy, at least to me. He treated me good."

The one thing Vonlee mentioned as the morning went on was all of the bleeding. Vonlee cautioned Don that he had to do something about the rectal bleeding—it was a sign of a much larger medial issue that could potentially kill him. Did he have colon cancer? Rectal cancer? Ulcers? There had to be an answer.

"I won't go to a doctor," Don said. "Won't do it."

He was one of those If-I-don't-know-it-can't-hurt-me guys.

Don had to realize he was dying a slow death from the drinking and the bleeding. Perhaps he didn't want to face a doctor telling him he had to give up the one thing he lived for.

Vonlee could not get the blood out of the carpet. There was way too much.

Billie Jean called.

Vonlee hesitated, but then explained what happened.

"But she was so distraught about her son and the accident that she didn't really care about it all," Vonlee later said.

At least not then. It would come up again, though.

Vonlee hung up with her aunt. Then she spoke to Don.

"I'll let her get all new carpets and have the upstairs remodeled and she'll be all right," Don said. Then he began talking about his life with his wife, which kind of shocked Vonlee. If what Don said was true, Vonlee didn't really know her aunt.

"He talked about lending [a family member of Billie Jean's] hundreds of thousands of dollars and not seeing any of it," Vonlee recalled. "And he really didn't have a say in it."

"What do you mean?" Vonlee asked. It was early morning. He was pouring his first glass of vodka of the day already.

"Well, she went down to the bank and signed off on it—I didn't know about it. She's my wife and they allowed her to do it."

"That's horrible, Don . . . ," Vonlee said. "Can't you do anything?"

He shrugged his shoulders and threw his hands up in the air. He was tired. Don didn't want confrontation.

Vonlee decided she needed to leave as soon as possible and go back to her life in Tennessee. Her aunt was a bad influence. She was obviously doing things Vonlee did not subscribe to. Sure, going out with her to the local casinos and drinking was fun. Spending some of her and Don's money was a good time, but this was not the way Vonlee wanted to live her life anymore.

"I'm going back home," Vonlee told Don.

"I don't blame you."

CHAPTER 7

DR. ORTIZ-REYES HAD BEEN waiting for Don's body on August 12, 2000, when it came into the OCME. Ruben Ortiz-Reyes, a medical doctor trained in pathology, had been told that he needed to be ready for an older gentleman with obvious signs of alcoholism and perhaps other, more chronic medical issues. There was "nothing abnormal" about the death scene, Ortiz-Reyes was told, and the "family had found him on the floor." For all intents and purposes, although sad, Don Rogers's death seemed to be a fairly common situation the OCME ran into all the time.

Ortiz-Reyes figured he'd conduct a routine examination on what he had been told was a "natural death." It would be one more of about two thousand that Ortiz-Reyes had been involved in during a career spanning some ten years by the time Don Rogers's body came across his metal slab.

The word "autopsy" means, essentially, "see for yourself." Many pathologists report that about 25 percent of all autopsies reveal some sort of surprise nobody ever saw coming. Doesn't mean there was nefarious behavior behind the death, but maybe the person did not know he or she had a bad heart valve or a growing tumor on the brain. Part of searching the body for answers is to give the family that much-needed closure at a time when they're trying to figure out what happened.

Getting started, Ortiz-Reyes first noted how Don was dressed in blue jeans, a T-shirt and undershorts. Perhaps most importantly at this juncture, Ortiz-Reyes reported: *There were no . . . obvious injuries on the body.*

There had been quite a bit of discussion about Don's alleged rectal bleeding back at the scene, Ortiz-Reyes had been told. Vonlee and Billie Jean had both mentioned Don bled a lot. Ortiz-Reyes took a quick look at Don's anus and found no dried blood, nor any sign of fresh blood. On Don's undershorts, where one might expect to find bloodstains, either old or new, Ortiz-Reyes did not see any.

It was a Saturday, so Ortiz-Reyes was limited by time. He had come into the office especially to accept the body. He conducted a cursory examination, making several notes, and decided to put an actual autopsy off until Monday morning, when he could devote more time and attention to it. (If the ME, Ortiz-Reyes's boss, warranted further examination and wanted him to cut Don open.) This was not highly unusual for a pathologist to do on a weekend. The guy had a life, too. He could not just drop everything to conduct a full-on autopsy on a Saturday morning. Sure, if there was some sort of serial killer on the loose and the autopsy was crucial in finding him or identifying a victim, he'd gladly drop everything and do it. If the TPD had requested immediate answers in Don's death, Ortiz-Reyes would forgo any plans he had and do his work. But it was apparent that Don, an older gentleman, had died of natural causes. Putting him in the cooler and waiting until Monday morning was not going to hurt anything. On top of that, what did his family want?

The one injury Ortiz-Reyes noticed as he wound down

his hasty examination was on Don's right eye. He had "an old injury" there. *Probably two days old*, the doctor later noted.

The one thing Ortiz-Reyes was obligated to do was come up with a preliminary finding; in other words, he needed to spend enough time with the body in order to determine a cause of death that he could put before the medical examiner on the death certificate, which the medical examiner would then have to sign off on.

Taken into account all Ortiz-Reyes had heard from responding officers and the OCME investigator sent to the scene, Ortiz-Reyes was comfortable with not proceeding with a formal autopsy on this day—i.e., cutting Don open and examining his innards, weighing organs, cutting open his brain with a buzz saw and initiating the lab to begin testing samples of tissue. Lab workers would come in early Monday, and if they weren't facing a backlog, they would test Don's blood and urine just to make sure there was nothing out of the ordinary as far as poisons or anything else that might cause alarm.

"When we have a body . . . [and] nothing out of the natural is related to the death of this person," Ortiz-Reyes explained later, "we usually see the body to check for any kind of injuries. If everything is within the normal, we don't do autopsy." Furthermore, Ortiz-Reyes added, because of Don's age being in the neighborhood "where most Americans die of heart problems, I thought he had died of heart problems."

As Ortiz-Reyes stood over Don, still taking notes, thinking about the situation and all of the factors involved, he told himself, *There is no need for an autopsy.* He then reflected, *This gentleman more likely died of problems in the heart . . . arteriosclerotic cardiovascular disease, meaning that the heart—that the vessels around the heart are in bad shape and do not give enough blood to the heart to support the life.*

It was an educated guess, based on Ortiz-Reyes's experience.

Generally, when a medical examiner thinks a human being died of a heart attack, the first thing he or she does is open that person up and have a look at the heart. But because Don was so old, by Ortiz-Reyes's swift estimation, he didn't feel the need to do that, at least not on this day.

Ortiz-Reyes took a sample of urine and blood from Don's body. He posted them to the lab for examination on Monday when they came back from the weekend.

"Heart attack," Ortiz-Reyes later said in court that he thought at that moment.

There wasn't a doubt in his mind.

Ortiz-Reyes took one last look at Don's body, finished his notes and told the weekend staff Don needed to be put in the cooler.

He then shut off the lights in the autopsy suite and left.

CHAPTER 8

VONLEE NICOLE TITLOW DECIDED to head back to North Carolina to pick up her new car, and then head home to Tennessee, where her former life was waiting for her. She could walk into the Waffle House and ask for her job back. She could explain she fell off the wagon and that she was now working with a clean slate and a clear head. She'd go back to AA. She'd clean up her life. It was a bump in the road. Everyone deserved a second chance.

The one lesson Vonlee took away from her time in Michigan with her aunt was that "I was seeing for the first time how Billie Jean wasn't the sweetheart that I had always thought she was."

Back in Tennessee as the middle of July 2000 came around, and Billie Jean was home in Michigan with her son, Vonlee went to see Billie Jean's sister, her other aunt. She sat down and had coffee and explained what happened in Michigan with Don coming into the bed and fondling her and all that bleeding. Vonlee was concerned that she didn't know Billie Jean and might have trusted her more than she should have. Vonlee was also asking herself a question: *Why is Billie Jean so interested in me now, all of a sudden?* Vonlee had not heard from her aunt in a decade, save for a phone call here and there. Why now, at this point, was Billie Jean so crazy to have Vonlee in her life?

"I don't want to go back there," Vonlee told her other aunt.

There was more to it than Billie Jean, Don and their marital and health issues. Vonlee still had that guy who'd signed over his house waiting for her. She wanted to end it completely with him, but she'd left without dissolving the relationship for good. So there were personal issues at stake here for Vonlee. She knew if she went back to Michigan, she'd be closer to Chicago and eventually go back to the penthouse and likely start dating the guy again. Temptation was the root of most evil, Vonlee knew. Seeing him might ultimately lead to her getting back into the escort service business and then the drinking and partying all night. She was exhausted just thinking about it. The way she saw it now: *Out of sight, out of mind.* Being back home felt good.

Billie Jean wasn't about to let Vonlee go, however. She actually came back into Maryville and tracked Vonlee down. Her son was doing better. Don was being a pain in the ass. Billie Jean pleaded with Vonlee that she needed her support.

"Come back, please."

"I don't know, Aunt Billie. . . ."

"You've got to come back with me, if not for nothing else but to settle things with [your man]," Billie Jean said. "You cannot just leave him hanging in the air, Vonlee. That ain't right."

"Billie Jean had a fit over this," Vonlee later recalled. She rode Vonlee, following her around Tennessee for a few days, until Vonlee caved in and agreed to go back to Michigan and stay with her and Don.

Back now in Troy, Billie Jean, Don and Vonlee were once again a quasi-family. Billie Jean's son was recovering, doing much better. Billie Jean was dragging Vonlee along to the casinos again. They were drinking and staying out all night.

Just like that, Vonlee was back to square one.

Vonlee still had not said anything to her aunt about Don fondling her breasts in bed that night. She thought Don did not even remember what happened. Yet, with Vonlee being back inside the Rogers household again, Don picked up his persistence that he and Vonlee get together. He became more aggressive and sexually explicit, according to Vonlee's memory.

"We'd be eating dinner, Billie would walk out of the room and Don would play footsies with me under the table and make eyes with me," Vonlee said later.

The passes continued as the end of July came around. It wasn't overbearing to the point where Vonlee couldn't manage, but more of a nuisance. Don would say things and make gestures. He'd grope at Vonlee. He was harmless in the sense that Vonlee never felt threatened that he'd do something forcibly. But Vonlee was constantly asking herself what in the world was she doing in that house. Why was she there? What purpose did staying at their house, subjected to this type of behavior, serve? Was it simply for the partying?

Vonlee sat her aunt down one day. "Billie Jean, listen to me, I have to leave. Don is becoming too much for me." Vonlee explained to her aunt that she had awoken one night back when Billie Jean was in California to find Don fondling her breasts. It was too much. Vonlee said she thought maybe he was just drunk, but now she knew he was seriously making passes at her.

Billie Jean's face pinched. Anger arose.

"He plays footsies with me under the damn table, Billie . . . ," Vonlee said again.

No sooner had Vonlee got those words out, than Billie Jean hauled off and slapped Vonlee across the face. Then she screamed: "You are a liar! Nothing but a liar. Liar! Liar! Liar!"

Vonlee was humiliated. "No, Billie, it's true. . . ."

"Liar. Stop lying to me."

Vonlee started to cry. This was, she recalled later, "like a scene out of a movie."

"Billie, I am *not* lying to you," Vonlee said through tears. "It is happening all the time now."

"Liar!" her aunt continued yelling.

Vonlee calmed her down. They spoke without yelling.

"Well, I don't believe you, Vonlee. Simple as that. Tell you what . . . I'm going to step out of the room next time and watch . . . see what happens."

"You go right ahead," Vonlee said.

The next day, as they were sitting in the formal room, Billie Jean gave Vonlee the eye and announced she was stepping out of the room and would be back in a few minutes. Don was sitting across from Vonlee.

According to Vonlee, as Billie did this and walked out of view, Don stood up, came over to her and laid his body on top of hers. He was rubbing on Vonlee, she claimed. Touching her all over, fondling her breasts again.

"Come on . . . come on . . . ," Don said, according to Vonlee.

Billie Jean came out of the shadows and stood over them, red-faced and alarmed. Don had been talking of divorce lately. He knew Billie Jean was bleeding his bank accounts dry with her gambling and spending habits, and he was threatening her with cutting her off of the finances. This was a definite threat to Billie Jean's way of life. Without Don, Billie Jean really didn't have anything. One could argue—and Vonlee would certainly be the one leading the charge—that Billie Jean married Don for a second time because she missed the lifestyle Don had provided. She married the guy for his money.

"You bastard!" Billie Jean screamed as she stood.

Don jumped off Vonlee, surprised by his wife's presence.

"You go right ahead and try to divorce me now," Billie Jean said. "You see what happens."

"Come on, Billie," Don pleaded. "I'm just playing around."

"I got something on you now, you bastard!" Billie Jean screamed.

Then Don changed his attitude. "You know what, Billie," he said, giving up on his let's-make-peace offering. "I don't give a shit *what* you do. I want to take her—your niece!—upstairs right now and I want to fuck her. I'll do whatever I want, damn it all! I want to fuck her," he said in his wife's face. "You hear me . . . I. Want. To. Fuck. Her."

Billie Jean was livid. "How *dare* you . . ."

"You're a bitch! A bitch from hell!"

Vonlee was horrified. She got up and walked away from the two of them as they continued screaming at each other.

Billie Jean tried to say something, but Don wouldn't allow her to finish. "You're a bitch from hell, Billie Jean, and your kids are spawn from the Devil—you're Satan. A fucking disgrace to women. I don't give a shit *what* you think. I would fuck Vonlee right here in this house while you're in it."

Billie Jean was fuming. She started to say something.

But Don wasn't finished. "I want my damn thirteen thousand dollars you owe me for the credit card bill.

You promised me that you would stop gambling. You know our agreement . . . you *promised* me." Don was right on her now. In her face. "If you don't stop, I am going to take the credit cards away from you."

Billie Jean had no comeback.

"I'm canceling the credit cards," Don said as he walked out of the room.

CHAPTER 9

ON MONDAY, AUGUST 14, 2000, after Dr. Ortiz-Reyes
returned to the office, he participated in the normal
morning meeting. The Monday meeting was designed to
review cases from the previous weekend and talk about
them. See where each needed to go, who needed to do
what and if there were any of those common surprises
that often dictated a pathologist's day. The chief ME, Dr.
Ljubisa Juvan Dragovic, was there, as well as all the toxi-
cologists and pathologists in the office, and even medical students and residents. One of the other reasons for
the meeting was to see if anyone had a problem with
what had taken place over the weekend.

When it came to the toxicologist to talk about his
findings in cases from over the weekend that he had
looked at earlier that morning, it was the first time
Dr. Ortiz-Reyes learned of what he later called a "surprise" pertaining to Don Rogers's death. The toxicologist
was concerned, he explained to everyone at the meeting,
about something found in Don's urine and blood.

As it turned out, the toxicologist told the team, Don
had a beyond-dangerous amount of alcohol in his
urine and blood. His opinion was based on two tests

that didn't take days or weeks to come back, but were immediate. Even for a chronic alcoholic, Don's bloodstream showed a whopping alcohol level of .44, way above even for a guy who might like to overindulge, as Don clearly had. This number indicated acute alcohol intoxication. Don had enough booze in his system, in other words, to kill him. Take a man of Don's weight—141 pounds—and height—five foot seven inches—and put that amount of booze into his system, and it was far beyond what could be called a dangerous and deadly amount. In fact, that ridiculous amount was enough to make a morbidly obese alcoholic stumble and pass out cold. For a guy that weighed 140 pounds, according to most blood/alcohol percentage charts, a .27 was enough to cause death—and Don had .17 more in his bloodstream.

So the question became: how did all of that alcohol get there?

Even a guy with Don's tolerance for alcohol would have passed out by about the .30 mark. According to the McDonald Center for Student Well-Being (formerly the Office of Alcohol and Drug Education), loss of consciousness occurs at about .25, with alcohol poisoning coming in near .39, and the onset of coma at .40, with death due to respiratory arrest near that same mark. Thus, Don was physically unable to put that amount of alcohol into his system by his own hand. It was impossible. He would have passed out before he was able to do it.

At .44, on paper, anyway, there was a pretty good chance Don Rogers was dead long before the level of alcohol in his blood reached the .40 mark.

The entire team around the conference room table was stunned by this revelation.

The urine sample, the toxicologist explained, was even higher: .47.

Ortiz-Reyes indicated that he would then have to go back and change his opinion regarding Don's cause of death and the hasty notes he had made on that Saturday morning. That was not a big deal; pathologists did this all the time. The simple fact was that yes, it could have been a heart attack that killed Donald Rogers, but acute alcohol intoxication was definitely a contributing factor. The guy didn't drink himself to death—that was not what the doctor meant by the change from "accident" on the death certificate to "contributory cause" of death.

In changing his opinion of Don's death, Ortiz-Reyes would have to issue an addendum to the certificate of death. He'd already written a certificate of death on Saturday and the medical examiner had signed off on it. Ortiz-Reyes had not yet filed it, however.

Don's heart problems could have been, as Ortiz-Reyes later explained, "contributory" to the root cause of death. However, they had a major issue now: how did that alcohol get into Don Rogers's system?

"We better do a complete autopsy," the chief medical examiner suggested at the meeting. "We need to find out if anything else is going on here."

Several in the meeting appeared perplexed by the proposition.

"What's the problem?" the medical examiner wondered.

Don Rogers's body . . . it was already gone.

CHAPTER 10

EVERY RECOVERING ALCOHOLIC KNOWS there's a sleeping dragon, a beast, hibernating inside his or her soul. Even if the person finds sobriety, dries out and goes on to lead a productive, alcohol-free life, one day at a time, that beast sits, patiently waiting, ready and willing to breathe fire once again when a vulnerable moment arises. Since Vonlee had returned to the upper Midwest to live with Don and Billie Jean, she not only started drinking again, but she'd rattled the sleeping dragon wide awake.

While she had been back in Tennessee at her grandmother's house, Vonlee later explained, she had given everything up. Vonlee had walked away, she said, from a "three-hundred-thousand-dollar town house" that her old boyfriend was willing to sign over to her in place of her going home to sober up. While living inside that bubble consisting of Denver and Chicago, and running an escort service, Vonlee considered that she had "hit [her] bottom."

"I was going to meetings. I was going to therapy. I was doing all of these things while back home." And through that, Vonlee said, she had "made an understanding with God," her higher power. She'd pleaded to God while immersed in her addiction that she wanted out of it all. "Okay, God, this is my bottom . . . ," Vonlee had told herself while ripping and running in Chicago before taking off for home. "And if this is not my bottom? Please, God, take me there."

The chaos her life had taken on since moving in with Billie Jean was perhaps that new bottom she had asked God for, Vonlee began to think as those days and long nights at the casino carried on. Maybe Chicago and Denver were not enough? Perhaps God wanted Vonlee to see another layer of living hell that would finally shake her into believing she had a drinking problem to begin with and that things could not possibly get any worse.

With Don dead, the police asking Billie questions, and Vonlee being around it all, feeling guilty and a part of what seemed to be, at the least, some moral culpability in Don's death, Vonlee asked herself, *Is this it? Is this my bottom?*

One of the main issues for Vonlee was that she had been blind drunk herself on the night they returned from the casino to find Don on the kitchen floor.

If I wasn't drunk, would he have had a chance? Vonlee wondered now.

The guilt ate at her.

"I was literally in another world while all of this was going on," Vonlee said. "I made an appointment to go to the psychiatrist because I just couldn't deal with it."

Don's kids, even Billie Jean's, were asking Vonlee what was wrong with her. She seemed so distraught. "Did you know Don that well, Vonlee? You are really taking this hard."

Anytime somebody said something to Vonlee, she broke down. She couldn't handle hearing Don's name.

"Someone would say, 'How well did you know Don?' and I would bust out bawling like a child."

There was a time a few days after Don's death when all Vonlee could do was pop Xanax her psychiatrist had put her on and wash those pills down with vodka.

"I'd get up off the couch only to take more Xanax, have a drink, and then [I'd] pass back out."

She couldn't believe what had happened—Don dying the way he had.

But if Don was dead when Billie Jean and Vonlee entered the house, why all the guilt? Why was Vonlee harboring so much responsibility for Don's death? What wasn't Vonlee sharing with anyone?

Billie Jean saw Vonlee on the couch one morning. "Look at you!" she said. "Pull your damn self together."

"I'm . . . I'm . . . ," Vonlee tried to say.

Billie Jean got down to Vonlee's eye level, put her hands on Vonlee's shoulders and stopped just short of shaking her, before saying: "Listen to me. You need to pull yourself together and move on. Forget about this. Forget it ever happened. Pretend it did not happen and get yourself back together."

CHAPTER 11

A.J. DESMOND & SONS on Crooks Road, a major thoroughfare cutting through the city of Troy, intersecting with the Chrysler Expressway, has the predictable look of a funeral home: its redbrick outer shell, white Romanesque columns lining the front entrance from ground to roof and its lavishly plush green lawn and lavish landscaping, with each blade of grass and boxwood bush clipped to utter perfection. This was where the dead lay in a state of repose while their loved ones come to pay final respects. Make no mistake, in the Troy region, A.J. Desmond has provided its first-rate services to those in grief throughout this community for over a century. Terence B. Desmond himself had signed off on Don's death certificate as the funeral service licensee when Don's body came in for its final examination and grooming. Interestingly, with regard to Don's death certificate, it had been signed by Desmond, Dr. Ortiz-Reyes and the Troy medical examiner, Dr. Dragovic, on August 12, 2000—yet, it would not be filed until August 17, 2000.

Don's wake took place a few days after his death. All considering, Don didn't look that bad lying in his casket all made-up, wearing his best Sunday suit. For many attending Don's wake, it was a celebration of his long and prosperous life. Most thought of Don as a good guy, someone who gave to his community, helped out the less fortunate when he could, but had kept to himself and, for the most part, left other people alone. In the end, a man shouldn't be judged by how much he drank. Don Rogers was a person of immense gratitude and humble beginnings, who appreciated what he had in life.

Toni Brosseau had worked for Don Rogers and his business partner, Don Kather, for the past sixteen years. She knew Rogers quite well and could vouch for how nice of a guy he was. She had seen Don Rogers, in fact, at about 2:00 P.M. on the day he died. Toni was the heartbeat of the company. Whenever Rogers prepared to leave the office for the day, he always made a point to stop by Toni's desk and bid her a fond good night. As it turned out, Don had spent about six hours at the office that Friday, August 11. To Toni, Rogers looked and appeared fine. He had no markings on his face or lips. He wasn't complaining about anything in particular, and he spoke of going home and staying put for the weekend. The last thing she would have expected to hear would be that Don had gone home and drank himself into oblivion, passed out and dropped dead on the kitchen floor. Don was the type of guy that went to work every day. He might not have stayed in the office all day long, and everyone knew he loved to watch television while in his office, but he showed up at 8:30 A.M. every day and did his work.

As Toni arrived for the wake and filed into A.J. Desmond & Sons, along with the line of mourners, she thought about her old boss. There was one conversation Toni had with Billie Jean the week before Don passed that now felt kind of strange to Toni as she went back and considered it. Billie Jean had called and asked to speak with Toni, instead of her husband.

"Mrs. Rogers, hi," Toni said. It was rather surprising to be talking to "the boss's wife." Toni had made a habit of not getting involved. But here it was, Billie Jean calling, looking to ask Toni a few questions.

"Toni, I need to know something," she said up front, holding little back. She sounded serious, but also anxious and maybe pissed off a little, too. "Has Don ever been improper with you in any way?"

It was altogether shocking and bizarre, this sudden accusation out of nowhere. Toni had met Billie Jean only a few times. She'd never heard from Don about any problems he and his wife might have had.

"Excuse me, Mrs. Rogers?" Toni asked.

"A pass . . . Don ever made a *pass* at you, Toni?"

"My goodness, no. No, Mrs. Rogers. Never."

This call had come right around the time Vonlee had mentioned to her aunt about Don and what happened when Billie Jean was away in California. That I-got-something-on-you-now charge Billie Jean had allegedly made to Don after walking out of the room and coming back to find Don on top of Vonlee. Apparently, if he'd done it to Vonlee, Billie Jean must have been thinking, maybe he'd done it at the office, too. It seemed Mrs. Rogers was in the mood to get all she could on her husband.

"Well, he's made advances toward Miss Titlow and . . . ," Billie Jean started to say to Toni.

"No, no, Mrs. Rogers," Toni insisted. "Not me. Not ever. He never, never, ever has done anything. He's never even used four-letter words around me. He is always a gentleman."

Billie Jean talked about Don's health. Toni had no idea how sick Don might have been. Still, Billie Jean mentioned to Toni, "He's been having problems with rectal bleeding lately—did you know *that*?"

"No, I did not," Toni said, wondering why this woman felt the need to share such personal information with her. "But maybe you ought to get him to see a doctor, Mrs. Rogers."

"He won't go. He just won't do it," Billie Jean said.

The two exchanged some small talk and hung up.

Scott Hadley (pseudonym), Billie Jean's future son-in-law, had never met Don or Vonlee, but he was in town from his home in Illinois, along with Billie Jean's daughter, to pay his respects. Scott had just asked Billie Jean's daughter to marry him in the weeks before Don had died. He was part owner in a software development firm in Illinois. He had some experience in finances and financial security, he and his wife-to-be explained to Billie Jean at the wake. Scott even offered to help the family wade through what could be temperamental financial waters after someone died unexpectedly.

The widow introduced Scott to Don's brother and sister. Then she found Vonlee and introduced him to her.

"We had just a small conversation," Scott said later. "Typical to what you would have with various people at a wake—just small talk about the family."

"How's Billie Jean doing?"

"Holding up rather well, considering."

"What a tragedy."

"Indeed."

Someone at the wake suggested that Scott sit at some point with Don's immediate family and Billie Jean to discuss Don's finances and what should be done with what was a rather large bank account he had left behind. It was unclear later on about who had actually suggested the meeting. But in any event, as of August 2000,

Don's net worth was valued at $1,778,603.11. Eighty-nine percent of that was in investments, with 1 percent available as cash, the remaining 10 percent or so being part of Don's fixed monthly/yearly income.

The guy had a nest egg, no doubt about it. Billie Jean was clearly looking to get this taken care of as soon as possible. She had to pay bills, run the household and make sure Don's partnership in the company was being fairly represented. She couldn't just curl up in a ball and be the grieving widow. That would not serve anybody well. And, to be honest, it had never been her way of dealing with problems and tragedy.

"I can help you," Scott told his future mother-in-law. "I lost my father several years ago, and having gone through it myself with my mom, I can assist you in everything. Help organize the finances. . . . I know the process."

Scott went on to explain that there was a lot of work involved in hunting down life insurance policies, getting Social Security documents changed, bank accounts situated, speaking with the financial institutions Don had his money invested in and anything else involved in trying to figure out a dead man's finances and how the family could do what was in his (and now their) best interests.

What could she say? The offer seemed to be a welcoming gesture. Billie Jean agreed—she was all for it. She definitely needed the help.

They would meet in the coming days, she said, and get it all situated.

Over in another part of the room, her daughter, Vanette Vereeke, whose father Billie Jean had been married to before Don (one of two marriages for Billie Jean before she met Don), ran into Vonlee. The last time she had seen Vonlee, Vonlee was a child. Vanette, like pretty much everyone else in her family, considered Vonlee eccentric and maybe even a little over-the-top in the way she dressed, did her makeup, walked and talked. Vonlee was a presence, certainly. There was some narcissism in there, too, with Vonlee always looking to be the focus and center of attention. There were reasons for this beyond Vonlee being a Southern belle and simply wanting and needing constant praise. But on this night, as they all celebrated Don's life and paid homage to him in mourning, Vanette noticed something else about Vonlee as she approached: Vonlee was wearing an enormous amount of what looked to be brand-new jewelry.

"Rings and bracelets, like diamonds," Vanette said later.

So much that it stood out among a crowd of people.

One ring in particular was of great interest to Vanette and some of the other women who were standing around and talking during the wake.

"Wow," Vanette said, staring at Vonlee's finger, "you're engaged?"

Vonlee had known the guy she was dating only about a month. He had given her the ring, though they were not engaged officially. She told him she was not ready to get married. He told her to keep the ring, anyway, and "maybe it will change" her mind. The diamond was huge. Vonlee said she'd be crazy not to accept it. She wore it on her wedding ring finger.

Several other women came and stood around as Vonlee and Vanette discussed the ring.

"Look at that ring, Vonlee. It's very noticeable."

Vonlee, who was obviously distraught and cooked up on pills and booze while at the wake, took the ring off and passed it to Vanette, who put it on and held it out in front of herself. "My goodness . . ." As were the other women, she was impressed with the sheer size of the thing. She took it off and gave it to another woman standing in the circle.

"They were all passing it around, like girls do," Vanette said later.

"Look at this . . . ," one woman said.

"Incredible," envied another.

"Lucky girl . . ."

As Vanette worked her way around the room, she walked over to where her mother was talking to a few people.

"Yeah, I came home around eleven and he was dead on the floor," her mother told the group, according to what Vanette later claimed.

Eleven?

The call to 911 did not come until around 4:00 A.M.

Maybe she simply forgot?

Her mother was being herself, her daughter later explained, while schmoozing with people at the wake. Her mom was very skilled in adversity. She could take a bad situation and enter into it with a straight face and generally a positive attitude. She was an expert at meeting stressful situations and handling them. People wanted to know what happened to Don, Billie Jean surmised—and so she was going to be open and honest and tell them what she knew. She didn't want people arriving or leaving with any sort of misinformation. That would only feed rumors.

"She could appear to have everything under control," one family member later said of her. "She didn't appear to be visually upset, but I'm sure inside her heart she was."

Well into calling hours, Billie Jean found Vonlee sitting down by herself over in a corner. Vonlee was crying.

"I can't do this," Vonlee said, looking up.

Billie Jean stared at her. She looked around to make sure no one was listening to them.

"I was so out of it at that point," Vonlee later recalled, thinking back. "I could not even function. I was so sick."

The situation, as Vonlee saw it then, was strikingly opposite to what she had been used to ever since moving in with her aunt and uncle. When Vonlee first got to the house, she noticed her aunt was depressed and always angry, down and out, lying around a lot, sleeping late, not doing much of anything. Vonlee, meanwhile, was a ball of fire like her old party self, wanting to go out and own the night. Now, after Don's death, it was as if they had changed places. "I became depressed and docile as Billie became lively and always up."

Billie Jean became agitated, according to Vonlee. "Stand up," she said, grabbing Vonlee by the shoulders.

"Billie, I . . . I . . . ," Vonlee started to say before breaking down crying.

"You *have* to pull yourself together," her aunt said. "Or you are going to have to leave right now."

CHAPTER 12

BILLIE JEAN AND VONLEE were at the Rogers household. It was midafternoon, August 17. "Vonlee, where are you?" Billie Jean said, looking for her niece inside the house. "Vonlee?" she yelled.

Vonlee was upstairs. "What is it?"

"Come with me, I want to go somewhere."

That afternoon, the two found themselves perusing the lot at Suburban Oldsmobile and Cadillac Buick on Maplelawn Drive in Troy. Don had not been dead a week and Billie Jean had her eye on a brand-new, flashy, fully loaded Cadillac. She'd always wanted one. Don would never part with the money. Now was her chance.

Ultimately, she chose a Cadillac Seville Touring Sedan (STS).

"Can we take it out for a ride?" the newly minted widow asked the salesperson.

She and Vonlee were gone for about fifteen minutes. When they returned, Billie Jean was all smiles. She said she wanted a sunroof put in and also "OnStar, with a one-year subscription."

Done and done, said the salesperson.

She also wanted the dealer rebate that was being offered.

"You got it!"

With a deal in place, Billie Jean took out her checkbook, wrote a check for one hundred dollars and handed it to the salesman. "I'll take it. When can you have it ready?"

"I'll call you," he said.

Four days later, on August 21, 2000, the dealer called to tell her that the car was all set; she could pick it up.

She arrived sometime later, once again with Vonlee. She handed over a cashier's check for the balance: $50,676. 80. This money was paper to Billie Jean, it appeared. The way she had been spending since Don's death was in itself a sign of a woman either in desperate and severe grief and mourning, or someone who had no concept of money. In the days before his death, Don Rogers was very active with his Merrill Lynch accounts, buying stocks and bonds and growth funds, working with his money to insure it continued to grow. And yet, no sooner did he pass away, than his widow began selling off the stocks and bonds in big numbers. Just days before showing up to buy the Cadillac, for example, four days after Don had died, she sold ten thousand dollars' worth of funds, of which she would be penalized for selling off early. What's more, between August 17 and the week after, Billie Jean had one hundred seventy thousand in cash transferred by wire to her bank accounts. In addition, on the day she bought the Caddy, she made a thirteen-hundred-dollar purchase at U.S. Jewelers, a store that Vonlee's boyfriend owned. In the days following that, she made another four-hundred-dollar purchase at U.S. Jewelers and spent upward of nearly two thousand dollars on clothes.

It certainly seemed Billie Jean was celebrating Don's

death and couldn't wait until he was out of the picture. Yet, when one took a close look at the credit card statement Billie Jean and Don shared over the past year, what emerged was a woman who liked to spend her husband's money all along. She had withdrawn thousands upon thousands of dollars in cash advances at two places: the MGM Grand and Motor City casinos in Detroit. Many times, on the same night, she'd withdraw five hundred dollars, which came with a $30.99 transaction fee, or one thousand dollars, which came with a $51.99 transaction fee. In many instances throughout the year leading up to Don's death, the transaction fees alone every month added up to thousands of dollars. Reading the statements, studying the times and dates, you could almost see her walking up to the window for the cash advance, telling herself, *This is it . . . last time tonight*—only to be back at the window an hour or two later after blowing through the five hundred or one thousand dollars. Don had a twelve-thousand-dollar limit on the shared card, and it was a good thing. Because as the year 2000 came, and Billie Jean continued to gamble, she'd hit that limit or close to it every month. It's clear that she hardly *ever* won any money. She was constantly withdrawing.

Don had taken lots of pride in his net worth. As a businessman, he had worked his ass off all his life to build it up, bolstering it with investments, until it grew into an amount he could retire comfortably with. Now his money was fading away at what seemed to be an uncontrollable pace. With no one there to monitor it or pester her about it, Billie could not get a handle on her spending in those days after Don's death.

While walking the lot, looking to buy Billie Jean's Caddy, Vonlee had spotted a Buick Riviera she liked. As they drove back to the dealer to pick up the Caddy, Billie Jean said, "You want me to buy you that car, Vonlee?"

Vonlee was a mess. She'd been back to drinking heavily and taking pills; she wanted to forget about what had happened to Don. In her mind, she kept going back to that night they returned to the house: *What actually happened? What could I have done?*

"Come on," Billie Jean added, "let me buy you that car. It'll make you feel better."

"I don't think anything is going to make me feel better," Vonlee said.

Billie Jean pulled into the dealer parking lot.

"I'm telling you, Von, just let me buy you a car—it will make you feel better. Pick out whatever you want."

Vonlee thought about it. "Okay," she said.

The Riviera Vonlee had eyed days before was still in the lot. The salesman asked Vonlee if she was still interested. He'd noticed Vonlee looking at the vehicle.

"We are," Vonlee said. After all, she did not have any money.

It was a used vehicle. When Billie Jean was finished inside the finance office, she walked out to where Vonlee and the salesman stood talking.

"She wants it," Billie Jean said.

When they returned to the lot to pick up the Riviera, Vonlee had a check for $19,834.90. The salesman looked at it. Billie Jean's name was on the check.

"You okay with this?" he asked, just to make sure. She was standing next to Vonlee.

"Of course," she answered. To Vonlee: "Now you forget about everything, you hear me? Just forget it happened. Pretend it never happened, Von."

The salesman stood and watched as Billie Jean drove away in her new Cadillac, with Vonlee following right behind in her used white Riviera.

CHAPTER 13

WHEN BILLIE JEAN WENT to Scott, her future son-in-law, for the money to buy the new cars, he explained as her financial advisor that she might want to wait. Maybe think about it some more. She was grieving. People did strange things in order to deal with the death of a loved one. Spending upward of seventy-one thousand dollars on two cars was not a sound investment. Sure, Don had a little over 1.75 million dollars in assets, but one could burn through that mighty quick if one wasn't careful.

"Why not lease the vehicles?" Scott suggested.

"No," she said.

"Well, you don't want to pay cash for them."

Scott could not convince her.

Not long after she bought both cars, she went to Scott and asked him for a check written out to Vonlee for twenty-five thousand dollars.

"Doesn't matter what it's for," the widow said when questioned.

Scott did as he was told.

CHAPTER 14

IN THOSE DAYS AFTER Don's wake, Scott continued in his role acting as the Rogers family financial guru. However, Scott later said he never considered himself the family's "financial advisor." Scott had convinced Billie Jean and Don's siblings that he needed to have, at the least, limited power of attorney. With everyone's blessing, Scott contacted Merrill Lynch and got the paperwork done so he could continue in his role as the family financial wizard and move Don's money around without issue.

"You should go home to Tennessee," Scott and Don's siblings suggested to the widow. "Spend some time with family. Allow us to take care of everything."

It was one of the reasons, Scott later explained, he was in favor of having limited power of attorney. She agreed and wanted to go back home to see her family for a few days, and there needed to be someone back in Troy who could sign off on financial issues and pay the bills.

So Billie Jean signed the paperwork, turning over power of attorney.

"You think I could get a look at the family records?" Scott asked.

Billie Jean wondered why.

"Well, Don has most of his money with Merrill Lynch, but I need to read through the life insurance policies and find out what else is going on."

Another important factor in handing over power of attorney to Scott, especially at Merrill Lynch, was that Billie Jean would need living expenses. She needed instant access to that money of Don's in order to go about her day-to-day life. She didn't want to have to call and wire money into her personal accounts. If her future son-in-law had the power, she could call him and have him get her cash or whatever she needed, whenever she needed it.

Before she left, she signed about a dozen checks in case anyone needed to gain access to the money in the bank and pay bills or purchase items the household needed.

As Scott dug into Don's financial records, it became clear right away that Don was a tedious and thorough man in terms of keeping records. He saved receipts for everything. For Scott, this made it easy for him to "track everything," as he later put it. Within Don's records, for example, Scott found life insurance policies dating back to the 1930s, 1940s and 1950s.

"One of my objectives," Scott later explained, "was to get Billie through this process with as little outside pressure as possible."

Peace of mind was Scott's goal as far as Billie Jean was concerned, according to what he later said in court. He needed to work with Don's ex-business partner and Don's accountant.

Just about everything, with the exception of the business, was in both spouses' names as marital partners. Billie Jean could say what she wanted about Don and his drinking and how they fought and there was no love between them, but in the end, Don had included her as his life's equal partner. Even regarding the business, as a probate lawyer advised, she would be required to make a decision about whether she wanted to continue in Don's role as a board member or sell out. But as Scott had explained over the phone to her, "You don't have to do that now." He wanted her to take some time. By the end of the year, November or December, they could revisit this part of Don's financial life and she could decide what she wanted to do then.

While she was in Tennessee visiting her mother, she contacted Scott and told him she was in the process of helping her mother purchase a home. She wanted Scott to transfer some funds from Merrill Lynch into her account so she could have access to it right away. Billie Jean wanted the money as soon as possible.

Scott asked her how much.

"One hundred thousand," she requested.

A wire transfer was made.

There was some discussion between them about her financial future. Scott wanted to make it clear to Billie Jean that she needed to make responsible decisions that solidified her future. She needed to invest. The worst thing anyone on a spending spree could do was to think only about today. Buying cars and giving money away to family was fun and exciting and generous, but she needed to think about her own future.

She asked what she could invest in. She knew nothing about investments. What was Scott suggesting?

Scott talked about his company. At the time, he later claimed, it was experiencing a major growth spurt. He needed capital to finance the company's progress, and the banks wouldn't invest because the company was so young.

Billie Jean indicated that she wanted to think about it.

Scott went to his future wife and explained that he

could use two hundred forty thousand dollars to take his company to the next level.

A check was written in that amount and signed by Billie Jean's daughter, according to Scott's later testimony in court.

Then Scott suggested that his future mother-in-law take all of Don's money in Merrill Lynch and put it into another company.

What company was that? she wondered.

A financial investment firm Scott's good friend owned.

Billie Jean, who had agreed to the nearly quarter-million-dollar loan for Scott, said, "What the hell, go ahead.

"Do it."

CHAPTER 15

LOOKING INTO DON ROGERS'S death, TPD detectives Don Tullock and Don Zimmerman sat down and listened to the 911 call Billie Jean had made on the night she and Vonlee reportedly came home to find Don Rogers dead on the kitchen floor. This call—and Billie Jean's demeanor, which had become somewhat of a discussion piece among investigators of late—was rather telling. It said a lot about her personality, despite family members claiming she was the type of person not to show much emotion.

In a matter-of-fact tone, she called and said: "Yes, this is Billie Rogers in Troy, and I was . . . I came in the house and I think my husband is dead on the floor."

No panic. No tears. No hurried delivery. Just plainly simplified and expressionless: *"I think my husband is dead on the floor."*

"Do you know what happened?" the operator asked.

"I have no idea. We were at the casino and he's supposed to go with us. And then he decided he wanted to drink."

Don had never wanted to go with them to the casino, Vonlee later said. At best, that statement was an exaggeration; at worst, a lie.

"Is he breathing?"

"I can't . . . I can't feel any breath."

As they are trained to do, the operator began asking questions intended to reveal simple facts. Things nobody would have a problem answering off the top of his or her head, even under stress.

"Okay. You just got home and he was home alone or . . . ?"

"Yeah, he was here by himself. I was with my niece. She's visiting us from out of town."

"Okay. I want you to stay on the line. I'm going to have you talk—"

Billie Jean interrupted, as though she had trouble hearing: "Pardon me?"

"Stay on the phone. I want you to talk to the paramedics, okay?"

Billie Jean said that would be fine.

They discussed the address. Then the 911 operator transferred the call.

"Community Atlanta, this is Carol. . . . Are you at 2090 Grenadier?"

Billie Jean said yes.

"And what's wrong?"

The caller now sounded frustrated for having to answer the same question twice. "Well, my niece and I just walked in the door and my husband's laying on the floor in the kitchen and it looks like he's dead."

"Okay. Can you see if he has a pulse for me?"

Apparently, she walked over, bent down and touched Don.

"No, he's kind of cold. . . . Yeah. I can't feel his pulse."

"Do either one of you want to do CPR?"

"No. I don't think he has any pulse."

"Okay, but do you *want* to do CPR?"

Vonlee took the phone from her aunt. "No," she said.

Then Vonlee said something about leaving the house, but the operator interrupted.

"I know you want to run away," the operator said, "but we need to do some CPR."

"Can you please just send somebody out here?" Vonlee pleaded.

"Sure, honey, we can do that."

Vonlee came across as panicked and anxious, like someone who had come home and found a man she knew lying on the kitchen floor, cold to the touch, with clear signs of death settled over him. She was scared.

"Please, just send somebody here. *Please*."

"Okay, they're on their way."

Vonlee and Carol discussed the address and where the house was located on the street so there would not be any confusion once the EMTs and police arrived.

The operator wanted to keep Vonlee on the phone until someone got there, so she asked, "How long were you gone?"

"We left like, uh, like . . . I don't know—like ten o'clock."

It was close to four in the morning. This was a surprising answer to the operator.

"And you're just coming home *now*?"

"I was at the casino."

"So he's been alone all that time?"

"Yes. I know he's dead. He is dead. He's dead." Vonlee was losing it. Her aunt stood by her side, calm as a river stone.

"Send somebody out here, *please*?" Vonlee reiterated one more time before indicating that she wanted to get off the phone.

"The ambulance is on the way."

"Thank you," Vonlee said, and hung up.

* * *

Was the fact that a woman who'd called 911 and didn't sound distressed, or that her husband's will left everything to her—and he might have died by unnatural causes—enough to suspect murder and then launch an investigation?

Perhaps.

It was certainly enough to look further into things, both detectives considered, a task that they were now firmly engaged in.

CHAPTER 16

ON AUGUST 24, 2000, after sitting down and thinking about all the events that had taken place since her father's death, Don's daughter, Rose (pseudonym), called the TPD and spoke with Detective Tullock.

"I don't think my father died of natural causes," Rose explained. "And it wasn't an accident."

Tullock asked her to tell him why she thought this way.

Rose said most of what she felt was instinctual, but certain things weren't adding up for her.

"Like what?"

She talked about how Billie Jean and Don had been married once and then divorced, then married again a few years after that. Billie Jean sought to have the will amended after the second marriage (eleven years prior to Don's death), allowing her access to Don's entire estate, which she had valued at nearly two millions dollars.

"Billie has always been emotionally distant from my dad," Rose added. "His body was cremated, I feel, to cover up evidence."

What was true about this statement was that Don's body

had been cremated after his wake. There was no body to exhume, if that's what the TPD had in mind.

All of this was speculation, although the cop was listening closely because he, too, had his own suspicions.

Then this from Rose: "The time Billie told us she came home is different from what she told others."

Tullock asked what Rose meant by that.

"She told us she came home with [Vonlee] at eleven—we know she told you and others it was more like four A.M."

That was quite true, Tullock considered.

The detective asked Rose to write out all of her thoughts and drop them off at the TPD. He'd take a look at it all. Get back to her.

"I've done that already," Rose said.

Rose provided the TPD with a four-page, single-spaced account of what she believed to be "skeptical" information surrounding the death of her father. The document was clear in its contempt for certain parties, but the information was extremely revealing.

Near the top of the document, Rose wrote, *Dad HATED Billie's kids.* From there, Rose painted a picture of these kids (from another marriage) always being a thorn in Don's side when money came into play. Rose recalled conversations with her father about the kids borrowing Don's money and his credit to sign leases on buildings for businesses that failed, leaving Don with the bill. She accused Billie Jean's kids of stealing money and jewelry; of charging up a "huge cable bill" while staying at the house; how Billie Jean's son, the one who got into the car accident, would need round-the-clock care and Billie Jean needed to pay for it; finally the kids were "the cause" of the divorce of Billie Jean and Don.

As far as the autopsy, Rose insisted, the fact that there "was no autopsy done" seemed suspicious in and of itself. Also, when Rose tried to ask for a copy of the will from Billie Jean's daughter, she was met with great scorn, and the daughter shouting, "You have been so demanding! You wanted a certificate of the death. It's not like we're going to change it or anything!"

Rose also said her stepmother lied about meeting with the attorney to get a copy of the will and told Rose "she couldn't remember when she met with the attorney." She had "no idea" if the will Don left, dated May 7, 1993, was his last will, or if his widow was actually hiding any amendments he had made. Just getting simple information from Billie Jean and her children about the will was frustrating and difficult. No one wanted to help them, not even the secretary from Billie Jean's attorney's office.

Rose talked about how Don would complain about his wife never being at home when Rose called to speak with her father. Rose would ask where she was and Don would say, "Back home, visiting her sick mother. . . ."

We knew what that meant, Rose wrote. *Billie has had numerous affairs.*

Rose went over to her father's office after the wake to look through his files to see if she could find anything of value. Don's partner allowed her in and Toni, the receptionist Rogers had loved like a daughter, even helped. When Rose found a file marked "estate," she was shocked to open it and find that it was "completely empty."

Tullock thanked Rose and told her they would look into all of the allegations. Then Tullock got together with Zimmerman and discussed what they should do next. It certainly seemed as though the case needed to be looked at more closely. A cop has to follow his gut. So Zimmerman and Tullock decided to head over and have a chat with aunt and niece. See where they were at, maybe they could offer more information.

"You mind if we come in and talk?" Tullock asked after Billie Jean answered the door.

"Yes, come in," she said. She seemed cordial and apparently wanted to help any way she could.

Both men entered the Rogers home.

As Zimmerman and Tullock started talking to the recent widow, they asked about her marriage to Don.

"We were married in 1985," she explained. "It ended in divorce." She said a few years after the divorce, about eleven years ago, they remarried.

The detectives asked about a will. Did Don have a will?

"Yes," she answered. She looked at the men quizzically: *What are they implying? What is going on here? Should I call a lawyer?*

There was nothing suspicious about the will Don had left behind. Don made his wife the sole beneficiary of the entire estate—eleven years prior.

The visit was mainly to let the widow know that the cops were becoming curious and she might have to answer some questions down the road. The TPD had been looking into this death and they kept coming to one conclusion: Don Rogers was murdered. The more they looked at the evidence they had currently, Billie Jean Rogers looked guiltier than ever of having done something to her husband.

Needless to say, as Zimmerman and Tullock left the house that day and Mrs. Rogers closed the door behind them, both parties believed the same thing: it was not the last time they would sit and chat about the death of Don Rogers.

CHAPTER 17

DONALD ROGERS'S BODY HAD left the examiner's office back on that Monday morning, August 14, 2000, two days after his death, and was whisked over to A.J. Desmond & Sons for the wake. But then after the wake, Billie Jean ordered her husband's remains to be cremated. After all, on that Saturday, August 12, the day after Don's death, the OCME ruled Don's death accidental. A death certificate had been issued. Billie Jean had every right to do what she wanted with her husband's body. And now Don Rogers's ashes were in a box. There would be no chance to cut him open and have a second look.

As they grew more suspicious of Billie Jean, the detectives realized the problems they had, however, didn't stop there—because that death certificate would now have to be officially amended. Dr. Ortiz-Reyes would have to write up a report or "inspection" addendum and file it with the certificate. This, of course, was not unheard of in the field; yet, it wasn't something medical examiners did every day.

On that inspection sheet that Dr. Ortiz-Reyes and his boss, Dr. Dragovic, had signed and dated August 12,

Ortiz-Reyes now included the "manner of death" as homicide. He also added another very interesting—albeit new—factor in Don's death. As for the "cause of death," Ortiz-Reyes was now claiming it to be "asphyxia by smothering."

If that was true, Don Rogers had, indeed, been the victim of a murder.

On the surface, this new accusation might have seemed to come out of nowhere. All of a sudden, a guy who had seemingly died of a heart attack, based on an overdose of alcohol, was now the victim of smothering? Moreover, in his report, Ortiz-Reyes indicated that Don's conjunctivae (mucous membrane lines inside the eyelids) were "unremarkable." His sclera (the white part of his eyes) "anicteric" (not yellowed). Nowhere did the doctor report any rupture or breaking of the blood vessels in Don's eyes, which is a fairly common factor when someone is smothered and choked, struggling for air.

This could mean two things: Don was not smothered; or he was smothered, but he was already in a coma or dead at the time from all that alcohol.

Furthermore, Ortiz-Reyes wrote in his addendum: *The body shows no signs of bruises, fractures, lacerations or deformities. . . .*

And then this: *The back is without note.* Meaning, there were no injuries and nothing suspicious found on Don's entire back.

That information was part of the initial report Ortiz-Reyes had written from his notes on his cursory examination on the Saturday morning Don's body had come in. On the addendum, after learning of the alcohol intoxication, the doctor now had several issues. There was no date or time on this sheet of the report, thus one was left to suppose it was written on that Saturday (but it had not been). Right at the top, in the first paragraph, both doctors—Ortiz-Reyes and his boss, Dr. Dragovic, the chief medical examiner—found a "brown spot" on the "base of the anterior surface of the neck," along with "small old bruises" on Don's right shoulder, left lower abdomen and right arm. They also now uncovered "multiple brown spots on the back."

Those injuries fell in line with someone placing a pillow over Don's face and putting pressure on it.

In the "evidence of injury" portion of the addendum (that third, added page, that is): *There is a healing bruise of the left eye socket. . . .*

His diagnosis, Ortiz-Reyes wrote, now consisted of: "Asphyxia by smothering" and "Acute alcohol intoxication."

In his now renewed opinion, Dr. Ortiz-Reyes was certain Don Rogers had been smothered after being plied with alcohol. The image one conjured while reading this report included someone knocking Don down, or waiting for him to pass out (as he normally would, according to both Billie Jean and Vonlee), pouring copious amounts of alcohol down his throat forcibly (maybe when he was so intoxicated that he couldn't mount a defense) and then placing that alleged pillow over his face to finish the job.

The decedent's body was found face up on the kitchen tile floor, the doctor wrote, *without any injury to the back of the head. . . .*

Now, if the doctors would have stopped there, one might ask how those injuries occurred. But the doctors then entered into speculative diagnosis—or maybe speculative *opinion*—when they followed in the addendum to the death certificate with the idea that Don falling on the kitchen floor should have been accompanied by at least some injuries to the head because they "would have been inevitable" when an individual fell fatally "from heavy intoxication."

But what if Don was so wasted he simply decided to lie

down and passed out on the floor? Maybe he put a hand
on the chair, used it to guide his drunken body down to
the floor, then flipped the chair over?

No one knew.

Certainly not these doctors.

What's more, the doctors added: *This finding is indicative of the repositioning of the body after death and the alteration
of the scene with the purpose to disguise this violent death as a
non-violent one.*

"Alteration of the scene"?

In other words, somebody staged the crime scene.

What a remarkable document, considering that the
certificate of death, under cause, had once reported
"acute alcohol intoxication" and "arteriosclerotic cardiovascular disease." A document that was then subsequently certified by the city clerk in the town of Troy.
Additionally, under item 29 on the original death certificate, where it asked if the medical examiner was notified,
Ortiz-Reyes answered affirmatively. So Dr. Dragovic was
told about Don's death and agreed with Ortiz-Reyes's initial findings on that Saturday morning. It was signed and
dated August 12, 2000. If one took this certificate of
death into account, it would appear that Don died of a
heart attack brought on by an "accidental overdose" of
alcohol.

Period.

So what happened to exacerbate this sudden change
in the OCME's opinion? This new judgment surrounding Don's death was the polar opposite to what it had
once been. There had to be more than a blood and urine
test leading these two distinguished men with nearly fifty
years' experience between them—not to mention thousands of autopsies—to draw this new conclusion that
would help to initiate an investigation into a murder?

And, of course, there was.

CHAPTER 18

IT STARTED WITH A phone call to the chief medical examiner by Detective Don Tullock on August 31, 2000. The TPD was having problems with Don Rogers's death, with or without the medical examiner's findings—there was something about the crime scene and information they were collecting that, for several experienced detectives, had a rotten odor to it. Even the officers present on the night the 911 call came in had issues with the way Don's legs were crossed, with a cup of water in the living room, as well as Billie Jean Rogers's overall demeanor. Usurping all of that, however, on the previous day, August 30, 2000, an explosive piece of information had come into the TPD, sparking the call to the medical examiner in the first place.

Bottom line: If cops did not sometimes rely on instinct, then very few murders would ever be solved. Here, now, the TPD not only had a "feeling" that Don's death was no accident, the information Zimmerman had collected on August 30 was enough to warrant an entire new look—by everyone—into the death of Don Rogers.

"We're investigating this case from a different perspective," Don Tullock, the lead detective, told Dr. Dragovic during a phone call to the medical examiner at some point after Don's death. "We'd like you to take another look at it."

"I can assure you that the lab does not dispose of the blood or vitreous fluid samples it collects. . . ."

"That's great. We are actively investigating this matter currently," Tullock concluded.

That phone call was followed up by a fax.

The fax was followed by a phone call from Tullock to the chief investigator for the medical examiner's office, Michael Dowd.

"Mike, listen, we have information . . . that foul play was involved."

"This is how it started," Dr. Dragovic later explained, "this whole process of reevaluation."

The TPD had been informed the OCME had signed off on accidental death due to alcohol intoxication. With the fax and the phone call, they were asking the medical examiner to go back and look again and take into account all that they had discovered (on top of that explosive information on August 30) and give a second opinion. Although it's not routine, there are plenty of instances when medical examiners change their opinions based on what investigators find out in the field. When a pathologist puts a death into the context of a law enforcement investigation and what cops have uncovered, some things that might not have made sense when initially conducting an autopsy now become quite clear.

After talking to the TPD, Dragovic found Ortiz-Reyes and sat down to have a chat.

"Listen, we have a very big surprise here and we are going to have more information regarding the Rogers case [coming in]." This conversation took place before Ortiz-Reyes had changed his opinion. "So hold on here with this for now."

Ortiz-Reyes said later the medical examiner, as often

happens when there are "surprises" in cases, then "took over."

Dr. Dragovic said he wanted Ortiz-Reyes to have a look at some of the police reports issued in Don Rogers's death. The TPD had developed some important information that was now imperative to the cause of death.

"They're telling me," Dragovic explained to Ortiz-Reyes, "that they have some information indicating that Mr. Rogers's death was not accidental or by natural causes. It was foul play. They even have a few suspects and they're investigating along those lines."

Ortiz-Reyes was obviously interested in this.

"I told them to continue and keep us informed."

Ortiz-Reyes said he understood.

The other possibility that Dragovic and Ortiz-Reyes talked about was that regardless what the studies showed and the "experts" reported regarding alcohol intake for severe, chronic alcoholics, Ortiz-Reyes later explained, "There are cases reported in which people were driving with higher than .5 of alcohol. So a .44 . . . it's like having a snack for them, for somebody that's used to drinking. . . ."

Ortiz-Reyes went on to agree that it was even possible for some with a .44 alcohol blood level to walk around on his or her own accord. Thus, if Don Rogers was drinking, as Billie Jean had told police, between one and two gallons of vodka per day, he was within this spectrum of those users. Don most likely woke up in the morning with a higher blood alcohol level than was legal to drive a car.

Dr. Dragovic told Ortiz-Reyes that someone would be by the office soon with photographs. The TPD wanted Ortiz-Reyes to have a look at photographs taken at the scene of Rogers's body. They wanted his opinion on a few things.

What was this new information the TPD had uncovered

the previous day, August 30, 2000? It certainly surprised
detectives, not to mention everyone else involved. In
fact, this "surprise" would not be the last one for law
enforcement involved in the investigation, which was
now substantially heating up around Don Rogers's so-
called "accidental death."

As additional detectives were brought in and the TPD
continued to investigate, learning all they could about
Billie Jean and Vonlee, what was to become a major
shock to all was about to emerge—and, boy, it would
change *everything*.

PART 2

In real life, unlike in Shakespeare, the sweetness of the rose depends upon the name it bears. Things are not only what they are. They are, in very important respects, what they seem to be.

Hubert H. Humphrey

CHAPTER 19

VONLEE'S "FIANCÉ" WAS A rugged-looking, somewhat overweight, dark-haired foreigner, who gladly bragged that he was the sole proprietor of a jewelry store. His shop, the one where Billie Jean made those large purchases in the days just after Don's death, was located in Oak Park, a twenty-minute drive south of Troy. Forty-year-old Danny Chahine was a transplant from Lebanon and had been in the United States since 1979. Danny had met Billie Jean and Vonlee at the Motor City Casino in late July when the two women started going out together, spending hours of their lives per week at the casinos in downtown Detroit.

Vonlee wasn't much of a gambler. So, as Billie Jean sat and gambled the nights and early mornings away, Vonlee wandered around, looking for something to do. That's how she met Danny. For Vonlee, there wasn't always a lot to do at the casino, besides drinking excessively. There were also many nights when Vonlee would have to pull Billie Jean off a slot machine or table or roulette wheel and literally drag her out of the place.

"Come on . . . let's go home," Vonlee would plead with her aunt.

"Just one more pull," Billie Jean would say.

"Please, Aunt Billie. Let's just go home."

Vonlee found herself "begging" her aunt on more occasions than not. Her aunt just didn't want to leave. It was always one more hand, just another dollar dropped down the throat of a one-armed bandit, one more go of the roulette wheel. One pull of the slot was too many, while a thousand pulls not enough.

"I didn't know anyone at the casino," Vonlee said later, speaking of those days before she met Danny Chahine. "I had only gone with my aunt because she wanted to go, and [Danny] was someone to talk to. . . . A lot of times, I would just sit and talk to him while he gambled. Sometimes I would gamble. . . ."

Since meeting in July, Danny and Vonlee dated regularly. Later, Danny would say he had seen Billie Jean and Vonlee at that particular casino about thirty times between June and August 2000, but it was clear he only saw Vonlee by Billie Jean's side during the latter portion of that time, because Vonlee was back home in Tennessee in June.

Danny liked Vonlee. She was attractive and fit the role of girl-on-your-arm, which he fashioned for her as they walked into the casinos together. Danny had the swagger of a regular, maybe even the clichéd, casino type: the cigar-smoking, potbellied, wannabe-rich man. Having a woman like Vonlee, whom he later referred to as beautiful as a supermodel, was one more prop for Danny's stage show.

For the most part, they'd go out to dinner and hang around Danny's place. For her, he was another guy in a long line that she viewed as caretakers—men to provide for the life she so much desired. Running the escort services in Chicago and Denver, Vonlee had gotten used to a certain lifestyle. She'd given it all up to move back home after the drinking and drugging got to be too much. Billie Jean, however, had indoctrinated Vonlee back into the nightlife game, and Vonlee now yearned on most nights to have her old life back, without making any attempt to drop everything and drive home. As it were, since living with Don and Billie Jean, Vonlee didn't have to work. Everything she did, the food she ate, the new clothes and jewelry she wore, even the car she now drove, was paid for by somebody else.

There was one night after Don's death when Vonlee took Danny out to a "very expensive restaurant at the casino," Danny later explained. It was a time when Vonlee (at least from where Danny saw it later) seemed to have more money than she knew what to do with it.

Vonlee looked at the wine list and ordered a costly bottle of the restaurant's finest.

They clinked glasses and smiled. It was romantic. Cozy. Nice. They were a couple enjoying a night out— at least in those initial moments after they sat down, that was what it seemed like. Vonlee liked Danny a lot, maybe even loved him.

"Good time, huh?" Vonlee said.

"It is."

"I have something to tell you," Vonlee announced, setting her glass down slowly, staring at her reflection. "It's about me." She took a sip from her wine, looked into Danny's eyes. Vonlee had been in this position before. She had a secret. It was time she shared it with Danny. He deserved to know.

"Vonlee, what is it?"

Vonlee took a pause and another sip of wine.

It was never easy.

CHAPTER 20

IT WAS LIKE GOING back to the old neighborhood where you grew up after not seeing it since childhood. Everything felt so much smaller, so much more crowded and cramped: the field where you played ball, it turned out, was just a patch of grass no bigger than a large garden; the biggest house on the block was a run-down, two-bedroom shack where five kids, a mother and father somehow managed to cram a life into; the road, which seemed like an expressway Mr. Frosty drove down after school every day in summers past, was only wide enough for one car; and your childhood home—it was so simple, so modest, plain and old-looking as you now stood in front of it wondering, *How the hell did we do it?*

That was how Vonlee Nicole Titlow felt: tricked by life's most treasured memories. She was someone else, always had been. She was a female trapped, screaming for someone to hear that she needed to be released. She was demanding that the soul inside the body with the penis and the hair growing all over it—which God had given her on the day she was born—wanted out.

Yes, Vonlee Nicole Titlow was actually born *Harry* Vonlee Titlow.

That was her legal name: *Harry.*

It sounded so manly, so masculine.

"Hey, Harry, stop by and take a look at my transmission."

"Harry, let's catch the football game on Sunday."

Harry.

Danny Chahine was about to find out, one could say, the hard way (although Vonlee would later say she had told Danny two weeks after meeting him). Both Vonlee and Danny recalled the story on this night the same, however: Danny was sitting, eating a nice dinner, sipping expensive wine with a person he believed to be the most beautiful *woman* in the entire building, maybe even the most gorgeous woman he had ever dated and had sex with.

"I'm really not a woman, Danny," Vonlee explained.

"What?"

"Danny, I'm a man."

The handful of times they'd had sex—which Danny later admitted (in court) included "intercourse"—had never caused any issues for Vonlee, she later told me. Vonlee insisted that she get on top and bounce on Danny. "I've had an operation for cancer. . . . You shouldn't look down there," she'd lie when they had gotten intimate the first time. "It's an ugly sight." From there, she simply covered her penis with blankets, and Danny had anal intercourse, which he mistook for vaginal, with a man he thought was a woman.

"Anal sex," Vonlee said later. "He didn't have a clue."

"There's nothing that I could tell she was a man," Danny explained in court later. "There's nothing. That's why I was very shocked."

Don Rogers died never knowing. The Cadillac dealer did not know. Neither did anyone at the casino Billie Jean or Vonlee had befriended. Nobody at Don's wake had a clue. Nobody ever asked. There was no reason to inquire. Vonlee wasn't one of those transsexuals you'd see coming a mile away: muscular calves, arms with the definition of a body builder, an Adam's apple, a masculine gait to her walk, hair on her arms and knuckles—wearing a dress and far too much makeup. She'd been on hormones for so long, Vonlee later said, she barely had a penis left at all.

"It shrivels up—it shrinks," Vonlee said. "Mine [was] basically gone."

And her breasts: a respectable, realistic large size—she had them done surgically many years ago. Every part of each breast felt and looked real, according to those who were in the know on that subject.

From head to toe, with the exception of—one could argue—the most important part, Vonlee came across as a female.

"Well, I've spoken to a lot of different psychiatrists," Vonlee later said when asked to clarify what a transsexual is, "and what they explained to me was, it's when a person is born in the wrong body or with the wrong gender and, therefore, they don't really call it a sex change. They actually call it a gender change, because you're actually changing your sex or your gender to become the sex that you are. So they look at you, as I am, a female, but with the wrong gender. So they're going to—when I have a change, it will be a *gender* change, instead of a sex change."

As they dined together in that posh restaurant, Danny's jaw was now squarely on the table. "No way," Danny said. "Uh-uh. I cannot believe it."

Danny stopped eating, he later admitted, "because I felt like throwing up. . . . I didn't believe her . . . because of what I had seen!"

"I'm a transsexual, Danny," Vonlee said. She tried to keep it together.

It doesn't match, Danny thought. "I don't believe you," he said again.

Danny noticed Vonlee was on the verge of breaking down into tears. He didn't want her to cry. The last thing he needed now was a scene at the restaurant.

"Danny, please believe me. I love you."

"Just hold on," Danny said. He could sense she was getting ready to cry.

As Danny soon found out, however, there was more to this night than Vonlee revealing that she was a trans-sexual.

She had another secret to expose.

"It's Don and what happened . . . the whole story," Vonlee said (according to Danny's recollection of this conversation).

It was the main reason why Vonlee had so much anxiety and emotional turmoil over the past weeks, or since Don's death. This was the reason why, she explained, she seemed to be so preoccupied and in a different place all the time. It was Don. Vonlee was carrying a heavy burden.

Danny was interested in what she was referencing. He'd had a feeling about Billie Jean ever since meeting and hanging out with the two of them. To Danny, the older woman was "cold." He said he "respected her" and she was a "classy woman," but there was something about her that Danny did not trust. "I have nothing against her. . . ." There was a time when Vonlee had told Danny that Don Rogers had expressed interest in adopting Vonlee and even putting her in his will, and Danny felt that it drove a wedge between the aunt and niece. But now this: something had happened to Don and it was no surprise to Danny that Billie Jean was involved.

"Just tell me the whole thing, Vonlee," Danny encouraged.

"I cannot take it anymore," Vonlee said. She then explained that she had just gone out to get her nails and hair done. "And I felt so bad spending Don's money."

"What happened?" Danny kept asking.

"I felt really, really bad spending his money. . . . I cannot do this anymore," Vonlee said. She had tears streaming down her face. She was nearly whispering.

"What do you mean?"

"My aunt Billie made me do it," Vonlee said. "I feel so guilty."

"What?" Danny persisted. "Do *what*?"

Was this going where Danny thought? Was Vonlee preparing to admit to something that would place Danny in a position where he was now involved, too? Danny had been in trouble with the law himself years before. He was trying to get his citizenship squared away. There was a lot at stake for him.

According to Danny Chahine's recollection of this conversation, Vonlee then said, "Listen, Danny, I need you to promise me something. I want to tell you the truth about everything. You cannot get upset or leave me, okay?"

"What's going on? Tell me. I won't leave or be upset. Von, what's happening?"

Vonlee said Don's death was not what people had thought it was.

This piqued Danny's interest even more. He had suspected as much. Yet, he changed the subject—and as they finished dinner, he was back to wanting to know for sure that Vonlee was a man. He still didn't believe her.

"Show me," Danny insisted.

"*Show* you?"

"Yes, I want you to take me out to the car and I want you to *show* me."

Vonlee gasped.

CHAPTER 21

IT WAS DIFFICULT FOR Vonlee to talk about the death of Don Rogers, especially what, in her view, actually happened inside 2090 Grenadier on that night. It was a tough conversation because Vonlee liked Don. Beyond a few personal issues with her own life, she had valued Don as a human being. She didn't see Don as the angry husband in desperate need of controlling his wife. To the contrary, in those days before Don's death, Vonlee was beginning to see Billie Jean as the domineering wife, addicted to gambling, pilfering her husband's bank accounts and spending all of their retirement money. Those passes Don had made at her? Vonlee shrugged off as a lonely and drunk guy simply wanting some affection from the opposite sex, craving a woman's attention that he wasn't getting from his wife.

Vonlee had indicated to Danny during dinner that Don might not have died the way in which her aunt said— that there was more to it. Thinking about it ever since Don's death, Vonlee told her boyfriend, she was sick to her stomach. It was all she thought about. Spending Don's money made Vonlee feel guilty. Vonlee wanted to leave and go back to Tennessee, but she felt she had to stay; Billie Jean didn't want her to leave.

"I felt sorry for her," Vonlee later explained, referring to her aunt during this period. "I couldn't believe that this person I had looked up to all my life had done something to her husband—and to me."

Billie Jean had a secret she wasn't sharing, either.

Vonlee was beginning to see that her aunt had invited her to Michigan to stay not as a thoughtful aunt looking to help out her niece, but perhaps so Billie Jean could, at the right moment, convince Vonlee to lie for her. Protect her. Provide an alibi Billie Jean might someday need.

Maybe even help her with the deed.

As far as Vonlee could tell, her aunt had a plan from the moment she walked into that Waffle House and convinced Vonlee to go back to Michigan with her.

A plan that involved getting rid of Don.

CHAPTER 22

VONLEE AND DANNY NEVER finished dinner. They were out in the parking lot walking toward Billie Jean's Cadillac. Soon as they sat inside the car, the only vehicle Vonlee and Billie Jean ever took to the casino, Danny started in on how he wanted a show-and-tell display. While Vonlee had been inside with Danny having dinner, letting him finally know about her manhood, teasing the idea that there was more to Don's death than what people thought, her aunt was gambling the night away, entirely oblivious to what Vonlee was doing.

"Show me," Danny insisted.

"No," Vonlee said. She wasn't some sort of sideshow or a carnival act. She was 99 percent female, just waiting to drum up the courage to go and get that final operation. She had her reasons why she had held off for so long—reasons that had nothing to do with the cost. But the "why" part of her decision was none of Danny's damn business. *He supposedly loves me,* Vonlee thought. *Well, here's a test to how much.*

"Most guys, when they found out," Vonlee explained, "didn't have a problem with it." Some had run, sure, but most were so impressed with Vonlee's looks that they were willing to wait it out and be there when she got the final operation. And Vonlee expressed what had been a definitive feeling inside her all her life that there was never any question about who she was. This wasn't a life crisis for her; she was a *female*. It was how she thought of herself. And everyone else that had known her thought of her that way, too.

"I can remember when I was, like, five, six years old and I was playing with dolls and wanted to dress in female clothing and I would get Christmas gifts like the Tonka toys or something, and I would immediately want my sister's Barbie dolls, instead. I've always just *felt* that way."

Vonlee never had a choice in the matter, according to her.

She agreed to allow Danny to touch her "down there," over her clothing.

He leaned in and put his hand on her crotch.

"But I didn't . . . I didn't feel anything," Danny later said.

Danny asked Vonlee about Don. If she wasn't going to drop her pants and show him the goods, he wanted to hear about Don and what Billie Jean had supposedly done.

Vonlee took a deep breath. It was time to come clean.

"We got home that night"—Vonlee began, according to Danny's later recollection of what was said inside the car on this night—"around eleven P.M. Don was lying on the floor in the kitchen, passed out."

It was getting chilly inside the car. Vonlee started it up and turned on the heat.

Continuing, she explained to Danny (according to his later testimony) that her aunt had told everyone they had arrived home about 3:00 A.M., the cops even a little later. She had mixed up the times: one to Don's family

(11:00 P.M.) and the other to her friends and the police (3:00 A.M.).

As they sat inside the car, Vonlee painted a somewhat vague picture of what happened next.[1]

"We got to do it now," Billie Jean said. She was standing over Don. They'd just come home from the casino.

"What?"

"It's a good time right now," Billie Jean continued. "He's on the floor."

If this was what Billie Jean actually said, in terms of Danny's choice of words to explain what Vonlee had allegedly told him, it would imply that there was a plan in place beforehand—premeditation. That one line— *"It's a good time"*—would imply as much.

"He's on the floor," Danny explained. "So [Vonlee] said they start pouring alcohol, vodka, in his mouth."

"Why are you wasting this good vodka on him?" Vonlee supposedly asked her aunt when she realized what Billie Jean was doing.

"The way they [did] it was one of them would hold his nose [and] he cannot breathe, [so] he opens his mouth," Danny said.

"Let's get some cheap vodka," Vonlee allegedly told her aunt.

"And he would not die," Danny continued. "She said that he would not die. When they were doing that, she said . . . he was playing with [Vonlee's] boobs."

"You've got to help me, Vonlee," Billie Jean said at that point. "You need to help."

At this point, with Don on the floor still alive and breathing, but totally out of it, Billie Jean allegedly told Vonlee that she would *"up the money from twenty-five thousand to fifty thousand."*

---

[1] I've chosen to put what was said in italics because there will be several versions of this narrative as this book continues. This one is Danny Chahine's recollection, as it was told to him the first time by Vonlee.

Money?

Danny gave the impression later that Vonlee said she and her aunt had made some sort of monetary agreement ahead of time: Billie Jean would pay Vonlee if she helped her kill Don.

"If he wakes up tomorrow, Vonlee, he'll know what we've done and there will be big trouble," Billie Jean said. *"We've got to do it right now!"*

As Danny later told this story in court, he explained how Vonlee, every time she tried to help her aunt, couldn't bring herself to go through with it. She'd hold his nose, but when he gasped for air, she'd let go and back away, scared and unwilling to follow through with a deed she apparently wanted no part of doing.

"I cannot do this, Billie. I just can't."

According to Danny, Billie Jean then got really pissed off at her niece.

"You're no help."

Danny said Vonlee told him that her aunt then left the room in a huff and came back sometime later with something in her hands.

A pillow.

While they sat inside the car outside the restaurant in the casino parking lot, by using her upper body to dramatize what happened next, Vonlee supposedly explained and demonstrated to Danny that her aunt had placed the pillow over Don's head and finished the job, suffocating her husband until he breathed no more.

"We threw the pillow and the empty bottles of vodka on the freeway," Vonlee told Danny. Vonlee was crying. She was upset. Yet, at the same time, she was quite relieved she'd gotten it off her chest.

"Come on, let's go back inside," Danny suggested.

As they walked toward the casino, Danny still felt that Vonlee might be lying about being a man. He had no idea why she would do such a thing, but based on what he had seen and the sex he'd had with her, it was hard for Danny to fathom that she was a male.

They found Billie Jean by a craps table.

"Give me some money," Vonlee told her aunt.

Danny stood by and watched as Billie Jean took out a bankroll, peeled off several hundred-dollar bills, then opened up a small notebook and marked inside how much she had given Vonlee, as if keeping tabs for some reason.

The next day, Vonlee met Danny at his house.

"Show me," Danny said. He was back on the male/female thing. It was clear he was serious.

Vonlee felt she had no choice at this point. She dropped her pants.

And he sat in total amazement, staring at a very small penis.

"You believe me now?" Vonlee said, lifting her trousers back up.

CHAPTER 23

DANNY CHAHINE WAS AT home a day after he learned not only that he had been dating (and had had sex with) a man he mistakenly thought was a woman, but also what he believed to be the truth about Don Rogers's death: the guy had been murdered.

Who was more culpable, Vonlee or Billie Jean? That was not for Danny to decide. What Danny needed to do was think about his next move. Danny had information about a murder. What he did with that information from this point forward would determine if he was involved or not. Furthermore, Danny had been trying to secure citizenship for almost two decades now. Whatever he did would impact the decision by the U.S. government. He realized he couldn't stay in the United States forever on a visa. Sooner or later, Uncle Sam would show up at the door with a plane ticket back to Lebanon.

Billie Jean had given Danny a bag full of several unlabeled videotapes after Don's death and told him it was porn and he could have it. She didn't want it in the house anymore. So, as Danny sat in his living room that day after having such a remarkable dinner with Vonlee, thinking about what his next move was going to be, he decided to relax and watch some porn.

He slipped one of the videotapes into his VCR.

Only it wasn't porn.

This one—out of what was seventeen tapes in the bag (sixteen of which turned out to be "adult films")—was a family video.

It was a wedding. A man who Danny thought was Don (he had never met Don in person) was having a great time with family and friends. "I see him playing with his kids, with his family . . . ," Danny said later. The video was nostalgic and emotional, Danny explained. He had lost his parents back home to murder and never knew why, when or where. He was only told they were victims of a double homicide. Watching "Don" and his family made Danny realize that the guy was a victim, a person whose life had been snuffed out for no reason. Don had people in the world who loved him. And Danny held on to information that could help answer some of the burning questions the family might still have.

"I decided I got to—I have to, for my conscience—I got to go and tell somebody about what I know," Danny recalled. "I mean, if I decided they're guilty—then they're guilty. . . . I had to go and tell someone."

Danny had a "friend" in the Bloomfield Township Police Department (BTPD), a nearby community to the west of Troy. They had met at a gas station Danny used to work at. They'd chat from time to time when the cop stopped in. Through that, they had developed one of those cop-citizen bonds. There were even times when people would try to pass bad checks at the gas station and Danny would have to make a report.

Danny took out the cop's phone number. Stared at it.

He'd know what to do.

So Danny picked up the phone and dialed the number. The one worry Danny had as the phone line rang was that he would be somehow implicated in the crime. Dragged into it by Vonlee and Billie Jean. After all, as Danny himself later admitted in court, "I got [a] . . . rap sheet." Plus, it was a bizarre story, to say the least. Danny had dated a man he thought was a woman, and that transsexual had just told him about a murder.

"So I was hesitant."

Indeed, it sounded like the makings of a trashy, true-crime TV movie from the 1980s, starring Susan Lucci.

Calling a friend, someone from within the community he knew and trusted, was enough for Danny to ask the cop for his advice regarding what he should do with the information. In the end, Danny believed that by doing the right thing and going to a friend who was a cop, that cop would vouch for him in some respects.

"I have a story to tell you," Danny began after the cop picked up. Then he proceeded to explain everything that had happened during the dinner he'd had with Vonlee.

"Wow," the cop responded.

Truly, what else was there to say?

"Can you tell them," Danny suggested, meaning the cops in Troy, "and see if they are interested in hearing it from me? If they are, I'll go in and talk to them."

"Yup, yup . . . don't worry. I'll have a detective call you. Don't go anywhere. Don't leave your house."

Danny said he'd wait.

After hanging up with Danny, the BTPD cop called the TPD. He explained what his "acquaintance" had told him.

"I know and trust him," the Bloomfield Township cop, who turned out to be a sergeant, told the TPD. "He has information about a murder that occurred in Troy during the past month that was made to appear to be a natural or accidental death."

CHAPTER 24

AS DANNY CHAHINE SAT and waited for the TPD to call him, he was both nervous and inspired by the decision he'd made to do what he believed was the right thing. He needed to relieve himself of this burden he felt Vonlee had placed on him without warning.

The phone rang.

It was TPD detective Donald Tullock.

"Can you meet with us here at the Troy PD?"

"I can."

Danny went down to the TPD. He sat inside an interrogation room. He asked if they were recording the interview.

The TPD told him no.

It was untrue. The entire interview was being videotaped.

Danny proceeded to give a detailed account, as he saw it, of the night he had gone out to dinner with his girlfriend/fiancée (or his boyfriend/fiancé?) and went home the same night thinking he knew absolutely nothing about this person. Danny focused specifically on what she had told him regarding Don's death.

"I can't believe it," he said in his broken English accent. "She's man."

Speaking with detectives, Danny came across as believable and trustworthy. Yet, when the TPD had a look at Danny's record, some credibility issues emerged. In fact, there was a time when Danny Chahine got into serious trouble for possession of cocaine. It was in 1987. The case was ultimately dismissed after the judge threw out some of the evidence against him. At the time, Danny had a green card, which meant he needed to stay out of trouble for five years in the country and work. The following year, 1988, Danny applied for naturalization. On the application, he was asked if he had ever been arrested. Danny said no.

"I didn't want to go back [to Lebanon]," he said later. "So I lied."

A year after that, in 1989, he was once again busted for possession of cocaine. This time, there was evidence and Danny pleaded guilty, and received several years' probation.

In 1990, when asked again, this time by the Immigration and Naturalization Service (INS), if he had ever been arrested, Danny lied a second time.

Despite all of these questionable actions, the U.S. government granted Danny Chahine citizenship in February 1993. Two years later, after the INS found out he had been lying to them, they charged him with illegally procuring citizenship and he pleaded guilty, receiving three years' probation. His citizenship was revoked. When he met Billie Jean and Vonlee, Danny was not a citizen of the United States, though he had reapplied and was waiting to hear.

As Danny got comfortable with the TPD, he talked about his life with Vonlee and the past several weeks. The day after Don Rogers died, Vonlee was upset; she was crying and hysterical. She called, Danny explained, and wanted to talk about what happened.

"Calm down and speak," Danny told his girlfriend. It was in those hours after the cops had left the Rogers house on the day Vonlee and Billie Jean claimed they found Don on the kitchen floor.

"I need to see you," Vonlee pleaded.

They made plans to meet the following day.

That next day, Sunday, August 13, Danny showed up at the Rogers household. He walked in and noticed that Billie Jean was rather casual, upbeat and even happy. She went about her business as if nothing had happened.

Vonlee was a wreck.

Danny looked at the new widow. He couldn't believe her demeanor. He thought: *What the heck? If my spouse had died the day before, I'd be very upset, crying. . . .*

"I need to get out of here," Vonlee told Danny. "I cannot be here. . . . I need to leave. . . ."

Off they went.

In those days after Don died, Danny and Vonlee had several conversations about the Rogers'es. According to Danny, Vonlee told him Don had "ten million" in the bank.

"How did he die?" Danny asked Vonlee during one conversation they had that same week of Don's death. The scene was still raw for Vonlee; she was terribly distressed.

"The police came and they were asking way too many questions, Danny," Vonlee explained.

"Why were they asking so many questions?"

"I don't know. . . ."

Danny was suspicious then, he later claimed. He asked Vonlee, "Why would the police come and ask all these questions? Have you or Billie done anything?"

"I'll tell you everything later," Vonlee supposedly responded.

As he thought about it over the course of that week, Danny was "shocked" that Don had died so suddenly. It wasn't his health. Danny, after all, did not know much about Don. He had never met him personally. During the time he had known the two women, Danny was under the impression that Billie Jean wanted to "get rid of Don."

Why?

"Billie will pay twenty-five thousand dollars to get rid of Don," Vonlee told Danny after he picked her up for a date, he claimed. They were heading out to dinner. It was a few weeks before Don's death.

There was another time, Danny told the TPD as he sat and recalled what had happened, when he picked up Vonlee and she seemed totally distraught, completely out of it. They sat in the driveway for a few minutes and talked.

"What's wrong?"

"Don and Billie are fighting."

Danny said that from outside, while they sat in his car, he could actually hear them screaming at each other.

"Over what?" Danny asked Vonlee as they pulled out.

"A thirteen-thousand-dollar credit card bill of Billie's—she used the money for gambling."

The detectives asked Danny if Vonlee had ever told him why she came up from Tennessee to be with her aunt. Was there a reason she had ever given?

"Yes," he said. "To help her 'do something.' Billie wanted a divorce from Don, but she didn't want to lose. Billie catch Don and [Vonlee] in compromising position and she will have something on Don."

The impression Danny gave was that Billie wanted Vonlee to set Don up with regard to him making a pass at her.

Then Danny told the TPD about the conversation he'd had with Vonlee over dinner the night before, and what she said after she admitted that she was a man.

Danny agreed to return to the TPD the following day. Walking out of the station house, he felt a bit apprehensive about a few things the TPD had asked of him. Danny was no rat bastard. He was turning in murderers, he believed. They must pay. He couldn't walk away from that dinner and not do anything. But what the TPD had asked of him, well, it was something Danny didn't really want to do. Yet, as he thought about it more and more that night, Vonlee's ("former") boyfriend felt it was his obligation.

It needed to be done.

CHAPTER 25

VONLEE'S GRANDMOTHER IN TENNESSEE was the one person in Vonlee's life whose opinion and advice Vonlee valued and respected more than most others. Vonlee had always looked up to the matriarch of the family, Annis Lee, a woman who never judged Vonlee, pushed her into doing "boy things" as a child or made jokes about Vonlee's gender issues. In fact, when she felt she was in trouble and didn't know what else to do, Vonlee went and spoke quite often to Billie Jean's mother.

Vonlee had called her grandmother and explained what she believed happened the night Don died. During the phone call, Vonlee went into detail, telling Annis what she remembered about the night, what time she and Billie Jean returned home and what her aunt had done. Vonlee was honest with Annis, telling her grandmother that she was pretty plastered that night and had drunk a lot of booze all day long.

"My grandmother was a very, very smart woman, very country, but very smart," Vonlee commented later.

She had called home to Annis because Vonlee was facing a moral dilemma: Should she go to the cops with what she knew and tell them what she could recall from the night? Or should she just allow time to take its course? Whatever was going to happen would ultimately happen, Vonlee surmised. Her aunt was involved in a lot of things post Don's death that Vonlee had no idea about. She had given Vonlee tens of thousands of dollars by this point and Vonlee felt that it was blood money. She was conflicted and confused, she later said.

"It all comes back to . . . you know," Vonlee later told me, "like, why I finally told Danny about my gender. I wanted to be honest. I thought that unless I start being completely honest with myself and totally honest about everything, I'm not going to get any better. I wouldn't get anywhere."

She was, mainly, speaking of her lapsed sobriety.

"Even Danny was telling me, right from the beginning, when I first met him, that he believed [my aunt] was not a nice person."

Now Vonlee wanted her grandmother's advice—what should she do?

The original call Vonlee had made to her grandmother, as Vonlee told her about the night of Don's death, didn't turn out the way Vonlee had imagined it might. Annis said, "You know it didn't happen that way. . . . You *know* it didn't, Vonlee."

Vonlee's grandmother didn't want to believe what Vonlee was saying about her daughter.

"I needed someone to understand what was going on with me," Vonlee recalled. "I was contemplating killing myself and taking it very seriously. I was thinking about, for the first time in my life, I'm done. I'm out. I couldn't take it anymore."

She was looking for someone to talk her out of it.

When Vonlee's grandmother failed to respond the

way in which Vonlee had assumed she would, Vonlee's mother, Georgia Pinkerton, got on the phone.

Vonlee told her mother what happened to Don, concluding with, "I am thinking about going to the police."

Georgia was shocked. "I'll talk to Billie," she said.

A day or so later, Georgia called and spoke to Billie Jean, a conversation Georgia relayed to Vonlee later that night.

Billie Jean took on a dark, cold tone with her sister after Georgia explained what Vonlee had said earlier in the day. "If you or Vonlee go to the police," she allegedly warned, "I will make sure that your son spends the rest of his life in prison. I'll make sure of it, Georgia. I have enough money now and enough influence."

"Your son . . ."

Georgia could tell that her sister was serious when she referred to Vonlee as "your son."

When Vonlee spoke to her mother later on, Georgia said, "Listen, Vonlee, she's capable of that."

Vonlee took this to mean: *Do not go to the police. Let it play out.*

"Why didn't anybody warn me, tell me about Billie before I came out here?" Vonlee asked her mother.

"Everyone did, Vonlee. But you acted like she could do no wrong. Y'all never listened to anybody, anyway— not *ever.* Even your uncle told you, 'Billie's the Devil.' You would *not* listen to him."

CHAPTER 26

WITH LIFE IN A dismal downward spiral for Billie Jean Rogers, with law enforcement now creeping and sniffing around, seeking information about Don's death, the widow pushed it all to the side on September 1, 2000, in order to satisfy what was, according to those who knew her best, a gambling addiction that had taken total control of her life long before Don's death.

Vonlee had not gone to the casino with her on this night. She was home waiting for Danny to pick her up. They had dinner plans. Vonlee had no idea, obviously, that two detectives from the TPD had wired Danny's truck with a transmitter underneath the seat, which was connected to a recording device. Vonlee trusted Danny. She was looking to talk to him, hoping that he would be there for her and help her through a really bad time.

"I looked to Danny as someone that was going to help me," Vonlee said later. "If he would have come to me and said, 'I'm going to the police, I need you to go with me,' I would have gone with him. He was a smart man. I thought, 'If I tell him the truth, he'll know what to do.'"

It seemed to Vonlee that Danny still had intimate feelings for her. Why else would he still be hanging around?

Before heading over to pick up his date, Danny stopped by the TPD so experts could wire up his truck, a black Suburban, with a digital recording device.

"Oh, look at you! Look. At. You!" Danny said, greeting Vonlee as she stepped into his truck, the recording machine picking up every word.

Vonlee was dressed to the nines.

"Had my hair redone. . . ."

"Look at you. Why you didn't tell me you going to be dressed up like that?"

They made small talk as Danny pulled out of the driveway and began the drive to the casino. Danny could turn on the charm when he needed. He said, "I can't believe the way you look. I swear to God, you just, you look like a model. What did you do?"

"I used to be a model," Vonlee said, lapping up the attention.

"I know. . . ."

Vonlee said she had finally stopped drinking. She was feeling so much better now. Her skin even felt smoother since she'd stopped.

It was a lie, Vonlee said later. "I was still drinking, just not quite as much as I was right after Don died."

"I went to the doctor," Vonlee told Danny.

"What doctor?"

"She put me on nerve medicine."

"*Nerve* medicine?" Danny said, surprised. "For what?"

"I'm a nervous wreck."

"You are a nervous wreck and I . . . You know what?" Danny sounded as though he'd wanted to say something, but then had changed his thought for some reason he failed to explain. Instead, he added: "If I was you, I would leave that house. I would *leave* that house."

"She's got me on Xanax 'cause I . . . haven't been drinking. . . . That drinking was *killing* me."

Vonlee later said she "was in another world as all of

this was going on." For her, going to a psychiatrist was a last resort. There were many nights when she sat at her aunt's house contemplating putting a rope around her neck and checking out. "I'm like . . . drinking and drinking . . . lying about it . . . and then the psychiatrist puts me on the Xanax." Everybody around Vonlee and Billie Jean—Don's kids, Billie Jean's kids—had been asking what in the name of God was wrong with Vonlee? She was so distraught all the time.

So withdrawn.

So docile and depressed.

Was she taking Don's death that badly? And if so, why? She hardly knew the man.

Inside the truck, as detectives listened, Danny tried to convince Vonlee that drinking again with him when they got to the restaurant would help her. She didn't need to quit altogether. Just slow down a bit. Danny was hoping that drinking would relax Vonlee when they got there and she would once again open up.

He said, "Drinking's helping you because—"

Vonlee interrupted. "It is *not* helping me. It is killing me. Drinking makes me even more nervous and more depressed."

"Yeah, you should, I mean, how—" Danny started to speak before she cut him off again.

"Fucking drinking drove me to kill somebody," Vonlee said.

"Drinking drove you to *kill* somebody?"

"Well, it helped," she added.

Later, Vonlee explained to me that what she meant was if she had not been drinking that night, she could have saved Don from what had happened. "I could have stopped it," Vonlee said. She felt morally bankrupt because of the booze and it was one reason why her aunt had taken advantage of her on that night. She had beaten herself up since Don's death: *If I wasn't drinking . . . I could have prevented what happened.* "I'm not saying that I shouldn't take responsibility . . . but was I wrong morally. Yeah, I was in a very fragile state." And her aunt knew this, Vonlee claimed.

Danny let it go. He realized that he did not need to ply Vonlee with alcohol in order to get her to talk about Don's death. A few minutes into their conversation and she had given him a money quote already.

"Drinking drove me to kill somebody."

Vonlee was feeling a fevered "hatred" for her aunt grow each day as she realized she had been used.

Danny took a breath. They were stopped at a traffic light. Then he blurted out: "No, it's not drinking that drove you to kill somebody—greed, I think, from your aunt."

"If I had not been drinking," Vonlee told him, "I would have never have been there in a million years. No way . . . no way. And my mother called and asked me about it today."

"What did she say?"

"I said, 'Well, you know, those detectives came over. The kids are suspicious and everything.' She said, 'I think everybody's a little suspicious.'"

"Everybody, I'm sure."

They continued to talk about Georgia Pinkerton and Billie Jean Rogers. Vonlee's mother was a bit apprehensive regarding her sister's true motivations in life. Moreover, Georgia worried about Vonlee being influenced by her aunt as she continued to live with her.

If her mother thought Vonlee had ever been involved with hurting Don in any way, Vonlee explained to Danny as he hit the gas and took off from the intersection, she'd have a "nervous breakdown."

"Oh, God," Danny said, trying as best he could to stay out of the way and allow Vonlee the space to bury the knife deeper into her back.

Vonlee continued about her family as Danny patiently listened.

"Do I look better?" Vonlee asked at one point. She pointed to her hair.

"You look much better," Danny said.

Vonlee mentioned how she had gotten the color of her hair changed. It felt good. And she was staying home now more and not going to the casino as often, not drinking, but still taking Xanax.

"Now you're rich woman," Danny said, indicating that Vonlee could do what she wanted at this point.

"Well, no. I'm going to quit killing myself," Vonlee said, before adding how she was even thinking about working out again. "I used to work out three days, three times a week, and everything."

"You don't need to work out. You got muscles like, uh, big muscles and, uh, you know," Danny said before stopping himself, realizing he was digging a transgender hole for himself he would have a hard time talking his way out of.

Vonlee kept returning to her family back in Tennessee and how her aunt didn't want much to do with anybody and hadn't, according to them, sent any money down there since she'd come into it. Vonlee couldn't understand why.

She didn't mention—because she didn't know—that her aunt had given her mother one hundred thousand dollars toward a house in those days after Don's death.

"I didn't get no money from her, you know," Vonlee said for some reason. "I'm not greedy." Vonlee was looking at Danny strangely. Sizing him up. She was wondering why he was asking certain questions. And why he had suddenly become so quiet.

"Maybe she's short on cash. Maybe she doesn't have cash," Danny said.

"Who? Billie?"

"Yeah . . . how much cash she got?"

"She has access to nine million dollars," Vonlee said.

"What do you mean—nine million dollars? She probably . . . It's all in stocks and bonds and stuff like that. How could . . ."

Vonlee leaned toward Danny and whispered: "She has over two hundred and fifty thousand dollars in her bank account."

"Cash money?"

"Cash! She wrote me a hundred-thousand-dollar check out of it."

"She gave you a *hundred*-thousand-dollar check? She gave you that check? It's in your bank account?"

"Yes, I have. I can . . . I have . . . It's in my name. . . ."

Danny said something along the lines of why couldn't her aunt help her sister down in Tennessee if she had all kinds of money to throw around, but Vonlee squinted an eye and stared at him.

She was thinking.

There was a moment of silence between them.

Then Vonlee asked: "You're not recording this or anything?"

CHAPTER 27

DANNY CHAHINE ALMOST DROVE off the road.

"No," he said. ". . . Are you crazy?"

Vonlee was looking at Danny with a curious eye. She paused.

Danny stared back at her.

"Are you going to blackmail both of us?" Vonlee asked. She was concerned that he knew what happened inside the house that night Don had died and was going to take the opportunity to crack his knuckles, flex his arms and maybe come up with a plan to want some money for keeping his mouth shut.

"No fucking way," Danny said.

As Danny thought about it later, the signs had always been there. He thought back to a few days after Don had died. He had gone over to the house to console Vonlee, who was "crying a lot . . . like she couldn't" at first "talk" to anyone about anything that had happened, without breaking down.

Vonlee had opened the door and let Danny in. Her aunt was home.

"Come, follow me," Vonlee said. Billie Jean was upstairs in her room. "See it?" Vonlee explained, walking in, pointing toward her aunt, who had one of Don's suits spread out on the bed.

"Hey," she said when she saw Danny. She seemed lively and excited and, well, happy, according to Danny.

"Hi, Billie . . . I'm so sorry about what happened to Don," Danny said, sharing his condolences.

Billie Jean didn't seem at all hurt or upset. She was okay.

Vonlee and Danny went downstairs. "She wants to do it right away," Vonlee whispered.

"Do what?"

"Cremate him."

"Oh, shit . . . so the suit is for him to be cremated in?"

"Yeah . . . and she's pushing for it to happen as soon as possible. . . ."

As they continued talking inside Danny's truck on the way to the restaurant, at one point Vonlee turned and looked at Danny: "Billie told me, 'Yeah, Danny will be [an] alibi for us, then he'll be fucking blackmailing us . . . !'"

Danny said, "I don't want to be no alibi to nobody, because I didn't see nothing. I didn't hear nothing."

"We were with you, though," Vonlee said, letting Danny know that he was involved.

"In the casino?"

"Yeah."

"Yeah, okay. I'm safe. Do whatever . . . you want. . . ."

They talked about money.

About her aunt and the cars her aunt had bought.

About Danny becoming someone who could, if needed, help them.

"I don't know why I trust you so much," Vonlee said.

"Don't trust me. Forget about this. Don't! I don't want to hear anything."

"Well, I do."

"I just want to go . . . to dinner."

Vonlee said her aunt's biggest problem with Don's kids was the fact that she had told them she and Vonlee had arrived back at home at 11:00 P.M., when the police report said 3:00 A.M. Vonlee was certain that one mistake was going to come back and bite her aunt.

"So why would she lie like that then?" Danny asked.

"'Cause she didn't think it was any of their business that she was at the casino."

Vonlee shouldered the burden of her life by drowning it in alcohol. She never once saw herself as "different" or less than; it was no mistake or error by God to have been born inside a male body. Rather, it was her life, complicated and important, as she understood it. Yet here she was in the middle of what appeared to be a murder, regardless of how it was packaged and sold to her boyfriend. If what Vonlee was saying during this ride to the restaurant was true, Billie Jean Rogers had murdered her husband—with Vonlee's help.

Danny explained that if they had told the police the right time that they had gotten home, they had "nothing to worry about." Didn't matter what they told Don's kids.

Vonlee said something about Don's body being cremated and the investigation being over, because of that. But now that Danny knew what really happened, they might have something to worry about all over again.

"But somebody like you comes along and tries to blackmail her," Vonlee suggested again.

"No, I'm not . . . gonna blackmail nobody. I don't

wanna blackmail nobody. I'm minding my own business. I want to go to dinner and have fun."

"You can't prove it," Vonlee said. She became passive and discreet. Then: ". . . I just want you to know I would never, ever, ever, hurt anybody. I don't know what in the fuck happened. I don't even really remember exactly what happened. I was so drunk."

Danny needed to pull Vonlee back around and steer her into talking about details.

"You do?" he asked.

"I know she got a pillow over his face," Vonlee admitted. "I do remember that. . . . She's the one that poured the vodka in his mouth. She did most everything and she even told me. . . . She said, 'I did all the work.'"

Danny said there was no way Vonlee could have helped her aunt because Vonlee was so wasted.

"Well, no," Vonlee corrected. "I kept letting go, I couldn't do it." It wasn't the booze, she insisted. It wasn't right, morally speaking, and she wasn't going to be part of it—that's why she stopped herself. Not because she was smashed.

"I couldn't do it . . . and I poured just a little bit of vodka down his throat, and she says, 'Oh, hell!' and just poured it up his nose. But it's sad and it's over."

"Please. Please," Danny said. "I don't wanna hear about this stuff. . . ."

"You're the only person I can talk to about it."

"I know, but it's just, it makes me feel sad that what happened, all that, you know. . . ."

Vonlee then explained how Don had fallen on the floor "by himself." They hadn't pushed him down or made him get on the ground. Earlier that night, after dinner, he was already really drunk and in the kitchen. "When we were there, we were sitting in the living room and he got up out of the kitchen and he just went. . . ."

"He was passed out?" Danny asked.

"Yeah."

Danny suggested that Vonlee bring her aunt with her to her therapist appointment scheduled for the following day. Vonlee's aunt needed to talk to someone about what was going on in her life; Danny added, "She's losing her mind and I think it's all because of what she did. She's losing it."

"Well, she kind of acts like it doesn't bother her, but, you know, it's got to bother anybody."

"I don't care how strong she is."

"I mean, at least, I mean, I don't have an excuse for what I did, but I was so fucking drunk that I don't even remember. I started drinking that morning and, sure, I drank all day. . . . She was sober."

"And I think she used you. I think she used you bigtime. I think the whole purpose of you coming over here . . . ," Danny said, before he called Billie Jean "sick." As he spoke, Danny tried to reconcile the woman that killed her husband with the woman he had known as nothing more than a gambler. At face value, the two personalities didn't seem to mesh; yet as he looked deeper into his memory bank, he could sense, when around Billie Jean, a devilish, devious person inside her just waiting to come out.

"But I've done it, too," Vonlee reminded him. "You have to realize that. So I'm not normal, either."

"You're not 'normal, either'?" Danny said, sounding as though Vonlee had made the understatement of the century. Then he got serious, asking: "You're not gonna kill me, are you?"

CHAPTER 28

THE TONE INSIDE THE vehicle during the drive to the restaurant took on an ominous air after Danny Chahine, however jokingly, asked his girlfriend if she and her aunt were planning to kill him now that he knew their secret.

Vonlee shrugged it off and was more interested in talking about how bad she felt. How deeply sorry she was that she had been involved at all. The way she described her contribution to what was, effectively, a murder, there was no doubt she felt responsible in some way and it was slowly beginning to control her every waking hour.

"I . . . I think about it twenty-four hours a day, seven days a week. If I feel one little bit of happiness, I feel guilty for killing him. . . . If I got struck down by lightning right now, I deserve anything I get."

Was it guilt? Was it worry and dread? Was it concern? Was she afraid of going to prison?

Danny didn't know what to say. "I hear you," he repeated four times before adding, "I'm an outsider."

"But I cannot go the rest of my life. I have asked God to forgive me and I've prayed every night and I know what I did is wrong. And I'm like, 'Whatever you feel is right, God, do it. I mean, whatever you need.'"

Danny kept saying he was an outsider looking in; he couldn't imagine how she felt. He only knew that a man had died and the victim's wife had been the driving force behind the death.

Vonlee started to cry as she broke into a lengthy story of her life and how things had never really worked out for her the way in which she had ever planned. She spoke of God and her belief that, inherently, she had been a good person. All she wanted was for her "life to get together." She talked about how she was constantly asking God for a way out of this latest mess. "Show me a way so I can have my surgery and have a normal life," she told Danny. Seemingly justifying the crime, she then added: "I asked God and so maybe He was getting ready to take Don, anyway, and . . . He gave me an opportunity to get my life together? I don't know. But that's what . . . kind of comes to me—because everything is falling into place for me."

Carrying on, Vonlee next explained how, since Don was gone, her life was falling into order in ways she could have never dreamed. Vonlee said she had just met a woman who wanted "to do the beauty salon thing with me." She wrestled with the idea that if she had done any-thing wrong, then "bad things should be happening to me. Not good things. But I have asked for forgiveness and, I mean, I think He knows that I'm . . . that I'm a *good* person. . . . He knows that what happened to me was that I was a victim. I really think *I* was a victim. I really do. Everything that was going on, I mean, she knew how bad I wanted my surgery. She knew how fucked up I was about telling you my situation. . . . You know, I mean, I was just crazy. I mean, she could've stopped it. She could've just said 'no.'"

Danny needed a narrative of what happened. Vonlee

was talking, and that was good. She was admitting her role in the crime and telling him—as she had suspected, he was recording everything—how the crime came to be, unknowingly drowning herself.

She mentioned how when her aunt first brought up the idea of killing Don, Vonlee believed it was a joke. "Then she says, 'I'll give you money' . . . and I, honest to God, just thought it was a big old joke at first. And then she got real serious, and then after she really got into it . . . [and said], 'Well, we can't stop now. He'll know we were killing him.'" Vonlee paused, then changed her thought and was back to asking Danny to support her: "Okay. But you just have got to not, I mean, you've got to understand, if we're going to be friends or whatever, that this is not something . . . I'm not that type of person. I mean, I'm not."

"I know you're not," Danny said.

The drive from Troy to Detroit with traffic was a solid hour. Vonlee had opened up. She spoke of her motives for not wanting Don dead, but also what the future without him held for her: a beauty salon and her full transformation into a female, totally complete, with the final operation.

Danny tried to convince Vonlee that she and her aunt had participated in a "mercy killing," as he put it.

Vonlee didn't think so at first, but Danny persisted.

Then she talked about how Don "was ready to go," anyway. She had even considered that he did have a heart attack that night, which might have been the reason for him falling onto the floor. Vonlee had even told Billie Jean how close to death she once thought Don was; he bled all the time, Vonlee said, quite clearly justifying his death for her own spiritual benefit.

They then got onto the subject of Billie Jean's true motivation and Vonlee tried to come up with a reason why her aunt wanted Don dead. Danny made a point when he asked why they had not waited until Don died, suffice it to say if he was so close to death? Danny was curious. Don was sick and bleeding from his rectum and knocking on death's door. Why push him over the edge and risk prison if Billie Jean only had to wait a little longer?

"She may have been tired of cleaning up blood . . . ," Vonlee responded. "She may have been tired of him trying to grab everybody's . . . my ass every time he turned around, or my tits, which he was. She may have been tired of him drinking to the point of where they couldn't go on vacation or anything. . . ."

"She lived with him for *sixteen* years," Danny said, making a good point.

"She put up with it," Vonlee said.

"You had to kill an old person?" Danny asked, raising his voice a bit. "An old person! He's dying! Why would you kill somebody that's dying? You see, you . . . Look what you're doing to yourself and look what she's doing to herself. The guy was dying!"

This comment made Vonlee mad. She said she didn't need any bullshit from Danny right at that moment. She was torturing herself enough over what had happened.

They argued about this for quite some time. Then Danny became impatient and said: "Let's find the restaurant, please. I need a drink. I'm ready to collapse. I need a drink."

Vonlee was talking more to herself when she then said: "I don't know why! It was not the money. I didn't even think I was going to get no hundred thousand dollars. I thought she was going to give me, I mean, I started, was like joking. You think I'd kill somebody for twenty-five thousand dollars? Fuck no! Twenty-five thousand dollars can't even buy you a car."

"I know."

"I can make that in a month . . . ," Vonlee said, meaning with her escort business.

"I know."

There was a lull in the conversation and they continued talking as Danny realized he was lost. Vonlee had been talking about what her aunt did after the police left on that day of Don's death.

"I'm lost. I'm lost. I need, we need to . . . stop at the gas station."

This was a new restaurant near the casino they had never eaten at before and Danny was having trouble finding it. Or so he claimed.

They found their way after stopping and asking someone for directions as a bit of an argument began. Vonlee said, "You can't flip out. And don't you tell *anybody* anything."

Vonlee was now paranoid. She began looking around the inside of Danny's truck, lifting up things and searching through the glove compartment to see if he was hiding some sort of recording device.

"I don't . . . trust anybody with anything. You got a tape recorder in here?" she asked.

"You're weirding out. You're just freaking out on me. You're freaking out on me."

Vonlee decided she didn't want to talk about Don's murder anymore. She wanted to go back home.

"I'm taking you to dinner . . . ," Danny insisted.

"I'm searching this truck to make sure there's nothing in here."

As Danny pulled into the parking lot of the restaurant, they discussed how "small" the place looked and Danny suggested that if they didn't like the look of the menu, they could go somewhere else.

Without warning, Vonlee then turned the conversation back to death. "Well, I've lost about—" she began to say.

"Five friends from drugs?" Danny finished.

"No, um, from AIDS."

"Oh, AIDS?"

"They died of AIDS."

"Now you're scaring *me* . . . ," he said.

"Why?"

"Shit," Danny said.

"I don't have it."

"Oh, God," Danny said, realizing he'd had anal sex with Vonlee on a number of occasions.

"You don't have to worry about it," Vonlee said reassuringly.

They both got out of the truck. Slammed the doors—and were now out of earshot of the recording/listening device strapped underneath the driver's-side seat of Danny's vehicle.

CHAPTER 29

HARRY VONLEE TITLOW FELT like a girl all her life. There was never any question about her gender in Vonlee's heart, mind or, for that matter, body. For as long as she could recall, Vonlee felt, thought and acted as if she had been born a female in a male body. Photos from early childhood depict a charming, cute baby. School photos from Harry's grammar school years show a boy with dirty blond hair, which was straight and thin and a little long, blue eyes, with a look of clarity and even happiness on his young face. Harry/Vonlee was one of those children you look at and can see either gender in the subtlety of his/her features. In the few school photos that still exist, Harry seems like a content child, smiling; his arms are folded in front of himself, his boyish qualities very much obvious because of the choice of clothing and hairstyle. Yet, you look closely and you see something different about this young person; there is something delicately effeminate and altogether natural. You see a girl inside.

Vonlee grew up in the town of Maryville, Tennessee, in a neighborhood known as Vestal of about two thousand souls, give or take. Just south of Knoxville, Vestal is low-rent, low-cost housing. It's a neighborhood atmosphere, where people hang out during the warmer months on their front porches, praise God on Sundays, bring food to the neighbors when a loved one passes and wonder what life is like for those with the means and money to live worry-free.

"Since she came from pauper roots," said one local who knew Vonlee well, "she had nothing but dollar signs in her eyes all her life. I'm betting the first time some dude paid her for her time as an escort, there was no stopping her. That was her way out and she probably looked up to Billie for making it out of this shitty little town. . . . I know people raised there in that same small community where Vonlee, her mom, and Billie were all raised, and it is still very much rough and tumble. Prospects for a life outside of Vestal are slim for a lot of people there, and Billie made it out probably like no other."

For the most part, Vonlee insisted, "My grandmother raised me." They lived in what she called a "very country setting." This was the South, where people spoke with a noticeable drawl, listened to old-school country music— Merle Haggard, Hank Williams, Johnny Cash and the like—and rode big green tractors to the neighborhood store when they didn't have a vehicle. Chickens. Gardens. Red barns. Fences in need of repair. Dirt roads. Blue jeans. Cowboy boots. Chewing tobacco. Rolling hills of acreage available for farming.

Every country cliché you can imagine packed into one setting.

That was Vestal and its surrounding communities.

It was hard later for Vonlee to answer the question of what she and the local kids did for fun, because there wasn't much to do in the area during the early 1970s when she was coming of age. Knoxville, although not far away, seemed to be in another world. And Nashville, forget it: off-limits to these kids living in modest homes passed down from generation to generation.

"We played house, dolls and dollhouses," Vonlee recalled. She'd never had a tool bench, a Hot Wheels car or a holster and cap gun; Vonlee had a Betty Crocker oven and Barbie dolls.

On some nights, the kids would all gather in a field somewhere and use glass jars to run around and capture fireflies.

"In the South," she added, "that's the big thing kids do—catch lightning bugs."

It was during this time, when she was seven or thereabouts, maybe a little older, when Vonlee began to realize not that she was different, but people that had not known her all her life were perceiving her as being different.

"I'm the mother," she'd say when one of the kids suggested playing house.

"Okay."

There was never any question, really, among the kids. It seemed right for Vonlee to play the role of the female.

She would always want to play the female in whatever imaginative game or situation they found themselves involved in.

It was a life back then, so different from today, when a child's world revolved around being outside all the time, not sitting on the couch, eyes glued to a computer, electronic gadget or video game. You made your own fun. It was innocence at its core. There were no rules. You were confined only to the scope of your imagination.

"We played hard and didn't go in until we were forced to."

Even back then, as a youngster, everyone called her Vonlee, she said. It was never Harry. Harry seemed so foreign and unlike a child's name, anyway. She had been named after a cousin "Vonray" and her grandmother

"Annis Lee," her mother taking the "Von" and "Lee" and putting them together.

"It stuck," she said. "Plus, it was a cross-gender name. I still love it."

One might wonder when it was Vonlee herself felt different, or had an inclination that there was something different about her.

"I have always just known," she recalled.

Vonlee said she believes her mother and grandmother "knew [from my] very young age" that she was a female living inside a male's body. The reason why she moved in with her grandmother around this time was not something Vonlee wanted to go into detail about, she insisted, although moving in with her grandmother, she said, was just easier. It was not that Georgia wanted to toss Vonlee out and despised her child for the way in which she was born, but rather Vonlee's grandmother was more accepting and understood Vonlee better. It took a while for Georgia to accept that Vonlee was not a boy and that she would likely go on in life and live as a female.

"Everywhere I went with them," Vonlee explained, "even as young as I can recall, people would say 'she.' 'Can "she" come with us? Can "she" come out and play?'"

No one in her immediate circle referred to Vonlee as a boy. But Georgia would "get very irate and sharp with the person" that referred to her son as a "she." This caused the beginning of a wedge to be driven between a mother and her child.

"She kind of went off on them if they said anything like that," Vonlee remembered. "And she kind of would take it out on me, too. Whereas my grandmother just *loved* me. She understood me. She let me play with the dolls. She let me grow my hair and wear nightgowns to bed. She let me *be* a little girl. Thank God I had her in my life."

Part of it was that Georgia was "one of these women where everything is going to be perfect," Vonlee explained. "You ever seen the movie *Mommie Dearest* . . . well, there you are. She was under the belief that there was a place for everything, and everything better fall into that place."

It wasn't that Vonlee wanted to come across as if she was disparaging her mother and the way in which she was raised. She loved her mother dearly, she insisted.

"But I just don't think she could cope with the fact that she knew who I was."

Vonlee's father had been in Vietnam when Vonlee was born and she was too young to remember him.

"I've never met him," Vonlee said. "I know who he is, but I don't . . . I just don't know what to say about that."

Her father wanted to see Vonlee, but Georgia would not allow it. He would come over when Vonlee was young and leave presents, but Georgia would always send them back. It was almost as if Georgia knew that Vonlee was "different" and didn't want the father to see her.

Living life as a girl when not in school was not a big problem, Vonlee said. There were obstacles, sure; but mostly, she had the support of her grandmother and her friends. Her aunts and uncles and cousins all accepted her and never made much of an issue about it. Vonlee wasn't the freak of the family in any way. She wasn't the secret everyone whispered about. She was Vonlee. It wasn't something they all spoke about, but it was there, out in the open. Still, nobody judged; nobody said much of anything. She wasn't running around the neighborhood in skirts and girl clothes and makeup. Vonlee wore mainly boys' clothes (to a certain extent), but there was a strong sense of her being a tomboy, as if she were a girl pretending to be a boy.

That certainly wasn't the case as Vonlee turned twelve and thirteen and entered middle school and then high school. It was then that she'd have to make a choice: Could she live the way she felt and pay the consequences of public bullying and discrimination and even homophobia (although, Vonlee made a point to say, she never once considered herself ever to be a homosexual)? Or could she go to school as a boy and wait until she was old and mature enough, out of school, to pick up her life as a female again?

What would she do?

CHAPTER 30

WHEN DANNY AND VONLEE finished eating dinner and returned to the truck, the recording device picked them back up. Why not initiate more incriminating conversation during the ride home? Danny figured. Danny felt as though he was totally immersed in turning in his former gal pal. He had taken it this far, she was suspicious and even checked out his truck, and yet Vonlee was still talking. Asking a few more questions would not aggravate the situation any more than it was already.

As they were getting into the truck, Vonlee said something about Danny being a "hardened criminal" himself, but then realized Danny had nearly fallen on the ground near the driver's door.

"You all right?" Vonlee asked.

"I don't feel good."

"Are you getting sick?"

"Maybe."

"What's wrong?" she said as Danny got into the driver's seat.

"I don't . . . I . . ." Danny had trouble finishing his thought. He started the vehicle as Vonlee sat down. Then he drove off.

As they headed home, Danny was still complaining about being ill.

"Pull up here," Vonlee said. "Pull up here."

Danny stopped the vehicle. They both got out. Danny seemed as though he was going to vomit. He said something about how sick the entire ordeal had made him—the idea that he had been dating a man, and that man was somehow involved in a murder. Hearing it all from Vonlee throughout the night had just been too much, he explained.

"I mean, I'm sorry this is going on right now, but it *is* going on," Vonlee said as they got back into the vehicle and Danny sped off, apparently feeling better. "I wish it wasn't going on, more than you wish it wasn't going on. Trust me. I mean, I'm a good person as far as that, and I'm going to get over this. What happened . . . *happened*. I think I'm going to get," Vonlee said, but then changed her tone: "I was a *victim*. I really do think Billie . . . ," she said, but stopped herself again.

Thinking about it, Vonlee considered that Danny's attitude and "sickness" were more about them than the crime.

"I think this has a little more to do with me and you. Am I right?" Vonlee wanted to know.

"No! No, no, no. It doesn't have anything to do with you and me," Danny said, giving Vonlee the indication their romance was still on track and the fact that she was a man did not bother him or have an effect on their relationship.

Vonlee wouldn't accept that. "What do you mean it can't have anything to do with me and you? It *has* to have something to do with me and you."

They went back and forth about this. Danny insisted he wanted to be there for Vonlee during her darkest hour and help her work through all of this.

"It's over," Vonlee said, referring to her speaking about

her aunt and Don's death and what had happened. "It's done with. I will never bring it up again. Can you do the same, please?" But Vonlee couldn't let the other subject go, however. "You finally meet somebody you really care about and she turns out to be a man!" she added sarcastically.

This comment sparked an argument between them.

Finally, "So you don't want to see me again?" Vonlee asked, feeling as though she had read through the lines of Danny's heart.

Danny hadn't said that, but he certainly was feeling it. He could not hide his disdain for what she had done with Billie Jean and the fact that she had lied to him about being a woman.

"No, I didn't say that. Did I say that? I'm just saying I'm weak today."

Why couldn't Vonlee cut the guy some slack? He'd been through a lot in such a short period. In the same conversation, on the same night, his girlfriend had confided in him her two deepest, darkest secrets—and each had affected him immensely.

"I'm sorry," Vonlee said. "I don't mean to do this to you. I mean, I don't want you to go through this. Please tell me you'll get over it."

Danny wasn't sure, he said.

"Well, I mean, do you think that we could work it out? 'Cause I really care about you. . . . I think I love you. . . . You know that I'm not a bad person."

"You're not a bad person. . . ."

"Are you going to call me?"

"Yeah, I want to."

They drove for some time and talked quietly and cautiously. Danny was all over the place, as was Vonlee. As the road signs passed, traffic whizzed by, a silence took over the inside of the vehicle. Here were two people, each hiding something from the other, each knowing that this relationship was doomed and that the Don situation was also going to blow up in the coming days. Still, Vonlee held on to the notion that if Danny just kept his mouth shut, and didn't say anything to anyone, everything would work itself out.

"Please, you would never say anything to anybody."

Danny shrugged. He'd said he wouldn't mention it.

"You said you wish somebody would shoot you," Vonlee said. To her, this meant Danny was done with everything. And his comment told her that if he was going down with the ship, well, she was going to drown with him.

"I wish somebody would shoot me, yeah," Danny confirmed.

"But a month from now, you're not going to wish that."

"Don't worry about it," Danny said.

Vonlee got back on the subject of her alcoholism. She kept working the conversation back to something Danny had said during dinner: that he felt somehow responsible for what happened to Don. If only he'd foreseen it and stepped in and told Billie Jean she was crazy for following through with it. He could have helped Vonlee avoid all of the problems she was facing.

"You've not done anything wrong," Vonlee told Danny.

"I know."

Danny pulled into the driveway. Billie Jean's car was gone. She wasn't home, Vonlee pointed out.

"I love you," Vonlee said as she got out.

"I love you, too." Danny took a pause. "Bye."

Danny drove off, staring at Vonlee in his rearview mirror as she struggled to get her key into the door. As he got farther down the road, the image of Vonlee dissolved smaller and smaller, until she finally vanished altogether, disappearing from his life.

CHAPTER 31

PART OF WHAT ALLOWED Vonlee to fall deeply into the person she believed herself to be, despite the body God had provided, was a steadfast sensitivity she'd established in the core of her soul: she was a female—nobody was going to change Vonlee Titlow into a boy. It wasn't a disease she had, or some sort of psychological problem she could go to therapy and work through. Vonlee was a woman, a Christian woman at that.

She grew up in the South, where most people rarely held back what they felt or believed religiously, politically or personally. And as Vonlee stepped into those formative, judgmental years of junior high and high school, it became apparent to her that life was going to be an uphill battle from this point forward. It was hard enough, she knew, for gays to come out and tell their families and admit in public who they were; but add gender to that and her days were now an unsettling, stressful, tumultuous journey of explaining who she was to those who did not know her, while putting up with the stares and the comments.

During her prepubescent years, Vonlee had dressed daringly for a young "boy" in the South; that is, cutoff blue jean short-shorts and half T-shirts, exposing his/her midsection. Vonlee's hair was kept "real long." Body hair was never an issue because Vonlee did not have much, anyway. Thus, "I looked like a little girl."

Fast-forward to those critical years of high school and that's where the problems—socially, culturally and emotionally—began. For one, as a child, Vonlee had no trouble looking like a girl. But as she grew into her teens, "I started to go through a real awkward stage. . . ." And as she changed and fought those changes, the people around Vonlee began to notice.

Vonlee's mother slowly accepted her more each day as she grew. There came a time when Georgia sold her mother's house (where Vonlee had grown up) and bought a different house for her. Vonlee then had to change schools. She left behind all those friends she had known her entire life—those who knew her best. Now she was subjected to a new group of kids that had never seen or met her. And that's when the insults and bullying started.

Heritage High School, home of the Mountaineers, was built in the shadow of the Great Smoky Mountains National Park. Standing in the school parking lot, one could look out onto what was a stunning display of American landscape, or "God's country," as some might be inclined to say. This part of the South is as picturesque and beautiful as any other in the country.

"I went to school with a lot of rednecks and back-country kids," Vonlee explained.

A person like Vonlee, who now tried as hard as she could to present herself as a boy, stood out. At first, she tried dating girls. It was one of the hardest things she ever did. Awkward and unsettling. Every bit of it, she felt, was wrong.

"I wanted to do their hair and makeup," Vonlee said later.

As a male, Vonlee had sex with a female. "But I felt gay, like I was a lesbian. It just wasn't comfortable for me."

After that stage, Vonlee went back to being herself, or as much as she could within the boundaries society had erected for her. She didn't want to walk the halls as a transsexual, not in high school, not in the South. Yet, she still couldn't hide who she was, either. It was always there, even if she tried dressing like a boy.

"Sissy," kids would shout at Vonlee as she walked down the hallway. "Wee-wee sucker!" And the ultimate derogatory homosexual insult: "Fag!"

These comments told her how much nobody understood who she was, or how she wanted to live her life.

As her days in school drudged on, it became harder to deflect the reproachful and hurtful comments, threats and ridicule. It was a daily ritual: wake up, get dressed, go to school and be subjected to harassment. As her sophomore and junior years came to pass, Vonlee grew severely depressed. She couldn't stop trying to be a female—it wasn't a choice. This was one aspect of being transgender, she explained, that people don't understand: she would never *choose* it.

Her grades began to slip.

"I hated school—it was horrible."

There was one day when Vonlee sat down with her mother. Georgia could tell that her child was having a hard time, not only with school, but life in general. For Vonlee, it was difficult just getting out of bed and going to class. She was sleeping in class whenever she could, because her nights were spent staring at the ceiling, battling anxiety.

"You okay?" Georgia wondered.

"I'm not."

Georgia sat near Vonlee and took her by the shoulders,

staring into her eyes. "Listen," a mother said to her child, "if you go and take the GED and pass, you can quit."

They hugged.

It seemed like the logical thing for Vonlee to do.

Not long after she started her junior year, now old enough to quit, Vonlee took the General Educational Development (GED) test and passed. So she quit high school.

The one thing Vonlee knew as she entered adulthood was that she needed to get out of Maryville. There was no way she could stay in a town, standing out like a Union flag, and live life on her own terms, openly being who she was.

There was a guy who had rented a room at Vonlee's mother's house during those difficult years. Vonlee soon found out he was gay. She had no attraction to this man. Dating men was not a same-gender relationship for her. Vonlee saw herself as a female and dating men to her would be considered a normal, heterosexual relationship.

"This guy, when I found out he was gay," Vonlee explained, "I began talking to him about the scene. He introduced me to the gay scene in Nashville."

It was hard for Vonlee to say she "felt comfortable" within the gay scene. But it was as close as she could get to feeling normal: meeting men who might be into her and living her life as a female.

"The gay community was accepting of me, which was why I embraced it," Vonlee later recalled. "But there were also bars in downtown [Nashville] geared toward transsexual life."

Vonlee walked into a club one night and there on the stage performing a "drag show" was a transsexual that looked "just like a Barbie doll." Vonlee felt at home for the first time in her life. By now, Vonlee was on a host of female hormones and her body was tightening up and shrinking. Her voice, quite effeminate to begin with, was changing remarkably. She looked and sounded like a female, now more than ever—as opposed to a male *trying* to sound like a female. Her body was changing and her mood and mind were fitting congenially into the mold of who she truly was emotionally. For what seemed to be the first time, her life was on track.

Staring up at the stage, drink in her hand, Vonlee looked at the drag queen and thought: *Oh, my gosh . . . a live Barbie . . . look at her! That's what I want to do. That's me. I'm home.*

Vonlee spoke to the drag queen after her set. It was liberating to hear the person speak about living life the way in which she wanted. No boundaries. No waking up feeling as though she had nowhere to go. No worrying about being insulted around every corner.

"You have to understand," Vonlee said, "back home, I would hide who I was in a lot of ways. . . . I would go into the bathroom and do my makeup. Then I would wash it off. So any chance I got to dress completely like a female, I would do it."

And now here was the opportunity not only to dress the part, but live it day in and day out.

Still, as time went on, meeting the Barbie drag queen, for Vonlee, "That was okay. But it wasn't who I wanted to be. I wanted to be a woman. Not a stage show."

It was 1984 through 1985, the height, one could argue, of the AIDS epidemic and crisis just reaching the gay community. It was not easy being different then.

But as she made her way through the Nashville scene, Vonlee made a decision. She was going to do something about her lifestyle. And the choice she was about to make would shock even her.

CHAPTER 32

ON SEPTEMBER 2, 2000, Danny was behind the counter rearranging some rings underneath the glass case when Vonlee walked into the store.

"Why the hell ain't you answering your phone?" Vonlee said upon greeting Danny.

Danny knew what she meant. Vonlee had called him that morning at 9:47, 11:06, and then that afternoon at 12:43. Each time, Danny watched the phone ring, but he did not pick it up.

"I just got into shop," Danny said. "Listen, I been going through a lot of emotional issues. Come on."

Vonlee was curious. Something was up. She could sense it.

"Everything will be okay as long as you don't talk to nobody about what I told you," Vonlee said. She stared at Danny.

"Okay . . . okay—" Danny tried to say something before Vonlee cut him off.

"If you have a nervous breakdown and decide to go to the police," Vonlee said (according to notes Danny made of the visit and conversation shortly after), "I will tell them I was lying and the only reason you're doing this is because I stopped seeing you!"

Danny looked around his shop. There were a few customers meandering, checking out necklaces and bracelets. He walked out from behind the counter. Put an arm around Vonlee's waist.

"Let's go outside there and talk," Danny said.

Vonlee appeared dazed and upset.

"It's okay," Danny said, sounding as reassuring as he could. He kissed her. "I need to work right now."

"If you want to go out with me, call me," Vonlee said.

"Okay, okay."

As Danny stood by and watched, Vonlee got into her vehicle, started it and took off.

CHAPTER 33

SHE STEPPED OUT OF the shower. Grabbed a towel, dried herself off. Fixed her hair and makeup. Then she gently tucked her penis underneath and in between her legs to hide it completely. She stood in front of the body-length mirror, staring at . . .

A woman.

"I just wanted to see her," Vonlee recalled, speaking of herself in the third person. "It's like she was in there . . . but I was constantly fighting on the outside to fit in somewhere."

Being transgender was a frightening thought. But there was very little Vonlee could do about it. She'd go through trends, trying her best to do "what guys are supposed to do," and then go back to being female. At one time, it was a continuous battle, rooted entirely in the way society viewed her.

Living in Nashville, going to the clubs that accepted her, Vonlee felt "the easy thing for me to do was to be a gay boy." She would not go against the grain and force herself onto a world that wanted to keep her confined inside drag queen clubs. Even in a city that was conservative but had liberal foundations, it was a constant struggle for her to live as a female outside of the box. Some did not want to accept the fact that there were people without a choice in the world, living lives they did not want.

"People really didn't understand transgender then," Vonlee explained about the mid-1980s. "So it was so much easier just to be gay, and date gay men."

But it felt wrong. She was fighting internally with herself. Vonlee had many of the parts of a female, except the one that mattered most. What stopped Vonlee all her life about getting the final operation was not the money, as some would come later to believe (she could go to Montreal, Canada, and get it done for twenty-five thousand dollars or less—and had already picked out the doctor and had spoken to him), but the finality of it all.

"Look, I knew who I was and who I wanted to be, but I thought then, okay, this is enough for me. I'm attracted to men. So I could dress up every now and then and just live as a gay man. I thought it would be enough. "

Every time she wanted to complete the transformation, she'd go back to the fact that it was irreversible, and that thought overpowered her feelings.

There was a chance that after the operation, Vonlee explained, she could lose her sensation of ever having an orgasm again (either as a male or a female), and it played heavily on her decision.

As she entered the gay scene, Vonlee was attractive to many of the more "manly" gay men that liked effeminate guys. She'd always go for "older men that happened to have a lot of money," she explained, but not as a shark on the hunt. It just happened that those were the men she was attracted to, she claimed.

"They took me on trips and showed me things I had never seen before," Vonlee said.

She found a happy medium, one could say. These guys did not mind her dressing up as a female from time to time, but all of them were unified in that they did not want her to ever change her body completely. They wanted her to stay male. Anytime she mentioned the words "transsexual" and "operation," she would get an argument.

"They wanted me to be a feminine *boy*," Vonlee said.

The claim that Vonlee sought out men with money and made it a routine to land them was, at best, far-fetched. "I never gravitated toward men with money," she said with a sarcastic laugh. "Men with money gravitated toward me."

The thing about Vonlee then was that she came across as extremely intimidating: Most insecure gay men were afraid to approach her. She had a visceral, almost glamorous quality to everything she did. It was evident in the way she dressed and spoke, the things she liked, even the exotic drinks in her hand.

"Why wouldn't you come up to me earlier?" she'd ask a man who had kind of lurked around her for hours in a club before introducing himself.

"Because you're beautiful and intimidating" was the common response.

The guys with money—the confident ones who were happy in their own skin—were less intimidated by her, however.

On top of that, "I did not want to date a bum," Vonlee said, again laughing at herself. "Why would I want to do that?"

As Vonlee forced herself to get used to the Nashville gay scene, she wound up working at a salon (she had gone to cosmetology school outside of Nashville after relocating from Maryville), where she did hair and nails. She also managed a few restaurants and bartended. She had no trouble making money and supporting herself.

Back then, life was comfortable and quiet, Vonlee explained. Still, living as a gay man, dating only gay men, was not what she wanted deep down. Vonlee yearned to live her life as a female, completely. That meant dating heterosexual males and getting the final operation.

A relationship she soon entered into with a gay man, however, turned into more: Vonlee fell in love. It was a time when she had amped down the female hormones, and the transformation was in a sort of holding pattern.

"I had these little bitty titties," she explained, "and was very . . . um, androgynous—people would look at me and say, 'Is that a girl or a guy?' Kind of like that Jodie Foster look."

But her body and attitude changed as she took her medication and soon got a job traveling, selling cleaning products.

"That job was perfect for me."

She was in New York one week, Los Angeles the next. Big cities. More accepting. Bigger scenes. Different people.

Then she traveled to New Orleans one time and met a man. He was gay.

Generally, whenever Vonlee went out, she did her makeup and hit the clubs as a female. One night, while in New Orleans, the power was out and she couldn't convert herself into a female, so she went out as a male.

A man walked up to her. He was manly. Gay, but truly a "guy's guy."

"Bill, good to meet you," he said. There was an attraction almost immediately between Bill (pseudonym) and Vonlee. An energy.

It was love, Vonlee said. Maybe not at first sight, but shortly thereafter.

They began a relationship.

"I really, *really* loved this guy," Vonlee explained. "The sex was good. We connected on just about every level." The problem was that "he did not want me to become a female."

Her hope was that after she explained that her life's desire was to complete the transformation, he would accept her and they could continue. But there was no way. He wanted to be with a guy. He was a homosexual.

Vonlee loved him enough not to go through with it. They moved in together. The years added up. Now heading toward her midtwenties, having lived in a gay relationship (as a gay male) for three years, Vonlee sat Bill down and got honest with him to see if perhaps he might change his mind.

"I cannot do this anymore."

"What?"

"Us."

"Us?"

"Yeah. I need to be who I am. . . . I need to get back on track."

They lived another three years together as Vonlee went back to focusing on taking the hormones and working toward the operation.

Bill finally said one night, "Look, I love you, but I will always look at you as a boy in a bra."

By this point, they owned a home together. Yet, when Bill mentioned how he would always view her as a boy, "something just clicked for me," Vonlee remembered.

They sold the house. Split all of their assets equally.

"And we stayed really best friends," Vonlee said. "I just . . . He never looked at me the way I wanted a guy to look at me—which was, you know, that look of me being the girl that I was."

Vonlee now faced a blank-slate future she could write for herself. This would require a substantial move. She had a friend who liked to dress up, but had not made the transformation with hormones like she had. They'd worked together.

"Denver," Vonlee's girlfriend suggested. "I used to live there."

Vonlee had heard there was quite the transgender scene in Denver. And on top of that, she needed to break away from her memories in Nashville. Also, she was thinking about starting a new business with several "girls" she had met and befriended, along with several more she was told lived in Denver.

"What kind of business?" one of the girls asked as they prepared to leave.

"An escort service," Vonlee said.

CHAPTER 34

"IT'S DANNY, WHAT'S UP?"

Vonlee had called Danny and he was returning her call. He didn't want to make Vonlee any more suspicious than she already was, so he'd decided to touch base and see where she was at. It was near the end of September. They had not spoken for seven days.

"Hey . . . hello," Vonlee said. She sounded strange—her voice, her tone.

"You got a cold or something?" Danny asked.

She said no, but she'd had some dental work done and wasn't feeling all that great. The entire right side of her face was still numb.

Danny was asking why he hadn't heard from her in so long. It had been a week, he told her, and she disagreed with how long it had been.

"Listen," Danny said. He sounded different. Hyper and anxious. It was like he wanted something, but didn't know how to ask. "You okay? You sound so different?"

"Yeah . . . ," she said. "You do not sound like yourself, either!" Danny wasn't prone to talking fast. She could tell he was nervous and—strangely enough—she had picked up on something wrong with him.

Danny was recording the call for the TPD, of course.

"What do you mean?" he asked.

"You sound *funny*," Vonlee said guardedly.

"Maybe the phone—"

"No . . . ," she said. It was more than that, but Vonlee couldn't put her finger on it.

"What do you mean?" Danny asked.

"I don't know. It's weird."

Vonlee talked about the dental work she had and Danny interrupted, asking if she had a new boyfriend yet.

"Hell no," Vonlee answered, her sassy Southern accent clear and pronounced.

Danny asked about Billie Jean. How was she doing? Had Vonlee and her aunt gone to the casino lately?

"She's down there right now," Vonlee said.

They talked about menial things: Vonlee's car, the casinos Vonlee and her aunt had been going to, how she was doing. Danny wanted to know if Vonlee was planning on going down to the casino anytime soon. He gave the impression that he wanted to meet her there.

Vonlee wasn't sure, she said, because she was taking painkillers for her teeth and she was tired and loopy all the time.

As they continued, Danny became more comfortable, and Vonlee opened up a bit about what was going on in her life. She was conflicted about her aunt, she explained. Billie Jean was spending like crazy. She was her same old self, going to the casino and gambling her nights away. Vonlee said she was thinking about getting an apartment and moving out, but worried Billie Jean might need her help around the house. She was torn over whether to leave or not.

"I think you helped her enough already," Danny said with a modicum of sarcasm. It was as if he were saying:

"What more does the woman want? You helped her kill her husband."

Vonlee was mumbling, probably because of the drugs. Then Danny asked what happened when "those people" (the cops) came to the house. What did they want?

"Oh, they wanted to ask about Don's best friend."

"They questioned his best friend?" Danny asked, sounding confused.

"Yeah. . . ."

"Why would they question his best friend?"

Vonlee explained that the cops wanted to know about Billie Jean's marriage to Don, the business, and why the kids (Don's) would say the things they were. Apparently, Don's kids had been putting pressure on the TPD to investigate.

"He [Don's best friend] told them," Vonlee explained, "that Don was slowly going downhill. He never had a problem with his marriage and the will was written when he was of sound mind, and that the kids were evil. . . . And [the cops] said that as far as they were concerned, it's over with. . . ."

The problem arose when Billie Jean had told Don's daughter that she and Vonlee had gotten home around eleven o'clock on the night they found Don, but the widow had told the police it was three in the morning. The discrepancy in times was enough to arouse some suspicion, according to what Vonlee had heard from Billie Jean recently. But Vonlee's aunt explained to the police that she only told Don's daughter that because she didn't want to admit to being out all night gambling.

"It don't matter," Vonlee said, when Danny mentioned how they would have to account for that missing time. "They have us on film down there [at the casino], and the detective said that Billie probably thought it was none of the daughter's business what she was doing."

"I just hope everything is okay," Danny said after the two of them chitchatted some more about Vonlee's car and how she and Billie Jean had wanted to return it to the dealer, but the dealer was fighting them and would not take it back. Billie Jean wanted "her money" back for Vonlee's car, Vonlee had told Danny earlier in the conversation. There were mechanical problems, along with warranty issues, and they were extremely unhappy. Vonlee was especially pissed off after the salesman, laughing, had said to her, "You think this is Kmart and you can get a refund?"

"You should have showed him how much money you gave and shown him that checkbook of yours," Danny said, laughing.

Vonlee laughed back.

They chatted about life in general and Vonlee's teeth and what time Danny was closing his jewelry shop. Then, after hanging up and calling each other back a few times, they made plans to meet for dinner. Danny claimed he needed to go home and shower after closing his shop. Vonlee questioned why.

After a bit of discussion about that, Danny agreed to close the shop early and not go home. Instead, he'd meet her at the casino.

CHAPTER 35

VONLEE TOOK TO DENVER as though the city had been built for her. Before the move, Vonlee had rented an apartment with some friends, a married couple that soon divorced after Vonlee had spent about three months there. She had purchased a salon with another friend, but that was failing horribly, she said. One day when she took a look at her savings account, she realized now was maybe her chance to start over and—along with the idea of Denver being new and fresh and accepting of her lifestyle—she took off.

The friends she moved in with in Denver were "never transsexuals," Vonlee explained, "but they [were homosexuals that] dressed up as females." They wanted nothing to do with "the change," as Vonlee put it, but liked being females when they went out.

"You are going to love Denver," her friend Mickey (pseudonym) told Vonlee as they traveled northwest from Nashville. "It is so much more accepting."

Not long after hitting the scene and taking in Denver, "I really started to come into who I was," Vonlee recalled.

Although the idea to start an escort service had been germinating for some time, it wasn't something Vonlee did as soon as she arrived in the Mile High City. What's more, she wanted to do it right: operate as a legitimate business—paid girls that went on dates with wealthy men. She never intended it to be a prostitution service.

While digging through the daily newspaper one day, Vonlee came upon an ad for a local club looking for dancing girls. The dirty kind.

A stripper, she thought. *Could I pull it off?*

By now, Vonlee had gotten silicone implants and had large breasts. She was taking massive amounts of female hormones and, with her long, curly blond hair and a burgeoning swimsuit figure, she was an attractive female. There was nothing about her that said "man." Her hands were feminine; her body hair was gone; her curves were real; her voice girly, but not overly so.

Vonlee walked in and applied for a job—a cocktail waitress, she'd decided. Turned out, Vonlee wasn't so confident that she could pull off being a female stripper in a strip club predominantly geared for heterosexual males.

She was offered a job, as was her girlfriend.

The strip club she worked at sold alcohol, so a requirement by the management was that all the girls wore two G-strings. This helped promote the rule that they were only to expose their breasts to patrons. If you were caught showing what you had downstairs, you were fired. The club could lose its liquor license if one of the girls exposed her vagina.

"You and Mandy want to make more money?" the manager asked Vonlee one night. Mandy (pseudonym) was a full-on transsexual herself, and she and Vonlee could have passed for sisters.

"How?"

"The stage."

Vonlee had never told anyone at the bar she was a

male. No one had ever asked. Vonlee knew about the G-string rule and figured it would be easy enough to hide her manhood, tucking it underneath.

"Why not?" she said.

Vonlee spent two weeks stripping. No one ever questioned her. She made lots of money, according to her. But, in the end, it was "far too stressful for me to continue," so she went back to waiting tables.

"Hey, Vonlee," the owner of the bar said one night while Vonlee was cashing out, "I got a friend who wants to meet you."

Vonlee wasn't seeing anyone. She was saving for her operation. She'd known a few transsexuals who'd gone up to Montreal and she was planning on doing it herself, once she had the money.

"Yeah," she said. "Okay."

She never told the guy she was a man. He had some money. He was looking for a place to live. All three of them—Mandy, Vonlee and Vonlee's new friend—decided to get a place together.

Vonlee and Mandy had moved out of the apartment they had been sharing with Mickey, the transsexual they had traveled to Denver with from Nashville.

"All she wanted to do was party all the time," Vonlee said about the other girl. "And she was way into the gay scene, bringing home all sorts of men . . . and we decided we wanted to move on."

So they left, and it pissed the girl off. As a result, Mickey called the guy they were moving in with and explained, "Hey, do you realize that they are men— Vonlee and Mandy?"

The guy had no idea.

"As it was, we were all going to move in as friends," Vonlee said.

It was a three-bedroom apartment. At this time of her

life, Vonlee viewed the world through a prism of always being on the defense. She got up and went about her days and was always on guard, waiting, anticipating, projecting that next insult would push her further into completing who she was. Thus, she saw people, whoever they were, as the enemy, no matter what they said or didn't say. She wanted acceptance; yet she wasn't prepared to accept herself completely. There always seemed to be a reason not to complete the transformation. By being a stripper, and not telling the owner and fooling the patrons, Vonlee was lying about who she truly was, or wanted to be. Essentially, she was living and working as a female, and yet lying about it still felt wrong.

CHAPTER 36

ON DECEMBER 4, 2000, Tony DeLeonardis, a detective sergeant for the Area Three Detective Division of the Chicago Police Department (CPD), sat in front of an apartment building at 1501 West Fullerton. It was cold outside his vehicle; the skies dark and gloomy; that infamous Chicago wind was whirling up newspapers and other garbage along the curb line of the street. DeLeonardis was sitting surveillance on a three-story building—the bottom and top floors occupied by businesses, apartments sandwiched in between— watching for a woman whose photograph DeLeonardis had in his hand.

It was 12:50 P.M.

Up the street, near Greenview, DeLeonardis had already spotted Vonlee's two-door white Buick Riviera. It was parked out in the open. He had confirmed it was Vonlee's by the license tag.

Vonlee had relocated back to Chicago, where she'd spent a considerable amount of time before leaving to move back home and sober up, to start a new life. She hadn't run to Chicago from Troy. Or taken off in the middle of the night because she felt the heat of the law,

as some had later suggested. Vonlee had decided it was
time to get away from her aunt and begin her life, once
again, in a place she was familiar with.

As DeLeonardis sat and watched, he witnessed the
"subject" walk out of the West Fullerton door of the building. Vonlee had her hair pulled back and tied up like a
rooster's tail. She wore a knee-length blue coat and white
shoes. She was toting a laundry basket full of clothes.

Vonlee got into her car and pulled out into the heavy
traffic on Fullerton. DeLeonardis followed, but he lost
Vonlee somewhere near Demon Dogs, a restaurant
several blocks from her apartment.

DeLeonardis drove back around and parked in
front of Vonlee's building again. Almost three hours
after losing her—Vonlee had still not returned—
DeLeonardis, as he noted in his report, "terminated" the
surveillance.

What this proved to the TPD, however, was that
Vonlee Titlow was living in Chicago, but not hiding out
in any way. She was out and about, doing laundry,
grabbing some food. She wasn't on the lam.

The next obvious task for TPD detectives Don Zimmerman and Don Tullock, who had taken over lead in
the case, was to put everything they had into a search
warrant and see what they could dredge up at the Rogers
house. They had most of Don's financial records already
and knew that a lot of money had been spent by Billie
Jean and paid to Vonlee. It proved nothing by itself. But,
in the context of a search warrant and what else they
now knew about Vonlee and her aunt, they could think
about dragging the two of them in for a little chat.

CHAPTER 37

TWO TRANSSEXUALS LIVING WITH a guy in Denver during the early 1990s—this was not the ideal domestic situation Vonlee had seen for herself in the crystal ball of her life. By this time (heading toward her later twenties), Vonlee was hoping to be settled down (with a guy), her operation done, hold a nice job, and maybe have a small slice—however different it was—of the American pie. Quitting the stripper job was probably a good move, she thought. But where would she go? What was she going to do for a living?

Just a few days after the three of them had moved in together, when the guy came home from work, he called Vonlee and Mandy into the living room.

"Sit down," he said. "Both of you."

"What's going on?" Vonlee asked. She could tell he was upset about something.

"I got a phone call at work today."

"Yeah . . . and . . ."

Vonlee knew this guy had ties to organized crime, or did at one time. He was not someone to mess with in any way. Or, in this case, they should not lie to him.

"It's time for a little show-and-tell, girls," he said. He wanted them to drop their pants.

Vonlee and Mandy looked at each other.

Shit.

Caught.

Mandy tried to say it was nothing but lies. Whatever the other girl had said was out of anger because Mandy and Vonlee had screwed her over and left without warning. She was just being a bitch and trying to make up stories about them. Both she and Vonlee were females. There was nothing to worry about. After all, didn't he meet them at a strip club?

Vonlee got up, walked into the kitchen, made a drink. She took a few pulls from the strong cocktail and worked her way back into the living room.

"Mandy . . . let me. Look," Vonlee said, addressing their new roommate, "the truth is, neither of us ever had any intention of having sex with you. It wasn't anything like that. I feel like we misled you. Sure. But if you want to back out of the apartment and leave, we understand. I'm really sorry."

They had a conversation. Mandy actually had a crush on the guy, but that was quickly suppressed once she and Vonlee told him that they were, in fact, men. He couldn't believe it, of course. Nonetheless, he decided to stay. They had been honest. They fessed up.

No more secrets.

Both promised.

As time went on, Vonlee said, "There was some sexual energy there between us." She and the guy had gone out one night and started drinking heavily together. When they got back to the apartment, Vonlee said she was out of cigarettes.

"Let's go," he said.

On the way back from the store, he pulled the vehicle

over and "just started kissing" her. No warning or lead-up. He just took her.

"One thing led to another, and me and him started fooling around," Vonlee recalled.

They never committed to each other as boyfriend and girlfriend, but as Vonlee told it, "It was like we were friends with benefits. We were living in the same apartment. . . . I loved him, but I wasn't *in* love with him."

Vonlee began working at a local chain restaurant after leaving the strip club. She wanted out of the stripper scene entirely. There was too much cocaine and drinking and dishonest business going on, and she saw herself, if she stayed, not coming out of it without a few serious bumps. She and the guy living at the apartment still had relations as the weeks turned into months, but it was all within that friends-with-benefits thing they'd started and never went beyond that. Vonlee and Mandy, meanwhile, became closer. Best friends, Vonlee said later. They always had told each other they would one day go into business together and were beginning to take that pipe dream seriously.

Working one night at the chain restaurant, a nicely dressed guy left Vonlee his business card and implored her to call him if she wanted to go out. As Vonlee sat home alone a few weekends later, she took out the card and dialed the number.

"And we just hit it off," she remembered.

They were inseparable after that first night out. Vonlee never shared her gender with him; she didn't feel she needed to. Their relationship just kind of took flight and she made the decision not to tell him.

Six months went by. They were in love. They'd had sex on a number of occasions, both oral and anal. He never questioned Vonlee about her gender. She'd always make an excuse: "I'm on my period. . . ." Or, "I have a yeast infection."

The time came to renew the lease where Vonlee, Mandy and their male roommate were living and Vonlee told her roommates she was moving out and getting a place of her own, but she would being staying with Jay (pseudonym), her boyfriend, until she found one.

After moving in with Jay, Vonlee and her girlfriend were sitting around talking one night. Jay was at work.

"I have to tell him," Vonlee confided in her friend. She'd been freaking out lately about it, stressing over the "right time." Their relationship had turned into something Vonlee never saw coming. They were deeply in love.

Both women agreed that when Jay returned, Vonlee's girlfriend would do the dirty work for her.

"Sit down," she told Jay when he walked in. Vonlee left the room.

"I don't understand," Jay said when the girlfriend finished.

Vonlee came into the room. She explained it to him as bluntly as she could.

"He was upset, confused and didn't believe it," Vonlee recalled.

Vonlee had always told Jay there was a secret about her he needed to know. She'd mentioned this many times. Jay had wondered, but never pressured her to tell him. He obviously didn't think the secret was that she was a man.

"Well, how in the hell did we have sex?" Jay asked. Vonlee could see that Jay was going back through his rolodex of memories and thinking, *Were there signs? Did I miss something?*

Vonlee explained how she carefully manipulated the situation and fooled him into having anal intercourse.

He had worn a condom, so there was no worry there for Jay, but he was still very disturbed by everything.

"I was scared to death of losing him. I wanted him to get to know me *for me*, as a person. I loved the guy. Is it deceptive? Yeah, of course. But, at the same time, if you walk around telling everyone, they are going automatically to judge you and not even give you the opportunity to get to know you."

Vonlee was going through an incredible personal inventory at the time of who she truly was, she said. She wore "gaff" underwear every day, which kept her manhood tucked underneath. Vonlee never had a small penis, nor did she have an overly large penis. Still, it was hard for a while to hide it—until she amped up the female hormones and her private parts shrank remarkably.

"At one time, another inch of shrinking and I would be a girl," Vonlee explained with a casual laugh. "And it works the opposite way, too: For a girl to take male testosterone, her clitoris will grow—I've seen them three, four inches long! But it's still easier to go from a guy to a girl. It's much easier to dig a hole than to build a pole."

Jay and Vonlee dated for another year. She wanted to be clear that Jay was not a gay man. He was heterosexual—a heterosexual, nonetheless, now faced with a personal dilemma: should he give up the woman he thought he was in love with, or stop dating a man?

"In the two years we were together, he had never seen my penis," Vonlee said.

Jay stayed with Vonlee, but he began to push her to get the surgery. He wanted Vonlee to be as completely female as she could be—or, rather, as surgically and humanly possible. When they talked about it, Vonlee was taken aback. It had been on her mind, clearly, for many, many years. What stopped her, every time, was the finality and how things could turn out. There were no guarantees with the operation. She could lose the entire feeling and sensation of orgasm—and every time she revisited getting the operation, it scared the hell out of her.

"I'm going to open an account for you," Jay said one night while they were discussing it. "I'll give you half the money, but you need to come up with the other half to show you really want it done, too."

Vonlee said she kept "derailing" the procedure. Any money she saved for the surgery, she'd go out and shop until it was gone.

"I don't know if I was a shopaholic or I was just putting it off," she later explained.

Vonlee had gone as far as meeting with the doctor, taking and passing the required HIV test, then scheduling pre-op meetings. The surgery in Montreal she was going to get was about the estimated twenty thousand to twenty-five thousand dollars, which included hotel and airfare.

"But I wasn't ready," she said. "This guy was everything I had ever wanted, too. He was the president of a company. Good-looking. He didn't use drugs. . . . He had taken me to meet his mother. She pulled me aside and said, 'He must really, really love you because he's never brought a girl home.'"

The second Christmas they spent together was special, Vonlee said. She decided to go all out on the guy as far as gifts. The surgery was on hold for now, but she'd promised to reconsider after the holidays. He seemed to accept that for the time being.

There was something different about Jay, though, throughout that entire holiday season. And Vonlee knew it.

"I've been reading a book," Jay said during the holiday that year. He was sitting in the living room. He had a mocking look on his face. Vonlee could tell something was on his mind.

"What book is it that you've been reading?" Vonlee asked.

"Didn't matter," he said. "But in the book, there was a guy going down on a girl and it really, *really* turned me on."

Jay was missing out on so much was the point. He couldn't experience the things he wanted to with Vonlee. There would always be a gulf between them. Operation or no operation, she was a man. Jay was having serious problems with it.

"You're never going to let up about the surgery, are you?" Vonlee asked.

They got into a fight.

During dinner later that same night, after another comment from Jay about something that only a guy could do to a "real" female, Vonlee "snapped," she said. She shoved her food across the table toward Jay. Stood. Then screamed: "I cannot do this anymore. I am not what you want me to be, and I am not ready to be that right now. . . ."

Vonlee ran into the bedroom and cried. Jay took his time, but he came in and consoled his girlfriend.

"You've taught me how to love, Vonlee . . . ," Jay said.

Vonlee tried to get up to leave, but he wouldn't let her go.

"I've never felt like this," he said (according to Vonlee).

As they began another round of yelling, the phone rang. It was Jay's work. The alarm system was going off and he needed to get over there immediately.

Jay grabbed his coat and, before leaving, said, "We'll finish this later."

Vonlee sat and watched Jay walk out the door. Moments later, she made a decision.

It was time to leave—with all of her belongings.

"And I never saw him again after that night. We had phone sex once, when he called, but that was it—we were through."

CHAPTER 38

THE NUMBER GLUED ON the brick portico had a contemporary slant to its decor: 2090. A white plastic lawn chair sat in the corner of the entryway, just underneath that street number and door, which went into Don Rogers's home. The blinds covering the side window attached to the door were closed, but it appeared someone was home. There was movement inside the house, Detective Don Zimmerman and a colleague noticed as they approached.

It was close to four o'clock in the afternoon on January 5, 2001. The holidays had come and gone. The TPD had left Vonlee and her aunt alone for a while, but now it was time to pick up the pace of the investigation again. Now that the TPD had Vonlee on tape admitting that she had watched as Billie Jean murdered her husband with a pillow—and might have even helped Billie Jean with the crime herself—but detectives figured why not confront Billie Jean with some of what they knew. See what she had to say.

Zimmerman knocked.

No answer.

So he knocked again.

A dog barked on the opposite side of the street.

The other detective with Zimmerman said, "They have a phone, don't they?"

"I can bang on the door again."

As they were figuring out their next move, somebody opened the door.

"Hi, Mrs. Rogers," Zimmerman said, extending a hand. He explained who he was before introducing his colleague.

The house alarm was going off in the background. It was loud and obnoxious.

"You remember me?" Zimmerman asked. "I talked to you several weeks ago when your husband died."

The other cop asked, "Can you make that alarm go off? You want to take care of that."

Billie Jean let them in as she walked away to shut off the alarm.

"Hi, Ms. Rogers," Zimmerman said when they got settled and the noise of the alarm diminished. "We need to talk to you."

After a few moments of small talk, taking over lead in the conversation, Zimmerman asked, "Do you know what happened?"

"Well," Billie Jean said, an obvious sharpness in her tone, "he died."

"We need to ask you about the missing stuff."

"The what?" She was confused about this statement. What was missing? There hadn't been anything stolen from the house—what were they talking about?

After realizing he'd made a mistake, Zimmerman explained: "You may probably know that [Vonlee] told somebody about what happened that night, okay?"

The other cop chimed in: "Don's been murdered."

"And there is a break in the case," said Zimmerman as the Rogers widow looked totally blindsided by the statement. "You remember Danny?"

"Who?" she asked.

They told her.

"Yeah," she said, looking at them.

Of course, she knew Danny: Vonlee's boyfriend.

"[Vonlee] told Danny what happened here that night. . . ."

"[Vonlee] . . . might say *anything*," she said with a bit of how-dare-she in her phlegmy, smoker's voice. "I don't know what you heard."

"We're here to get to the truth."

"Okay," she acknowledged, as though she didn't have a problem talking to two cops without her lawyer present, both of them coming across as pushy and accusatory.

For cops looking to figure out who was the driving force behind a murder such as the case in front of the TPD (after all, they understood that Vonlee could have lied to Danny and planned and carried out the murder entirely by herself), there were two ways to approach an interview like this: One, lay everything down the way it happened and see if the subject drops her shoulders, takes a deep breath and, caving into her own guilt, admits everything. Or the second way, play one perp against the other and lie about certain details in order to allow the truth to rise to the surface by itself. With a subject like Billie Jean Rogers, considering her history of gambling (i.e., taking chances), it might be better to go with the latter.

One of the detectives said the TPD wanted to give her "the opportunity to tell us the truth about what happened," adding grimly, "[Vonlee] painted a pretty gruesome picture of you to us, and she has indicated that this entire thing that happened was all your doing, and that she's really a minor part of that—and she's putting basically *everything* off on you, okay?"

Billie Jean was obviously surprised by this breach of

trust. One could almost hear her thinking: *How dare that bitch. All I did for her!*

The second cop added, "Um, we looked at her . . . criminal history—or his?—or *her* criminal history, whatever. What do you refer to her as? Your niece or your nephew?"

Billie Jean started to say something, but they cut her off.

"But we, we looked at . . . her criminal records. She's got a criminal record."

"She *does*?" the aunt asked, seemingly surprised.

"Yeah. And we've looked at yours and there is none. So Vonlee . . . we've come to think that Vonlee might've helped put you up to this, or at least she did it and you helped do it. We know that you were there and we have plenty of evidence . . . to say what's going on, and Vonlee has told us things . . . but we know [she] told somebody everything that happened that night. They told us."

Don Zimmerman mentioned how they had it on good information that Vonlee had since moved to Chicago, and Billie Jean confirmed Vonlee had indeed left the state. It might have appeared, or these cops certainly made it seem, as if Vonlee had taken off in haste and had run. But she had told everyone where she was going and where she was living. It was no secret.

"You know, now maybe you know what happened that night, and we're here to find out the truth," Zimmerman added.

They walked from the living room into the kitchen for a moment as she poured herself something to drink. "I know nothing happened that I *know* of," she explained, before blurting out, for no reason, what seemed to be an odd statement: "I did not asphyxiate my husband. I wouldn't. . . ."

"Well, you know, why would [Vonlee] say that you did?"

Billie Jean said she had no idea why Vonlee would accuse

her of such a heinous crime. She had no explanation for that. Did she need one?

"She said that she *assisted* you in that endeavor . . . and that you paid her money."

"No. No," Billie Jean insisted.

"Did you pay her any money?"

"I gave her some money to get a, uh, for a sex-change job."

"Yeah, you bought her a car, too."

"I wrote the check for the cash," the aunt explained. She was having trouble with the idea that any of this was a crime. Could she not give her niece money—especially after suddenly coming into a fortune because of a death?

They talked about money and how the widow had been spending frivolously. Then Zimmerman gave her a chance to ease her way out of what they were projecting to be seriously suspicious behavior on her part lately.

"Well, what we're trying to get at is the truth here. If you only had a little part to do with this, we want to know that—and you can tell us what part Vonlee had in it."

"I had *nothing* to do with it," Billie Jean said right away, firmly. She walked back into the living room and sat down. She was feeling cornered and pressured. These cops were being overbearing bullies, following her around her own house, peppering her with questions that seemed to point a finger, all because her niece had said a few things. She didn't understand it. Why were they doing this? They kept going back to Vonlee and how she had claimed her aunt paid her for her help. Didn't matter what Billie Jean was saying now, Vonlee was apparently tossing her aunt to the wolves.

"We don't know the exact story what happened," one of them said, "but she is telling us one and it makes you look pretty bad, okay?"

Billie Jean explained that Vonlee, throughout her life, had always told lots of tall tales. She was known for this in the family. What she was saying now meant nothing to Billie Jean, she said.

Zimmerman claimed they had spoken to Vonlee and that she was willing to "take a polygraph to say, you know, what she said is the truth. So it's probably going to happen."

The aunt didn't seem too concerned about this: "Whatever," she said.

They asked her what time she got home that night.

She wouldn't answer. She'd already told them, she explained.

It seemed they had reached an impasse when Zimmerman suggested, "Now, you're going to have to . . . tell us what actually happened, or we're going to have to go with *her* story."

Billie Jean took a sip from her cup and stared at them. Checkmate.

CHAPTER 39

VONLEE TITLOW WAS AT a crossroads in her life once again. This time, she sat back and licked her wounds from that last relationship with Jay. She'd put two years into it. The only thing Vonlee could think of doing next was perhaps to leave Denver. Get the hell out of town and find her roots back home in Tennessee.

So she packed her car and left. Unlike many people, if Vonlee understood one thing about life, it was that you could always start over. There would always be another sunrise. Maryville was home. Family would always be there for her.

Along the way, Vonlee stopped and called Mandy, just to let her know that she'd thrown in the towel and had taken off.

"Where you at?" Mandy asked.

"I don't know . . . halfway between Denver and home, I guess."

"What are you *doing*, Vonlee?"

She started to cry. "I don't know. I am going a little crazy."

"Well, you turn your ass around and you come back here!" Mandy insisted.

What made this so difficult for her was the belief that she "was truly, *truly* in love with this guy. Everything I thought I wanted in a person, he had," Vonlee said. The demise of the relationship, however, made her feel like she "wasn't good enough. And I knew that after I had the operation, the next thing for him was going to be 'We cannot have kids,'" Vonlee wisely stated.

As she saw it, with Jay, maybe with any heterosexual guy, there was always going to be that one thing she couldn't give him: never being a complete woman.

"[Jay] was the kind of person that wanted kids, and the type of person that wanted kids that looked like and sounded like him. It wasn't ever going to be enough for him and I could see it."

The decision to transform into a female—that final operation—was a process that she needed to take her time at, Vonlee explained. If a guy did it when he was eighteen or twenty, or even midtwenties, it was far too early, Vonlee maintained, speaking for herself. However, being that young, he might not have known any different.

"You need to live your life as you see it . . . ," she elaborated. "I needed to be sure. My mother said to me, 'Wait until you're at least twenty-five.' I promised I would."

Then there was the possibility of never experiencing an orgasm.

"Look, I've heard stories of girls having no trouble after the operation having a 'female' orgasm. And I've been told by others that they could stab their new 'vagina' with a fork and not feel a thing. So it was always a big decision for me, because I valued and liked sex so much."

Vonlee drove back to Denver after talking with Mandy.

"And I began to date guys that actually enjoyed being with a 'she-male.'"

Once again, Vonlee rolled with the changes of her life and thought she could find happiness in something new.

The escort service was next. Vonlee opened it in Denver. Yet, after going home for a visit, she decided she wanted to leave Denver and move to Chicago. It was during that brief visit back home when Vonlee ran into Billie Jean and, after not seeing each other for almost a decade, the two sparked up a relationship. Vonlee mentioned to her aunt how she was going to be moving to Chicago in the near future and that she would be close to Michigan, where the Rogers couple was living.

"Y'all better come and see me," Billie Jean suggested.

"Of course, I will, Aunt Billie."

Vonlee was taken by Billie Jean during the visit. Her aunt had made Vonlee feel as though she could do anything in life she wanted. She gave Vonlee hope. She planted within Vonlee the idea that anything she wanted was within her own potential, her own grasp. She taught Vonlee to go for it, if she truly wanted it.

"My aunt was classy, beautiful, one of the most gorgeous women I have ever seen. But that entire time, while in Denver and then after I left, I had zero contact with her until I went back home for that visit. Growing up, though, I always thought of Aunt Billie as a movie star—she was so glamorous and just, well, she had that star quality about her. I wanted to be like her. I loved her."

Billie Jean and Vonlee's mother, Georgia, grew up in a family of eight kids. Billie Jean stood out from the pack—always. She "had to have the best of things," Vonlee shared. "She was also different, someone that was very smart. She had this aura about her that once you were around her, you just wanted to *be* around her. She was funny and she was talented, and I never had anything bad to say about her."

Contrarily, certain family members said Billie Jean had this "evilness" about her that only those close enough could see and actually feel. One family member claimed later that Billie Jean had asked him to kill Don once and she even drew a map of the house. The family member went to police with the map and told them the story. According to Vonlee, "Not long after that, he was beaten to death by a couple of men with chains . . . and I almost believe she had something to do with it."

After starting out with an escort service in Denver, Vonlee decided it was time to move to Chicago. She had met a new guy and he allowed her to stay at one of his town houses in downtown Chicago. Barton (pseudonym) wouldn't be living there (he had his own), but he wanted her around. He had even once told Vonlee that he'd pay all her bills and give her a stipend if she was there for him. By now, though, Vonlee was making so much money with the escort service, she didn't need anybody else.

There were no secrets between the two of them. Barton knew Vonlee was a transsexual and he didn't have a problem with it. It was around this time that Vonlee began to meet a lot of men that preferred transsexuals, many of them straight men.

"You have to understand," Vonlee explained, "these weren't 'gay' relationships. When we were together, I was the woman [and] he was the guy. . . . You know, it was there—I don't know how to say it. Some guys, you have to recognize, are into it. They find the whole penis thing as being part of the package extremely attractive. Those 'chicks with dicks' videos are the most popular in the porn shops. There's an entire market out there for it."

Why not capitalize on that market, then?

"After moving to Chicago, I still had three escort services I was running—transsexuals, gay, straight. The transsexual phone lines rang off the hook."

She had five transsexuals and she would turn dates herself if needed.

Vonlee's Telegrams, as she called it, began in Denver. It was an escort service, but Vonlee set it up with a tax number and she paid herself a salary. She hired an attorney to tell her what she could and couldn't do. All of her "girls" had to sign waivers that said they would not solicit customers for sex.

But come on now . . . business is business.

"I knew it was going on," Vonlee admitted later. "But I couldn't . . . Well, I was trying to be as legal with it as possible. Look, it was about making money."

When Vonlee took calls herself, there were only certain things she would do.

"Limits," she explained. "I never once had anal sex or kissed one of these guys—I just wouldn't do it. Honestly, though, most of them just wanted to 'do oral' . . . on me. They had always fantasized about it and it was something they always wanted to do. These guys weren't attracted to men. They were straight. Many of them were married. They would all say the same thing. 'I'm not attracted to men, but I am *very* attracted to transsexuals. I love the way you look. I always wanted to give one oral sex.' It was always the same story. They claimed they had never done it before. They were always scared and a nervous wreck. It would last about fifteen, twenty minutes and they'd pay five hundred dollars."

Moving to Chicago for Vonlee was her way of trying to get away from the escort business, though she kept doing it, running businesses in both cities at the same time. The money was too good. And by now, she was drinking a lot more than she ever had and dabbling in hard-core drugs.

And so, with her new lifestyle caving in around her, the idea that one man wanted to "keep her," Vonlee

decided finally to bail on it all and go back home, get
that job at the Waffle House, and then try to clean up
her act. She thought she could leave it all behind and
bury it for good.

But then Billie Jean walked into the Waffle House and
laughed at her niece, ultimately offering her a life in
Troy, Michigan, with her and Don—a life that Vonlee
Titlow, apparently, could not turn down.

CHAPTER 40

BILLIE JEAN ROGERS HAD two pushy cops sitting inside her home, pressuring her to answer questions about her husband's death she thought she'd answered already. Did she need to remind them that Don's body had been cremated and there had not been an "investigation," which she was aware of, into his death? The ME, moreover, had ruled Don's death a result of natural causes, and had found nothing out of the ordinary. What were these two cops doing, anyway? Trying to make a case out of nothing?

As she listened to their questions, she certainly believed so.

After Don Zimmerman asked Billie Jean to go through that night once more, she balked at first, but then explained, while pointing, how she had walked in "that door" right there and saw him lying on the floor in the kitchen "right there."

This would become a major issue for cops as they thought about it and looked at the layout of the house, studied the crime scenes photographs and delved deeper into Billie Jean's financial woes. It was that glass on the table and those shoes in the living room. One could not sit in the chair where that glass and the shoes were located and *not see* Don on the floor inside the kitchen.

"Vonlee," Zimmerman's partner said, "has indicated that both you and she has participated—"

They were now pointing a finger directly at Billie Jean.

"Now," Billie Jean said, interrupting, stopping just short of asking them to leave her house at once, "I know *nothing.*"

The cop then finished what he was trying to say, adding, ". . . in *smothering* your husband. Now she says that *you're* the one who did it. She says it was all *your* idea, and you had been wanting to get rid of your husband for some time past. Now, um, we have been in the police force over twenty-five years," he said, pointing to himself and Zimmerman. "We know there's two sides to this story, okay. We know that [Vonlee] has a little bit of a sordid past. You don't have no criminal history . . . [but] the truth is that your husband was *smothered* to death. . . ."

"I did not smother him," Billie Jean said.

Zimmerman cleared his throat. It sounded almost like a fake cough. "So . . . I'm getting the impression that you knew something happened that night?"

This was a question, not a statement.

She became irate. *"Impression?* What's the matter with you?" she snapped. "Now you're . . . you're twisting my words."

They wouldn't let up. "We know that this happened that night here. It wasn't . . . that he just, uh, had too much alcohol. He obviously had a little bit too much alcohol."

"Well, if it happened here, somebody came in and did it when I was gone," the widow said.

"Two people . . . 'cause Nicole's saying *she* did it with *you.*"

Billie Jean said there was no way they should believe

anything Vonlee said—*not ever.* She was making it all up.
Vonlee was known in the family to tell all sorts of stories.
She'd get drunk and call back home and spew lies and
make up things about people—only to turn around the
next day and say none of it was true. She had been intoxicated.

Zimmerman asked why she would do that in this situation. What could possibly be Vonlee's motive to drag
herself and her aunt into a murder? Why even tell Danny
anything? It was as though Vonlee had wanted to set up
a story by telling Danny that her aunt was solely responsible for the murder. She had, in effect, put herself in
the same context of being responsible—at least in some
respects. Why would she do that if it was not true?

"Why would she tell [her] boyfriend . . . that this happened that night if it *didn't* happen? Why would anybody
ever do that? She told this guy, and we heard her telling
this guy that this happened. . . ."

Billie Jean walked toward the kitchen, stopped, turned
around and walked back to where both cops sat. "I don't
know," she said.

They tried to convince her that her niece was singing
loud and clear, and that it was going to be in her best
interest in the end to come clean. Here was her chance.
Right now. At this moment. Give it up and they might be
able to help. Hold back and she was on her own from
this point forward.

Classic cop chess move.

But Billie Jean wouldn't bite.

So they tried to appeal to her moral compass.

"[Vonlee] can't live with it anymore," one of them
said. "She cannot deal with it on her conscience anymore, and you're going to have a problem with it on *your*
conscience."

"I have nothing on my conscience," she said clearly

and without hesitation. It came out as sincere. If she had been involved, the truth was that she *didn't* care.

"I think you do," the more assertive Zimmerman said.

"Well, I think I *don't*."

Both cops kept going back to what Vonlee had told Danny, but Billie Jean didn't seem too jarred by it. She had a definite attitude: *So what? Vonlee said this and that. Big freakin' deal. Where's your evidence?*

"I was very good to that man," Don's widow explained after being accused of not caring about her late husband.

"I know," Zimmerman said. "You married him twice, right?"

"And he and I had a *good* relationship."

"Do you have like videotapes of you and him on honeymoon or anything like that?" Zimmerman's partner asked in a tone that indicated he already knew the answer.

"No."

"Why, though?"

"We didn't have anything like that."

"Yes, you did," Zimmerman said snappishly. "'Cause you know why? 'Cause I have them. 'Cause you threw them away shortly after he passed."

She stared at the cop: *And that is your evidence of murder?*

They got stuck on this videotape thing. Billie Jean said she and Don had taken off to Vegas to get married and were "not into" videos.

The detectives disagreed.

"You threw them out several days after his death and Danny picked them up. . . . Now, why would [you] throw out those videotapes if [they were] so important to you? I understand he was a very sick man. A lot of work for you. You did a great job with him."

The conversation stayed on the videotapes as the two

cops could not let it go. Billie Jean seemed genuinely confused by this. She couldn't recall if or when she supposedly threw out a bag of videotapes and Vonlee's boyfriend took them.

As they kept on it, however, Billie Jean admitted that perhaps, yes, she and Don might have videotaped their second walk down the aisle, but what did it have to do with killing him? Then, trying to steer both cops off the videotape thread, she offered, "I swear on my life [Vonlee] had nothing to do with it—and neither did I."

"[Vonlee] *did,* because [she] is *admitting* to having something to do with it."

Both cops hinted that Vonlee could be in custody (she wasn't), while not allowing Billie Jean a moment of reprieve. They continually badgered her about the situations that led them to change their focus from a simple death investigation into a complicated murder investigation.

They had Vonlee on tape accusing Billie Jean and admitting her role.

Danny Chahine backed it up.

They pointed to all the money Billie Jean was spending.

They talked about the drinking and gambling.

They knew about the debt Billie Jean had created by gambling.

There were cars and jewelry.

The marriage had been in a bit of shambles.

Vonlee had no reason to lie about any of this. They had not confronted or sought her out. She had essentially admitted this to them without knowing they were listening.

Then it was back to the drinking, this time focused not on Don, but on Billie Jean.

". . . I don't know if you drink or not?" Zimmerman wondered.

"I *don't* drink," she said, contrasting what everyone else involved was telling police about her.

"Okay," one cop started to say, "so . . ."

But he wasn't able to finish. Billie Jean had an admission to make—something she needed to share regarding not only her alleged drinking, but also Don's death.

Both cops waited.

She stared at the carpet and took a sip of water.

CHAPTER 41

BILLIE JEAN ROGERS STARED at both cops. She was ready to say something important—perhaps finally admit her role in this alleged murder.

"I have a liver problem," she began. Then: "I . . . I may not live . . . another six months." She allowed it to hang in the space between them for a minute before adding, "Why would I want to do something like that?"

In other words, if her time was up, why would she ever want to get involved with killing her husband? It made no sense.

Or did it?

Maybe Billie Jean wanted to live it up before she left the planet and knew that killing her husband wouldn't matter. She was dying, anyway.

What came across as interesting about the revelation of Billie Jean perhaps having only months to live was how these two cops reacted to it, responding as if she had made it up. Billie Jean said she was dying, and they missed the opportunity to ask her if she wanted to live it up on Don before she went—hence a motive for taking him out. Instead, they chose to ask her if she had a gambling problem.

"How's your gambling habit? Is it pretty bad?" one of them asked.

"It's not a habit," she insisted.

"I mean, you *had* a problem. . . . Your husband had a problem with your gambling, didn't he? I mean, he was onto you about the gambling money?"

"Well, he . . . well, every once in a while, he was."

The interview went on and on and on. The detectives kept going back to the money, the insurance claims, the cars Billie Jean bought, the money she gave Vonlee, the casino, how Billie Jean did not seem at all bothered by the fact they were there questioning her.

Follow the money, these cops knew. It always told a story.

She shrugged it off: *You have nothing!*

In a way, this was true. If they had anything, she would be answering these questions in metal bracelets downtown. But here they were inside her house, drilling her on everything they'd supposedly developed during their investigation. From where she sat, she looked pretty damn solid.

Didn't matter what Vonlee said.

Didn't matter that they had Vonlee on tape.

Didn't matter that Billie Jean had spent her husband's money.

Didn't matter where she got that money: from a cashed-in mutual fund or his bank accounts.

What mattered was evidence—old-fashioned evidence of murder—where was it?

She became frustrated: "Okay . . . I just don't know what's going on here."

For another hour, they peppered her with questions about the money and Don's bleeding from the rectum and his drinking and her gambling. They went back and forth, tit for tat, as she answered every single question they put in front of her. It was exhausting just listening to the interview.

Finally, near the end, she said, "You know what? Get realistic. If I was going to do anything like this, listen. If I was going to do something like this, it *certainly* wouldn't be with her. . . ."

"Well," Zimmerman said, "according to her, it was. . . ."

Billie Jean didn't know how to respond to that.

"Let me ask you this. Honestly, straightforward, honest answer. Have you ever spoken to [Vonlee] in any way, shape or form [saying] that you would pay somebody money to get rid of your husband?"

"No!"

"You never told her that?"

"No."

"Not even as a joke?"

"No. Never! Absolutely did not."

They asked again and again.

No. No. No.

Then it was back to the money.

"This is your opportunity. If [Vonlee] did it and you're covering for her, this is the time to tell it. Because let me tell you what [she's] going to do. . . . She's going to get prosecuted, then she's going to turn around and she's going to be a witness against you, because she has the minor part in this thing, okay? She's going to testify against you and put you away as the main culprit in this whole deal. When she is the main culprit, you're sticking up for her and you're going to do the time for it and she's going to be out getting her sex change. Okay?"

Billie Jean said repeatedly that she didn't do anything.

They tried for another half hour and got nowhere.

Zimmerman wanted to ask her one more question as they were preparing to take off. "Billie, you willing to take a polygraph test?"

"Sure," she said.

They scheduled it for January 6, 9:00 A.M.

She never showed up.

"Billie, are you coming?" Zimmerman asked after calling.

"Family members advised me to get a lawyer before submitting to the test."

Hanging up the phone, Zimmerman knew there was only one thing left for him to do at this point.

CHAPTER 42

SOME CONSIDERED IT AN unlucky number, but thirteen law enforcement officials were on hand at 11:25 A.M., on January 6, 2001, when a search warrant was issued for Billie Jean and Don's Grenadier residence. With that type of personnel power, you'd expect a meth lab or bomb-making factory to be uncovered in the basement. Yet, this mighty show of force was there to go through and find any incriminating evidence against Billie Jean Rogers (and perhaps Vonlee) inside the home she shared with the husband she had supposedly murdered.

Detective Don Zimmerman and a partner knocked on the door. Zimmerman handed her the warrant, saying, "We're here to search your home for items associated with the homicide of Donald Rogers."

She let them in.

Zimmerman asked if it was okay for the entire team to come in.

She took a look outside.

Man, what a crowd.

"Yes, come on in . . . ," she said without much ado.

The TPD was now all over Billie Jean and Vonlee,

though Billie Jean did not seem too concerned as the investigation took on an entire new level of intensity. Where Vonlee stood on it all was anybody's guess: she was still in Chicago.

In his twenty-nine-item search warrant, Zimmerman outlined the case he believed the TPD had against the two women. Mainly, it consisted of Don's daughter, Danny Chahine's recorded conversations with Vonlee and the money trail that alerted the TPD to a possible homicide, which from there tipped the scales of the medical examiner to say, *"Yeah, you know what? Maybe Don was murdered, now that I think about it."* Detectives Zimmerman and Tullock had met with the medical examiner again and talked about Don's death in more frank, focused detail during those days after Danny Chahine had come forward. Now that they had the information from the conversations Danny had recorded, it was easy—from their perspective—to put together the scenario that had vaguely shown up on the initial autopsy. Things made sense, in other words, now that they had all the pieces of the puzzle in place: the slight bruising on Don's lips; the amount of alcohol in his system; the fact that one leg was crossed over the other.

Essentially, the TPD needed the medical examiner's office to change its stance on the cause of death. In order to proceed with criminal charges, Zimmerman said later, the cause of death needed to be homicide. It didn't mean the medical examiner's office or the TPD was forcing anything, or trying to convince each other there had been a murder. The fact remained: more information about Don's death had become available—namely, a confession by someone who was there when it happened.

For Don Tullock, he later said in court, Don Rogers's legs being crossed had always bothered him. He thought it to be very odd from the first time he saw it. With twenty-five years on the job, Tullock had relied on instinct. And in this case, his gut said that Don Rogers's killer staged that scene to make it appear as though he had fallen out of a chair onto the ground and died.

Executing this search was an important moment for the TPD, especially for Detectives Zimmerman and Tullock. It meant a judge had agreed that there was enough probable cause to execute a search of Billie Jean's home and, most important for these cops, Don's financial records, much of which they expected to find inside the house. Whenever a spouse kills his or her significant other, it is generally motivated by money or revenge. Documents are the best source for detectives in finding the roots of that motive.

The Rogers widow was cordial as she let everyone in.

One of the first things Zimmerman looked for was Billie Jean's checkbook and ledger. Zimmerman wanted to see what she had been spending her money on, whom she had paid money to and what other interesting factors the ledger might reveal.

"It's right here," she said.

"It was a financial record, number one," Zimmerman commented later. "And number two, I was aware that checks pertaining to this case were issued through Bank One. . . ."

Indeed, they had a check made out to Vonlee for $70,260 and signed by Billie Jean. It was dated August 24, 2000. The TPD believed that check was payment either to keep Vonlee's mouth shut or for her participation in the murder—or maybe both.

The TPD had already known about the cars, and the checkbook verified that information and the amount Billie Jean had paid for each.

As Zimmerman looked at the back page inside the cover of Billie Jean's checkbook, he noticed something else. A handwritten note, presumably by Billie Jean: *Vonlee—$100,000.*

Other items they secured included: *one plastic drinking glass from kitchen; last will and test[ament] for Don Rogers; death certificate . . . misc. Cadillac papers; two dining room chairs; cardboard box containing misc. documents relating to Donald Rogers.* All of this was taken, along with other nonforensic-type evidence, which amounted to nothing.

For Zimmerman and Tullock, despite the lack of locating any smoking gun that would undeniably nail Billie Jean and Vonlee, it was a matter of time before Billie Jean Rogers would be under arrest for the murder of her husband.

CHAPTER 43

FROM THE POINT OF the search warrant on, the investigation took on a familiar checklist type of routine for Detectives Don Tullock and Don Zimmerman. The documents they uncovered led them to witnesses and other people who knew the Rogers couple and interacted with them on a daily basis. One business associate Tullock spoke to, in particular, added a bit of insight into Don Rogers's life and what he was thinking about in the days before he died. Essentially, the TPD needed whatever it could get at this point. Because when all was said and done, the best case they had was based on circumstantial evidence.

The guy, who had worked for Don and his partner at the machine shop, told Tullock that Don had said to him one day, "Some people are just waiting for me to die so they can get my money."

"He ever say who?" Tullock asked.

"No . . . and in all fairness to Mrs. Rogers, Don could have been talking about [other family members]."

Tullock wanted to know about how Mrs. Rogers acted after Don's death.

"Toni [the company secretary] asked me to go over

and help Mrs. Rogers remove some things from the home. I hauled out approximately one hundred large plastic garbage bags at the direction of Mrs. Rogers. Don was a pack rat and opted not to discard most of his possessions."

Still, just days after Don's dead, here is his wife getting rid of any memory of the guy. It seemed far too soon to be cleaning the house of Don's lifetime worth of personal belongings, in the detective's opinion.

"You know what was in the bags?" Tullock wondered.

"Clothing, bedding materials, personal stuff. That type of thing. I also hauled away old furniture."

"Tell me about Billie Jean," Tullock said. "How has she been?"

"I've only seen her on a few occasions . . . but since his death, I found nothing unusual about her demeanor, other than she appears to be sedated or medicated whenever I see her."

Tullock asked about Vonlee.

"I did meet [her]," he said sheepishly, almost embarrassed to answer the question. "Mrs. Rogers's 'niece,' I was shocked to learn from a recent newspaper article, is male. I even saw her once wearing a 'see-through' nightie and could see her very large breasts."

And that was all he had.

CHAPTER 44

ON JANUARY 16, 2001, Vonlee was inside her Chicago apartment getting ready to go out for the night with a friend, Thomas (pseudonym). They had plans to party and gamble aboard a riverboat casino. Vonlee's friend was in the process of having some remodeling done on his apartment and needed a place to crash, so he had been staying with her. As Vonlee applied her makeup in the bathroom, Thomas walked in.

"Hey, can I borrow your car to go to the ATM?"

"Of course."

He said thanks and left.

Vonlee decided to lie down and take a quick nap, knowing it was going to be a long night. She drifted away quickly, but was soon startled awake by a rap on her front door.

"Yes, yes . . . just a minute," she said. The knock on the door had an urgent, impatient tone to it. Vonlee wasn't expecting anyone and wondered who it could be.

"Who is it?" she said, opening the door to a man she had never seen before. There were several other men and one female standing behind him.

Cops, great, Vonlee thought when she figured it out.

"Do you know a man by the name of Thomas?" the man, now identifying himself as a detective, asked.

"Why, yes, of course. He's a friend."

"Does he have permission to drive your vehicle? We just stopped him in your car." They had him in custody.

"Well, yes, yes . . . he has permission," Vonlee said. *What in the hell is going on here?*

"Listen, can we come in?" the cop asked.

Vonlee said fine as she opened the door and "that's when they all came rushing in." A swarm of law enforcement. The first domino was about to fall for the TPD. The Chicago Police Department, acting on a warrant issued by Troy, were there to arrest Vonlee on murder charges. Detectives Zimmerman and Tullock, Vonlee said, were there with them. But this was CPD's collar.

"You remember us?" Zimmerman walked over and asked Vonlee (she later recalled). Zimmerman, she said, had a smug look about his face. He was being sarcastic. Smarmy.

"Uh, yeah," Vonlee said. "I remember."

"Well, you are under arrest for the murder of Donald Rogers. . . ." He said the words as though he'd been waiting for this moment since first meeting Vonlee.

"Have y'all arrested my aunt?" Vonlee asked.

There was no answer.

It wasn't hard to secure an arrest warrant for Vonlee considering that she—in a recorded admission—claimed to have participated in Don's murder. The TPD had a statement and a recording from Danny Chahine, and Vonlee certainly gave enough incriminating information against herself and her aunt to make any judge suspicious enough to sign a warrant. The trick for the TPD was going to be holding on to Vonlee once she was in custody.

Later on, when she went back and revisited it in her memory, Vonlee said, "You ever watch a movie, and they show somebody walking out of a house, lights flashing, cops in uniform all around, and the person is in handcuffs and it's in slow motion? Well, I swear to God, it was just like that."

Vonlee said her life stopped at that moment and began to move at a "snail's pace." It began when they were in the living room. Vonlee hadn't even been dressed when they came in. She was wearing a robe. The shoulder of her robe kept falling down, and the female officer there to supervise the arrest kept telling Vonlee to pull it up. The detectives had to keep reminding Vonlee to get dressed, since it was time to go. She was milking it, Vonlee later admitted, thinking that every moment she stalled was another moment free.

"Well, this is a first," one of the detectives said, according to Vonlee.

"What do you mean: 'This is a first'?"

"The first time we come to somebody's house like yours and don't find anything illegal."

To Vonlee, the judgments began with that comment.

As they walked around the apartment, Vonlee recalled, Zimmerman and Tullock were taken aback by the "things" Vonlee owned. If there was one truth about Vonlee's character she would readily agree to without a fight, it was that she liked expensive material possessions.

"How can you live like this? How *do* you live like this?" one of the detectives asked, referring to all of the nice things Vonlee had inside her apartment.

"Extravagant," Vonlee said later. That's what they were insinuating—that she lived in the lap of luxury. And it was some sort of a crime for her to do it. As they walked around and wanted to know how she could afford to live the way she did, without working a regular job, Vonlee inferred from the conversation that they were disgusted by it.

Most of the things Vonlee had, she said, "I had my

whole life. I designed my own bedroom set. I had it forever. I had antiques . . . and it might take me three or four years to pay for the things, but I wanted them and paid for them myself."

What she later suspected had set them off were some of the dresses and blouses with the price tags still attached, which she had hanging in her closet. They were expensive.

"And they were just trying to chastise me for being able to afford such things," Vonlee added.

By nine-thirty on that same night, Vonlee was in custody at the CPD, being booked and processed. But the Chicago police had a major problem: where were they going to hold Vonlee until the TPD could get her into a Chicago court and ask a judge to extradite her—if Vonlee agreed, that is—back to Troy?

CHAPTER 45

WHILE IN CUSTODY AT the Chicago Police Department, waiting to go before a judge and face extradition to Michigan, Vonlee was "scared to death," she said. It's no secret that a transsexual like Vonlee, as good-looking and seemingly "female" as she appeared, would be a good candidate for excessive and violent rape while in lockup.

Vonlee recalled how big the story was: "If I didn't imagine this, I swear that while I was being taken into custody and led out of my apartment and into a patrol car, there were helicopters overhead . . . because it was on the news instantly."

She sat in a small room at the CPD, her hands hand-cuffed to the chair. Left with her own thoughts about what would happen next, all she could do was think about the stories she'd heard about Chicago lockup. It was one of the worst places a person like Vonlee could be housed.

"You want to just go ahead and just tell us what happened?" one cop came in and asked Vonlee.

"Well, why don't you tell *me* what happened?" Vonlee

snapped back. She'd been down this road before. She knew the drill.

"You might as well go ahead and confess, because we got it all on the recording," one cop explained—Vonlee could not recall who it was, whether it was Tullock or Zimmerman.

"If y'all got it on the recording, well, you don't need me to tell you what happened."

They looked at each other. This was not going to be as simple as they'd hoped.

This sort of psychological impasse went on for hours. They'd come in, ask a few questions, leave Vonlee for a few hours to wrestle with her own thoughts, then come back and ask her what happened. They'd inquire if she needed to use the restroom, want a cigarette, coffee, soda, food, whatever.

But Vonlee was not going to talk about anything. That was made clear to them right away, she later claimed.

Because Vonlee wouldn't eat anything, she said, "I guess that was their plan—to wait until I was really hungry and then use the food to make me talk. But I never got hungry."

She could not recall how long, exactly, she was with the CPD inside that room, handcuffed to a chair, "but it seemed to go on for days. . . ."

It was about twelve hours.

As she sat and thought about her situation, Vonlee considered that all she had to do was call them in and say, "Look, I understand that this was said, and that was said, and it is recorded, but I was afraid of Danny . . . and I was afraid of what he would do if he found out . . . because he knew that my aunt had killed her husband and he used to warn me all the time that she was a mean person, who could do such a thing, and I just decided to play along with him and that story. That story got out of control and . . . well, I told him what he wanted to hear."

Sitting, contemplating what to do, Vonlee thought, *I could just lie about all of this, because they have nothing. I know they have nothing. That recording is nothing.*

Still, as she considered her options, Vonlee later said, "There was just something inside of me that just wouldn't allow me to lie about it all."

Finally, after a rather long stalemate, Vonlee called them in and said, "I'm going to tell you everything you want to know."

She said they gathered everyone together and sat down with a recording device placed in front of her. All of the cops seemed excited.

"You're not going to like what I am getting ready to say," Vonlee explained after they asked a series of specific questions: name, address, where they were recording the interview, time of day, that sort of thing.

"We know it's hard, but it's the right thing to do," one cop told her.

"Okay, y'all ready . . . ?"

They waited on baited breath.

Vonlee nestled up to the microphone and announced, "I want an attorney."

She smiled, sat back, crossed her legs.

"Get her the hell out of here," one of the cops yelled to a uniform outside the door.

CHAPTER 46

VONLEE WAS IN LOCKUP. From her point of view, it was as though she had walked into the Roman Coliseum, with lions and tigers pacing back and forth in front of her, ready to pounce.

According to Vonlee, with no corroborating evidence to support her claim, the abuse started the moment she got into the elevator with a cop to head to lockup.

"I was offered alcohol by a guard, first thing—that is, if I showed him my boobs," Vonlee said. "They offered me weed to have oral sex with a white guy I was put into a bunk with. . . . I was raped . . . abused. . . . It was absolute hell."

Vonlee weighed about 140 pounds at the time, long blond hair down to her waist, the curves of a woman.

"I was going to the tanning beds all the time then, and I had this little Playboy bunny sticker I would put on my skin so when I tanned and took it off, I had this Playboy bunny there."

She claimed she was forced to "strip twice in front of a whole group of guys and they were just freaking the hell out."

When she squawked about being put into the pen

with all of these men who were hardened criminals, ready and waiting to do her harm in the most vile ways, according to Vonlee, she was told, "Look, we have to treat you the same as any other man—we were sued by a transsexual and that's the way it is! We cannot discriminate."

She wound up in the maximum-security portion of lockup. When she was being escorted in, a series of "large, *very* large, black and white men" looked on, whistling and shouting obscenities and what they were going to do to her when they could get her alone.

It was only when she was forced to shower with all of them that a courageous guard stepped up and said, "There's no way I am putting her in there with them."

So from there, after a lengthy discussion, they put Vonlee in the psych ward.

"I mean, it was crazy. It was full of crazy people. It was like, if it was quiet, they turn on music for them, but if it got rowdy, they'd turn the music off. . . ."

After a time in the psych ward, they went to Vonlee and offered her protective custody, but she had to sign for it.

Some of the inmates in protective custody could shimmy their doors open enough to get out of their cells, Vonlee said. As she was walking by one particular cell, a guy grabbed her and pulled her in, then closed the door behind them.

"You don't have to do this," she pleaded with the man.

He came at her, forcing himself. She screamed.

"I kicked him as hard as I could in the nuts," which slowed him down. She got up, threw him against the wall and went for the door.

It was open. She ran out, slamming the door behind her.

"That place was crazy," she recalled.

Whenever she took a shower, Vonlee put up a sheet as a curtain so no one could see her.

"Well, this little black kid came up and ripped it down one day," she said.

"Don't you do that," Vonlee said to him. They were on the second tier of a two-tier facility.

"Bitch, you talk back to me and I will throw your ass over that balcony," he said.

After several days of this and an appearance in court, Vonlee was offered the opportunity to be extradited back to Michigan and she jumped at it.

"I would have been killed in Chicago."

CHAPTER 47

DON TULLOCK WAS WITH Vonlee at the TPD station house while she was being booked. Of course, the obvious first question was her name.

Vonlee said she was a male, and her actual given name was Harry, but she had never used Harry. She went by Vonlee or Nicole. They could take their pick.

The conversation was short. Tullock asked, "Have you experienced the death of a loved one recently?"

"Yes," she said.

"Who? When?" Tullock countered.

"My uncle was killed."

On the medical intake form associated with Vonlee's arrest and booking at the TPD, an interesting aside played out. Under the question of whether the arrested individual was at that time seeing a physician, Vonlee reported she was. Asked to explain, she wrote, *Sex change.*

Was Vonlee finally going through with the operation at the time of her arrest?

As Tullock sat and read through it, a report of a search done on Vonlee's Riviera indicated cops had found a duffel bag of "misc. clothes," a pair of glasses in a case, two CDs, a wallet, laundry basket, "misc. gay literature," a sweater, several miscellaneous items, inconsequential to the charges, and one "nine-inch cock/dildo."

When they searched Vonlee's apartment in Chicago, they found nothing. As to her involvement in a murder, Vonlee thought, where was the corroborating evidence to back it up?

Vonlee was housed in a special section of the jail, where she could be alone and away from other men. The jail in Michigan was sympathetic to her situation, she said later.

While in lockup that night, Vonlee placed a collect call to Billie Jean. She happened to be home.

Vonlee wanted to find out if her aunt had secured a lawyer for her. After having trouble hearing each other, Vonlee said, "Well, I'm here."

"You're in Detroit?" Billie Jean asked, seemingly shocked.

"I'm in Troy."

"When did you get here?"

Vonlee said about "thirty minutes" before the call, explaining how they had flown her from Illinois into Michigan earlier that day after she went to court. She did not get into anything that happened back in Chicago.

Vonlee had a scheduled court hearing the following morning to be arraigned and formally charged in Michigan. She wanted to know if her mother had sent money to a lawyer and if he was going to be showing up to represent her. Had Billie Jean heard anything about that?

"If he knows you're there (in Michigan now), which I'm sure he does," her aunt indicated.

The court had contacted Vonlee's attorney for her and he had explained to them very candidly not to question her any longer. Vonlee told this to Billie Jean, before adding, "Can you believe this bullshit?"

"Well . . . all my money's tied up," her aunt said defensively, as if Vonlee had asked her to cough up legal representation funds or else.

"Huh?" Vonlee said, confused.

Her aunt said something about having only "twenty dollars" left "to her name."

They discussed lawyers and Vonlee asked if Billie Jean's attorney was going to be representing her all the way through the process.

Her aunt said she didn't know because she didn't even have enough money to pay a lawyer for herself, which she presumed she was going to need sometime soon.

This was untrue—Billie Jean Rogers was in the process of hiring one of the most expensive and top defense attorneys in Detroit.

Vonlee then pleaded with her aunt for legal help, asking if there "was any way, please. . . ."

Billie Jean promised she would look into it.

After some small talk, back and forth, Vonlee said, "Billie, I don't think they really have a case. I mean, we didn't *do* anything. You know."

"I . . . I know that."

"They tried to get me to call you and say . . . you did, and stuff. I mean, I told them, 'How can I say something that *didn't* happen?'"

"They tried to get me to do the same thing."

Vonlee told her aunt the TPD wanted her to believe Billie Jean was going to turn on her and the only way out of it was to take control and get her aunt to admit her part first. It was an old police tactic, Vonlee knew: play each side against the middle.

"Well, they haven't arrested you yet, so that's good," Vonlee said.

"It's only a matter of time."

The conversation then moved from topic to topic. Vonlee focused mainly on the idea that cops had very little to charge either of them with, and Vonlee talked about how "facts are facts" and the cops needed to stick to the "facts of the case."

Bottom line for Vonlee: what could they possibly have against either of them?

Billie Jean kept talking about how all of her money was tied up and she had no access to it.

"So, if I get a bond, there's no way you can help me out, is there?" Vonlee wondered.

"I? No. I have not got a dime. . . ."

"How can they tie that up?"

"You've got money in *your* bank," her aunt said, changing the subject.

"Huh?"

"You've got money!"

Vonlee said she only had seven or eight thousand left.

They then talked about family stuff and how Vonlee wondered if her aunt's lawyer could access her money for her.

Billie Jean didn't think so.

At one point, Billie Jean said she'd "die" if the TPD came for her. Vonlee was very sympathetic to that comment, saying how she had explained to detectives that it was not a good idea to lock up her aunt. She said she also told them they were "crazy" for accusing either of them of this crime, especially her aunt, who had taken care of Don "for twenty years" and counting, at the time of his death.

Vonlee then spoke of how, when she got out of jail, she was going to sell off everything she owned: car, jewelry, furniture, "anything. I will give you back the money."

Billie Jean suggested Vonlee should have someone do that now. As the widow talked, it appeared she knew a lot of details surrounding what was going on. She spoke of how Danny Chahine was being "checked out" and possibly working with a detective.

"Well, see," Vonlee said, "they told me they thought *you* did it."

"*See,*" Billie Jean countered, "they play people."

"They said, 'Oh, we know she had eighty percent to do with it, and you probably had twenty percent, but she's going to blame it on you.'"

Billie Jean said the cops had said the same thing to her.

Both women, it appeared, had no idea the conversation—like most prison calls—was being recorded. But Billie Jean did mention how she believed that "they've got my phone tapped." To which, Vonlee replied she didn't really care, because neither of them had done anything wrong and they had nothing to hide, anyway.

Then Vonlee mentioned the only "evidence" they actually had was "Danny. But it's circumstantial. . . . It's hearsay. It's . . ."

Billie finished for her: "A story!"

"Huh?" Vonlee asked, not hearing her well.

"I said it's a made-up story."

"I know. It's just lies. A drunken lie."

There was no crime scene, Vonlee suggested. Nothing more than a man with felonies of his own who came to cops with a story and then recorded her saying some things.

Vonlee latched onto details about that night. She wanted to clear the air between her and her aunt. Vonlee said she believed that when they left for the casino that night, Don was alive; and when they returned, Don was dead. It was that simple. She asked Billie Jean about the coroner's report. What did it say?

Her aunt said, "Suspected murder. . . ."

Vonlee mentioned that she was done with booze and drugs for good this time. She was "never, ever going to take anything again." This entire situation had taught her a great lesson.

The conversation kept moving back to the money.

Her aunt was saying how she was strapped and had no control over any of it.

Vonlee came back with how Billie Jean might have to sell off everything she owned to defend herself, before asking her for a promise that she would help her as much as she could.

Her aunt said she'd do whatever she possibly could.

"And promise, Billie," Vonlee said seriously, "please don't, like, lie."

"Vonlee, have I ever lied?"

"No, you haven't."

They continued to circle around the same subjects: Danny, lawyers, money. And as they talked for another fifteen minutes, it was clear that their relationship had turned fragile and fractured. Billie Jean was scared of being arrested, while Vonlee was trying to comfort her aunt by saying the cops had nothing against either of them.

The message: stick together, tell the truth, allow it to set us free.

"You know there are innocent people in prison," Vonlee said.

CHAPTER 48

DETECTIVES STILL HAD SOME work to do. Making an arrest was one thing; getting Vonlee to talk and then obtaining more than circumstantial evidence against Billie Jean was quite another. When it came down to it, the TPD had very little on Billie Jean. A few recordings from an ex-felon and financial records that did not indicate anything other than a woman spending her dead husband's money on whatever she wanted was not enough to convict Billie Jean Rogers in the murder of her husband. Any prosecutor knew that. Add an amended death certificate to it, and no real autopsy on a guy who had been cremated, and it was hard to tell if the TPD could gather up enough for an arrest, to begin with.

On March 2, 2001, Detective Zimmerman made contact with Don's ex-wife, Doris. They'd split up in 1975, Doris explained. That was a long time ago. Since then, Doris added, she'd only met Billie Jean when Don and Doris's daughter had gotten married. Beyond that, she didn't know either of them that well.

Zimmerman pressed Doris. Could she recall *anything* about her ex-husband's widow?

There was one story of Billie Jean having a boyfriend, she said. "Jack . . . I think his name is. He's a truck driver. I also heard that she might have had a boyfriend in Tennessee, too."

Billie Jean Rogers was preoccupied with Don's money, Doris further explained. Everybody knew that. In fact, she wouldn't marry Don a second time unless she was given access to all of his assets.

"Did Don know about her alleged affairs?" Zimmerman wondered.

This was a potential motivating factor—maybe a good thread to pursue.

"He never told me he did. But I think he knew, because he would roll his eyes whenever I asked him where Billie was, [whenever] she had been gone."

CHAPTER 49

WHILE IN TPD LOCKUP, Vonlee thought about her life back in Chicago. It was the first time in a long while she had been able to live the lifestyle she had chosen. The Troy region wasn't a bastion for the homosexual/transgender scene. She also had friends and an apartment of her own in the Windy City. Moving back to Chicago before her arrest, a place she had lived for three and a half years previously, Vonlee felt as if her life was getting back to normal—as normal as it could ever be, all considering.

"It's a lot larger community, as far as transsexuals and gays or the alternative lifestyle, so I just felt that I would fit better there."

While she sat alone, not being able to smoke, waiting to go to court so she could hopefully make bail, there was that one other issue Vonlee didn't want to face: Billie Jean was desperately ill. That hadn't been a lie to police when she told them that.

"She'd developed a liver problem," Vonlee said later, "from years of drinking."

It was actually more than that. Vonlee's aunt was battling cancer.

And she was losing.

Her prognosis became grimmer as the year 2000 closed and she sat home wondering when the troops were coming through her front door to arrest her. Billie Jean didn't seem to be paying too much attention to her illness, but before Vonlee left for Chicago, she could tell her aunt was a lot sicker than she had let on.

The more Vonlee considered what had happened on the night Don had died, the only conclusion she could come to was that Billie Jean had killed him. She didn't want to share her thoughts with her aunt, obviously; but as she had hinted to Danny, in Vonlee's opinion, her aunt had cold-bloodedly murdered Don. There were times, Vonlee thought, while back at the Rogers house when Don was alive, when it seemed Billie Jean wanted nothing less than for Don to be out of the picture for good. But was there anything to indicate, before Billie Jean took matters into her own hands on that night, that she had wanted her husband dead? Could Vonlee find premeditation somewhere? Or had Billie Jean, by Vonlee's estimation, acted on an opportunity?

During many evenings, they would sit around the living room, drinking: Don, Billie Jean and Vonlee. There was one night, Vonlee recalled, after Billie Jean had put in brand-new wooden floors throughout the downstairs, including the kitchen, that stuck in her mind now. As it were, her aunt had routinely asked Vonlee about a "hit man" she believed Vonlee knew in Chicago—if he could do a job. It was always portrayed to Vonlee as a joke; but now, that joke, as Vonlee considered it in this new context of their lives, might have been a disguised request.

Don had "his chair" in the living room. He kept his vodka in the freezer portion of the refrigerator. When he finished a drink (he'd never ask his wife, because she'd never do it for him, Vonlee said), Don would get up and fetch another. As a habit, Don never wore slippers or shoes inside the house. Always "black socks," Vonlee said. In fact, Don had died in black socks.

It happened "almost every night" while Vonlee was there—that same routine of Don in his socks walking into the kitchen to get a drink. Don got up one night, though, and as he walked into the kitchen, he slipped on the new wooden floors and fell on his butt.

Billie Jean laughed.

Vonlee jumped up. "You had better be more careful, Don," she said, helping him.

"Yeah," Don said. "I think Billie put these floors in here so she could kill me."

Don got his drink and went back into the living space, where his wife was sitting.

Billie Jean eyed him.

"What?" Don wondered.

"Next time, I'll just spend the damn twenty-five thousand and hire someone," she joked.

Vonlee laughed. "I assumed she meant the floors cost twenty-five thousand dollars," Vonlee said later.

But now, as Vonlee thought back to it, she wondered if her aunt was trying to say something to her without coming out and actually stating it bluntly. All those subtle cues—"How much would it cost? . . . Do you know anyone?"—were followed with a laugh. Vonlee now had to consider: was Billie Jean serious all those times?

CHAPTER 50

THE LEAD-UP TO DON'S death had actually started in the weeks before. Vonlee had always viewed her presence in the household, particularly during those last days, as the "peacemaker" between the two of them, she explained to this author. There had been some serious issues regarding money and Don lending a substantial amount to one of Billie Jean's family members and that person not paying him back, according to Vonlee. This became a focal point for both Don and Billie Jean; it was something they fought about all the time.

"There was a lot of animosity going on there between them," Vonlee explained.

Vonlee had spent August 10, 2000, at Danny's house. They'd had a night out at the casino, gotten pretty drunk, and then had sex when they returned. The following morning, August 11, 2000 (the last morning Don Rogers would awake), Vonlee woke up and asked Danny to take her back to the Rogers house. She wanted to go home and sleep off the previous night's bender.

"I'm hung over as shit," she told Danny. "I need to go."

"Yeah, yeah . . . no problem. I take you home," Danny said in his broken English.

Vonlee grabbed a bottle of cranberry juice from Danny's fridge, poured half of it down the drain, and then added a few inches of vodka from a bottle Danny kept in an entertainment center near his television.

Armed with her morning drink, she told Danny, "Let's go."

Vonlee didn't speak much as they drove. She drank the cranberry and vodka, hoping to bite the hair of the dog that had mauled her the night before.

Inside the house, Billie Jean was preparing to clean. As Vonlee walked through the door after kissing Danny good-bye and saying she'd call him later, her aunt implored Vonlee to help.

"I need another drink first," Vonlee said. She'd consumed the vodka and cranberry. There was no way she could get on her hands and knees to scrub floors, clean toilets and vacuum without getting rid of what was still a dreadful hangover.

So Vonlee made a Bloody Mary, one of about "four or five" she'd have throughout the day. On an average morning, Billie Jean would get up around five and see Don off to work. Then she and Vonlee would have a few drinks, decide whether to go to the casino, or hang around the house and drink the day away. Don would come home around 3:30 or 4:00 P.M., and then start drinking with the two of them if they were around, or by himself, if not.

Vonlee was feeling much better as she and her aunt cleaned the house and drank throughout that afternoon. In fact, by the time Don walked through the door after work, Vonlee was feeling pretty damn lit all over again.

Just before Don walked in, Vonlee pulled her aunt aside and asked, "Why don't we all go to the racetrack tonight?" Vonlee knew Don loved the track: the excitement of the dogs, the crowds, the drinks, the food. It was a good night out. Being the arbitrator inside the house between the two of them, trying to convince Billie Jean to head out to the track, instead of the casino, and to bring Don was just another step to see if she could convince them to get along.

"Sometimes you have to give in and do what he wants to do. Simple things make a man happy. You can still gamble there, Billie."

"Yeah, sounds good," her aunt said.

Don walked in, fixed a drink, and Billie Jean made dinner. The three of them sat and ate peacefully, Vonlee later explained. Don had a few pops of straight vodka before dinner and he was feeling those. During his final days of drinking, Don did not require much to get loose.

After dinner, the two women sat in the family (or "great") room, as Vonlee sometimes referred to it. The TV was on. By that point, Vonlee recalled, she'd had at least "seven or eight" drinks since finishing her breakfast of vodka and cranberry. Vonlee was now well on her way to a good drunken evening.

Billie Jean looked into the kitchen, where Don was sitting by himself after dinner, drinking. This was not his usual spot to drink. Don liked to idle in his recliner in the great room and pound straight vodka until his body told him he'd had enough. But he obviously wanted away from his wife on this night because they had been fighting again.

"You see there," Billie Jean shouted to Vonlee after she saw how out of it Don seemed. "I knew we wouldn't be going to no fucking racetrack tonight. He cannot stay sober long enough to go *anywhere*."

"She was highly upset with him at this point," Vonlee recalled.

"He's too damn drunk again," her aunt added as Vonlee sat and listened. "I'm not taking him *anywhere*." She made it clear to Vonlee that this was another letdown on a long mental list she had been keeping. Vonlee said this was a common narrative inside the house while she was there: Don getting drunk and screwing up most of the plans Billie Jean made with him.

It was well into the early evening by now. As she and her aunt were talking in the living room, they heard a loud "plop" (Vonlee's word) from inside the kitchen.

Billie Jean shook her head. She knew what that sound meant.

"Fucking passed out *again*," Billie Jean said more to herself, shaking her head.

"Don had gotten up to fix himself a drink and he had fallen on the floor," Vonlee explained. "I heard a chair flip over."

Vonlee stood up from her seat. Her aunt didn't move. Yet, in defense of her aunt not jumping up out of her seat to help her husband, Vonlee recalled, "This was not at all surprising—the fact that Don fell out of his chair. It wasn't like she was being cold, Billie not rushing to his side. This was normal. He passed out almost *every* night."

Vonlee walked toward the kitchen and saw that Don had fallen on the floor and was now lying on his back. Standing between Billie Jean (who was still sitting in the living/great room) and Don in the kitchen, Vonlee said, "Hey, he just passed out on the floor."

Billie Jean shrugged.

"I'm going to help him up, Billie, and get him off to bed."

"You might as well," her aunt said without moving.

Before tending to Don, Vonlee later told law enforcement, she walked around Don and into the laundry room area, where she had some pants in the dryer she was planning on wearing that night. They were dry. So she took the pants out and folded them. Then she walked over to Don and knelt down, shaking his shoulders, hoping to "wake him up" enough to get him off to bed.

"It almost looked like Don laid down on the floor," Vonlee remembered.

Don didn't respond to Vonlee's nudging. In fact, still as a brick, he didn't move at all.

"Don!" Vonlee yelled, hoping to rustle him awake enough to pay attention. "Come on, get up now. . . . Let's go upstairs."

Vonlee stood, walked over to the entryway between the two rooms, and told her aunt that her husband was not getting up. "I cannot wake him up, Billie. . . . I think something's wrong."

Normally speaking, Vonlee explained, "it was not hard to wake Don up after he passed out." They generally shook him a little bit, called out his name, then helped him up onto his feet and guided him to bed.

But not on this night. Don was not moving.

Billie Jean stood.

"He's not responding at all, Billie," Vonlee reiterated. "Help me out here. . . ."

Her aunt walked toward the kitchen.

Vonlee stood in the back of Don's head. Billie Jean came into the kitchen, grabbed the bottle of vodka from off the counter, and then she stood by the side of Don's face for a moment, staring down at him.

"I'll get him up," she said.

Vonlee recalled a nefarious, chilling aura coming over Billie Jean. There was something different about her, Vonlee explained, and the look she had on her face scared Vonlee.

CHAPTER 51

BILLIE JEAN KNELT DOWN near Don's head and poured a shot of vodka into Don's mouth, according to Vonlee's recollection.

Don suddenly came to and spit it out.

"Hold his mouth and hold his nose," Vonlee claimed Billie Jean told her at that moment.

"No," Vonlee said.

"I am extremely inebriated by this point myself and I'm thinking, 'Okay . . . she must do this all the time.' He responded, after all—he spit out that shot. I thought this was how she woke him up when he was *really* out of it."

Billie Jean handed Vonlee the bottle and said, "You pour a shot in his mouth."

Vonlee took it and did what she was told, thinking that following her suggestions would help wake Don up and out of his stupor.

Nothing happened.

Billie Jean went back to trying to get Vonlee to hold her hand over Don's mouth. Her aunt had pinched his nostrils together so he couldn't breathe out of his nose.

"Do it," she said. "Put your hand over his mouth."

This would cut off Don's oxygen supply, Billie Jean

explained, and Don would begin to choke for air and subsequently wake up. The way Vonlee saw it, Billie Jean had done this routinely and it had worked.

Still, Vonlee did not want any part of cutting off Don's oxygen completely. It didn't feel right.

"No! I'm not doing that, Billie. I'm afraid of hurting him."

"Well," her aunt said, "come on. Just hold your hand over his mouth."

Vonlee thought about it. She felt comfortable placing her hand on Don's mouth and spreading her fingers out with gaps in between each so as not to close off Don's mouth totally to oxygen. Vonlee said later she could feel that Don was definitely breathing at this time.

She understood it was hard for most people to comprehend why she would take part in doing something like this, Vonlee later said. She related this particular portion of the night back to childhood. There had been a man who rented a room at her grandmother's house. He would pass out drunk from time to time. Vonlee was just a child. When he would pass out, she and the other kids would "do things like holding his nose and mouth." Mess with him, in other words. "Pinch his nose, cover his mouth . . . and make him wake up. We'd stick straws up his nose. Tickle him. We played with him." It was akin to a frat house using a Sharpie on a passed-out fraternity brother and painting up his face.

Childish games.

"What she was doing to Don, it was kind of like that to me," Vonlee explained later. "It was like the same thing. At least, for me—that's what I was thinking."

Not once, Vonlee said, was she thinking, *Billie wants me to help kill him.*

"Not in a million years. I don't even think if she would have said it at that moment, I would have believed it. I would have probably thought, 'Oh yeah, I'd like to kill a lot of people' . . . a figure of speech."

After a few seconds of holding his mouth with one hand (with those spaces between her fingers), the bottle of vodka in the other hand, after pouring a shot into Don's mouth, Vonlee let go and backed away, telling Billie Jean, "I'm not doing this. I can't do it."

Her aunt then grabbed the bottle from Vonlee's hand and poured a shot of vodka, according to Vonlee's recollection, up Don's nose.

"I never held his mouth to where he couldn't breathe," Vonlee later insisted. "I was very, very intoxicated, and I was thinking that it was just . . . I don't know. I didn't know. . . . She did this all the time. . . . This is how she wakes him up. I really wasn't thinking."

And she was drunk.

When Vonlee saw Billie Jean pour the vodka up Don's nose, she took a step back from the situation. "My whole demeanor changed," Vonlee said. Something happened in that one moment. She saw evil come over her aunt. Vonlee now knew that she was on a mission. What might have started out as a playful way to rustle Don out of a drunken sleep had now turned into Billie Jean making sure Don did not wake up.

"Oh no, Billie, this isn't right!" Vonlee said.

Billie Jean looked at her.

Vonlee grabbed the bottle from her aunt. "Listen to me! You leave him alone. You are going to end up hurting him, Billie. You need to stop this right now. Go get dressed. Let's get out of here and go out."

In her mind, Vonlee considered that if she could just get her aunt out of the house and over to the casino, everything would be okay.

"Come on now, Billie. Just get dressed and we'll go to the casino."

Billie Jean stood. She appeared to back off and

emerge from whatever fog she had gone into while trying to basically drown Don in vodka.

Vonlee felt as though her aunt was finished with whatever she had been doing. She placed the bottle of vodka on the countertop and poured herself a stiff glass.

"I'm going to get ready," Vonlee told Billie Jean. "You do the same, Billie."

Vonlee left the room.

CHAPTER 52

WHILE SHE WAS INSIDE the bathroom, getting ready to go out, Vonlee took a few pulls from her drink and calmed down. She was using the restroom off to the side of the kitchen, not too far from where Don was lying passed out on the kitchen floor. The door was closed. Vonlee stared at herself in the mirror. She applied lipstick, puckering up, and teased her hair with some hair spray. She thought they'd likely go out to the casino and have another night of drinking and gambling. Billie Jean would be fine after some time at the tables and slots. Once that woman was inside a casino, gambling, she was an entirely different person, totally wrapped up in the action.

Vonlee sprayed a bit of perfume on her neck, took one last look at her reflection, then walked out of the bathroom. Immediately after opening the door, she saw the backside of Billie Jean, whose front side was facing and kneeling down near Don's head. So Vonlee walked around to the opposite side to see what she was doing.

Upon figuring out what was going on, Vonlee became horrified, seeing clearly what Billie had now planned.

"What the fuck are you doing?" Vonlee yelled.

According to Vonlee, her aunt had a throw pillow from the living room in her hands and she was covering Don's face with it, smothering him.

"And that's when everything, from that point on, went downhill," Vonlee later said.

The look her aunt had on her face while she was suffocating her husband, Vonlee claimed, she would never forget.

"Possessed. Determined to do this. A woman on a mission" was how Vonlee later described it.

There was no turning back. Don was not moving. He wasn't struggling for air, gasping, kicking and fighting. There was no telling how long Billie had the pillow over his face because she must have begun doing it when Vonlee went into the bathroom.

"Billie . . . what the fuck are you doing?" Vonlee yelled again.

But her aunt was done. She stood. Turned toward Vonlee.

"I had to do it."

"What the fuck do you mean? You 'had to do it'?"

"You want that money, don't you?" Billie Jean asked.

Vonlee was confused. "What money, Billie? What are you talking about?"

"You need the money for your surgery, don't you, Vonlee?"

"What?" Vonlee said. She then gasped.

Oh, my . . .

According to Vonlee, in that moment, Billie Jean said to her, "Listen, I'll give you twenty-five thousand."

"Billie, no . . . no . . . no. Are you crazy?"

"You want fifty thousand?"

"No, Billie. No. No, no! And I am not going to jail for you."

"Yes, but you . . ."

"No! Billie, listen to me: I am *not* going to *hell* for you."

Vonlee walked over and bent down next to Don. She felt for a pulse. Put her ear to his heart.

He was not breathing.

Standing up after realizing Don was gone, Vonlee announced, "I'm calling 911, Billie. Do you realize what the fuck you've done here?" Vonlee walked over and made another drink. She took a long, slow swallow. "Do you understand what you have done, Billie?"

Vonlee thought about doing CPR, but she had no idea how to do it.

Call 911 kept playing over in her head.

"You had better not," Billie Jean said after Vonlee indicated she was going to phone the police.

The scene became "surreal" for Vonlee as she paced inside the kitchen, with Don's body now going cold. Billie Jean just stood, expressionless.

"I became numb," Vonlee added. "I remember this so clearly. I could almost see myself in the kitchen . . . from another place watching it all happen. From the time I pinched his nose, until I realized what she'd done. It really wasn't me there—it was like it was someone else."

After some time, Vonlee switched gears. She needed to make sure they did not get caught for this. She felt she needed to "take over." Her aunt couldn't do it. And one of them needed to.

"You have to understand something," Vonlee explained to me years later, "I still feel responsible for this. I accept . . . I feel . . . that it's my fault. I should not have been involved. I feel that it's my fault he's dead."

Vonlee stared at her aunt. She didn't say it, but Vonlee was certainly thinking: *What have you done?*

"If I hadn't killed him," Vonlee claimed Billie said in this moment, "he would have *known* what we were doing earlier."

"Earlier"? What is she talking about? Vonlee thought.

So she asked Billie: "What do you mean by 'what *we* were doing earlier'?"

As Vonlee remembered it, when Don was on the floor in the kitchen passed out before she went into the bathroom, "We were trying to wake him up. . . ." The way Danny Chahine later described this, per Vonlee telling him, they were fooling around with Don—a sort of "drunken play," Vonlee had called it.

"Danny Chahine later made it out to be me saying, 'Stop wasting the good vodka,'"—which Danny would later tell police Vonlee had told him she said to Billie— "but that's not true. I was just trying to get Billie to leave Don alone."

After Vonlee mentioned for a second time that she was going to call 911, Billie Jean said, "Whose word do you actually think they would believe, Vonlee? I'm in my sixties . . . never had a parking ticket. . . . You are, Vonlee, a transsexual. You've been arrested for prostitution. . . . Come on, honey. Get real."

Vonlee was stunned by this. "I froze . . . ," she told me.

Billie Jean walked over to Vonlee. "Come on, sit down. Let's talk."

"No," Vonlee said.

"Vonlee, listen to me. . . . I can give you money. Twenty-five thousand dollars."

"No. I do not want your money, Billie."

As Vonlee explained this part of the night to Danny Chahine, she said to him, "And I remember crying and telling Billie . . . 'I did this for you! I did it for you! That's the only fucking reason I did it is I did it for fucking you!'"

It was holding Don's nose, Vonlee later explained she meant.

Not murder.

Taking over, after going around and around with Billie

As a child, Harry Titlow
seemed like any other boy
growing up in the Deep South:
cute, happy, content.

During his grammar school years, Harry began to feel that something was very different about him.

The Orchard Hill section of Troy, Michigan, where Don Rogers lived with his wife, Billie Jean, was considered exclusive. *(Photo courtesy of author)*

Don Rogers spent most of his time at the home he shared with Billie Jean. *(Photo courtesy of author)*

Don Rogers was a business owner and celebrated member of the Troy, Michigan, community, where he lived most of his life.

Billie Jean Rogers and her niece, Vonlee Nicole Titlow,
spent most nights at the Motor City Casino in downtown Detroit,
drinking and gambling. *(Photo courtesy of author)*

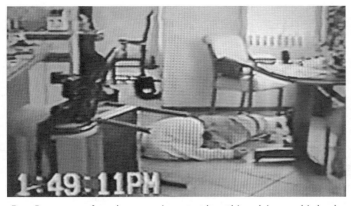

1:49:11PM

Don Rogers was found unconscious, not breathing, lying on his back,
his legs crossed at the ankles, during the early-morning hours
of August 12, 2000. Paramedics determined that he was dead.
(Photo courtesy of Troy Police Department Records Division)

Danny Chahine was Vonlee Titlow's boyfriend. After hearing a story that led him to believe that Don Rogers had not died of natural causes—but might have been murdered—Chahine sat down with police and told them what he had learned.
(Photo courtesy of Troy Police Department Records Division)

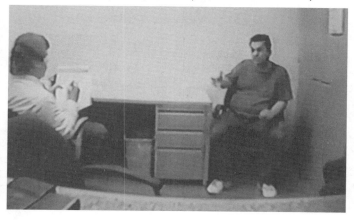

A beautiful woman, Vonlee Nicole Titlow enjoyed the party scene while living in Denver and Chicago in the late 1990s, before moving in with her aunt and uncle, Billie Jean and Don Rogers.

While living in Denver and Chicago, Vonlee Nicole Titlow worked as a stripper and even started her own escort service, catering to men with unique fetishes.

While living in this Chicago apartment building, Vonlee Nicole Titlow
was watched by the Chicago Police Department and finally
arrested and charged with the murder of Don Rogers.
(Photo courtesy of author)

Before her arrest on murder charges, Billie Jean Rogers, Don's wife, seemed to enjoy the simpler pleasures in life.

To the Troy Police Department, this check for $70,260, made out to Vonlee Nicole Titlow and signed by Billie Jean thirteen days after Don's death, appeared to be a payout for Vonlee's help in Don's murder.
(Photo courtesy of Troy Police Department Records Division)

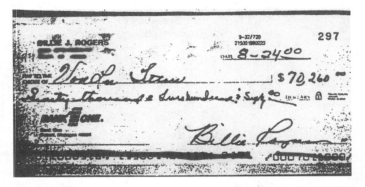

This notation on Billie Jean's checkbook indicated to law enforcement that Billie Jean had agreed to pay Vonlee a total of $100,000.
(Photo courtesy of Troy Police Department Records Division)

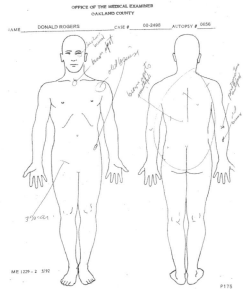

OFFICE OF THE MEDICAL EXAMINER
OAKLAND COUNTY

NAME DONALD ROGERS   CASE # 00-2498   AUTOPSY # 0656

The medical examiner's report indicated that a crime had taken place.
(Photo courtesy of Troy Police Department Records Division)

The Troy Police Department, headquartered in this building, initiated the investigation into Don Rogers's suspicious death.
(Photo courtesy of author)

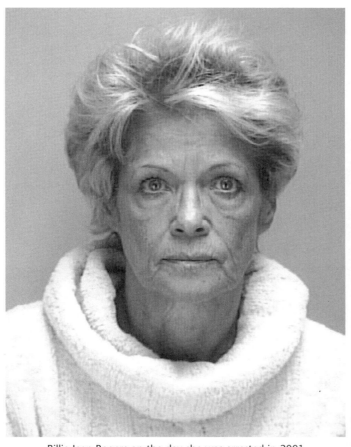

Billie Jean Rogers on the day she was arrested in 2001
for the murder of her husband.
(Photo courtesy of Troy Police Department Records Division)

Vonlee Nicole Titlow in 2001 shortly after she was arrested and booked for murder. *(Photo courtesy of Troy Police Department Records Division)*

In the months after her arrest, Vonlee had reason to smile after she passed a polygraph "proving" that she'd had nothing to do with murdering Don Rogers. *(Photo courtesy of Troy Police Department Records Division)*

In 2013, Valerie Newman argued Vonlee Nicole Titlow's case in front of the United States Supreme Court.

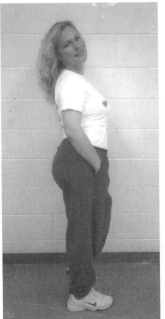

Vonlee Nicole Titlow in 2015.

Jean about calling 911, Vonlee switched into cover-up mode.

"Grab that pillow and that bottle of booze," Vonlee said she directed her aunt.

"I am thinking now that there's no way I am going to jail for this."

In Vonlee's mind, she didn't kill Don and had no part in what she described as a cold-blooded murder. And so as she thought about it, while standing in the kitchen hovering over Don's dead body, Vonlee decided to help Billie Jean. It was her only way out of it all, Vonlee now believed.

Billie Jean drove. Vonlee had the bottle and pillow on her lap.

"And I don't know why we did this," she said later, "but I threw them out the window on the way to the casino."

Vonlee did not recall being at the casino, though she knew they arrived and walked in and drank and gambled. She even vaguely recalled seeing Danny Chahine there on that night.

The next thing Vonlee could recall was arriving home very early the next morning. Then her aunt called 911 and both of them talked to the police after they arrived.

Of course, Don Tullock, Don Zimmerman, the TPD and eventually the prosecutor's office had a problem with this: Because as one recorded conversation between Vonlee and Danny ended, Vonlee said at this point during the early-morning hours of that day of Don's death, she told her aunt, "I know that you're not going to live long and I know you want . . ." She just stopped short of saying, one might speculate, that she knew Billie Jean wanted Don's money. "He was dying," Vonlee told Danny. "I mean, he was definitely, definitely dying. I know that for a fact. I mean, the man wouldn't go to the hospital. He was bleeding everywhere. Every day he splatted blood all over the place. . . . He'd get up and fall face-first. He had a black eye, where he had [fallen] down. I mean, you'd have to help him up. . . . [He'd] come home from work and drink to the point he was so miserable. I asked myself, after it happened, 'I would rather somebody had killed me than to let me go through *that* every day.'"

Was Vonlee justifying a murder she claimed her aunt had committed?

"I mean, basically," Vonlee concluded, "they said his whole insides were just. . . . He was fucked up."

Speaking to Danny, she paused. She thought about what she had just said.

Then, perhaps pulling back, added: "But, I mean, *nothing* makes it right."

PART 3

Justice is an essential element of the divine economy;
otherwise, we would be too easily reconciled to the human
capacity for betrayal, and even atrocity.

James Carroll, *Christ Actually*

CHAPTER 53

BILLIE JEAN ROGERS WAS a beautiful woman. Even with the deer-in-the-headlights look she had on her face as the TPD snapped her mug shot on March 13, 2001— after she was finally taken into custody and booked on murder charges—Billie Jean displayed signs of a once-elegant and attractive woman. She revealed smaller traces of a younger, sexier Billie Jean: her piercing blue eyes, whitish blond hair, fairly healthy-looking frame, perhaps marred by time and personal demons. Had she taken better care of herself over the years, had she lived without succumbing to her vices, had she overcome the anger for her husband spreading inside her like the cancer she had, she could have transformed her natural beauty into untainted grace. From decades of smoking, however, Billie Jean had those creased lines above her upper lip, as well as age spots and deep wrinkles on her face mapping a hard-core life. Billie Jean was sixty-one years old on the day she was charged with first-degree premeditated murder. If convicted, Billie Jean Rogers faced life in prison without the chance of parole.

The Oakland County Prosecutor's Office (OCPO) had the job of making any charges against Billie Jean and Vonlee stick. This task was not going to be easy, considering the lack of evidence in both cases. Billie Jean might have been a lot of things, she was already saying from prison, but a murderer? Good luck proving it, she warned.

Vonlee was preparing to celebrate her thirty-fourth birthday behind bars, unable to convince a court to allow her to go free on bond. Because of Billie Jean's terribly deteriorating health situation, she was free on a hundred-thousand-dollar bond. Newspaper headline writers had fun with the story, many of them following along the salacious headlines initiated by the first Associated Press (AP) story: WIDOW CHARGED IN MAN'S DEATH IN ALLEGED PLOT TO GET CASH FOR SEX CHANGE.

With that, Billie Jean's lawyer, Walter Piszczatowski, lashed out: "The codefendant, [Vonlee] Titlow, made a statement to a third person who he was romantically involved with. There is no evidence whatsoever tying Mrs. Rogers to the crime except that statement."

This declaration, in all of its perceived desperation, was very true. Where was the *evidence* linking Billie Jean Rogers to the murder of her husband?

Handcuffed and being led into court for a preliminary hearing on March 21, 2001, Vonlee looked as though she had not showered or gotten any sleep in days. Though she cut a rough, somewhat slim figure, her face looked swollen and bloated. She had obvious bags under her eyes; her bleached-blond hair was a bit wiry and wild, black roots now visible, most of it pulled back into a flimsy ponytail like a rooster's tail. She wore clogs, white socks, police-blue slacks and a black-and-yellow sports jersey, which made her look heavier than she was. In a photo the AP snapped of Vonlee sitting at the table with her lawyer, she stared directly into the camera, a look of sheer defeat and disgust on her face. Not in a legal sense, mind you—but one rooted more in the sheer rawness of her gaze—it was a look that said she was at the end of a long road paved with a war on addiction.

Billie Jean was there, too, seated not far from her codefendant. A probable cause hearing is basically a way for the court to decide if, in fact, there is enough evidence to send a case (or cases) to trial. Not all cases end up at trial. Almost all are pleaded out before, during, or after the preliminary hearing phase. Unlike a grand jury proceeding, which is held in secret, during a preliminary hearing (overseen by a judge), the defendant has a chance to defend him- or herself.

Piszczatowski was there to represent Billie; attorney Richard Lustig was on hand for Vonlee. John Skrzynski, the assistant prosecuting attorney (APA), sat studying his notes and preparing to lodge his case on behalf of the state of Michigan.

It took a mere two minutes after the morning opened before the state called its first witness, one of the police officers responding to Don Rogers's home on that early morning when Vonlee made the 911 call. And throughout the day, three witnesses in total—two police officers and an EMT—were summoned to the stand to endure direct- and cross-examination questioning, consequently describing a scene at the house that at first appeared to be a natural death. However, as they thought about it and conversed with detectives over the course of the morning, and the days and weeks that followed, they concluded something along the lines of *"Well, you know what, yeah, there was something strange going on in that house on the night Don Rogers died."*

Retrospect is an eye-opener; hindsight an easier way to see guilt. Anybody knows this. And here, as each witness testified over the course of that first day, he or she had the advantage of going back over behaviors and comments with a new outlook. The new perception was now backed up by a coroner and investigating officers who, after going through the case again themselves, believed that Don had been murdered.

On March 22, 2001, day two of the hearing, the state brought in the medical examiner and chief medical examiner to explain how they had first decided Don died of acute alcohol poisoning and a heart attack, but then changed that determination after the TPD called and explained several extenuating circumstances, one of which was a man who had come forward with new and striking information.

Concluding the second day, that man, Vonlee's former lover, Danny Chahine, was called to tell his tale of Vonlee admitting to him what had happened to Don.

Danny Chahine laid out to the judge his account, focusing on how "bad" he felt for Don and his problems with alcohol and how Billie Jean had treated him unfairly by spending all of his money at the casino. When he heard from Vonlee that Billie Jean and Vonlee had potentially killed him, he was taken aback because he felt Don was on a collision course with death, anyway, and these two "women" had taken it upon themselves to hurry that up.

Vonlee's attorney objected repeatedly during Danny's direct testimony, as most defense attorneys will do during a preliminary hearing. It wasn't going to do any good, however. As she listened, what became clear to Vonlee was that the judge was going to drop the hammer and send them both to trial. As much as they are touted as fair legal processes, a balanced alternative to a grand jury proceeding, perhaps, preliminary hearings are absolutely biased against the defendant. Judges rarely side with defendants in preliminary hearings. The thought is: if there's enough evidence to warrant a preliminary hearing, there's enough to take it to trial.

By the end of the second day, all the attorneys agreed there would be nobody else called by the state, and the defense would need only one day to call its witnesses. So the judge talked it out with both sides and agreed to meet back in court on April 5, 2001.

When that day came, attorneys for Vonlee and Billie Jean called Don Tullock, Dr. Dragovic, who was the chief medical examiner, Danny, and Don Zimmerman. Billie Jean's and Vonlee's lawyers both conducted direct questioning and focused their questions on the noticeable ambiguity of the entire case, from the way in which the body was found to the cause of death to the way Billie Jean and Vonlee were later questioned by TPD cops. Both women were presumed guilty at some point by Zimmerman and Tullock, and then both cops, the defense lawyers argued, tried to fit their theories into that context by talking to various witnesses—all of which was built around what Danny Chahine had recorded. They did not investigate the case with the possibility that the women could be innocent, in other words. The attorneys maintained that, in turn, the TPD as a whole had viewed the women as guilty and worked its investigation from that perspective.

The words "speculation" and "hearsay" became rather popular during this part of the proceeding, but again, as Vonlee sat and listened, she felt the wind of that hammer coming. There was no way this judge was going to rule against the state. Vonlee could sense it. She knew that no matter what she said, or what Billie Jean said, these cops were never going to view it any differently than through the static-filled prism Danny Chahine had provided them via that choppy, at times inaudible, tape-recorded ride in his truck.

Piszczatowski made a good point when he asked

Danny if at any time he ever thought Vonlee might be joking or kidding around and making up stories when she talked about that night Billie Jean had supposedly coerced her into helping to kill Don.

"No," Danny said.

Billie Jean's attorney wanted to know if at any time Vonlee had told him that if she didn't get her hormone shots on time, and on a routine basis, that "it made her crazy."

"No," he said.

After all, the attorney pointed out, Vonlee had tricked Danny into thinking he was a female. She was obviously good at conning Danny.

"And did you have sex with her on more than one occasion before this revelation [of her being a male]?" Vonlee's attorney asked Danny.

"Yes."

By the end of the day, the lawyers made their final arguments to the judge. The APA said, quite simply, putting the People's case into a legal opinion, "The crime of aiding and abetting of a murder has occurred—[Vonlee] clearly assists defendant Rogers before the smothering with the intent that the crime of murder should be accomplished. And her aiding and abetting of the murder, therefore, is accomplished even before the smothering occurs."

The judge listened to both sides before he went through the testimony he had heard—each witness, one by one—as if describing his observations would explain the decision he was about to make. The judge found all of the witnesses to be believable or, as he put it, "credible." In fact, beyond Danny Chahine's statements and the recording, the judge explained, the medical examiner proved to the court beyond a reasonable doubt that a homicide *had* occurred. And if a murder had taken place inside that home, there were only two people that could have committed the offense.

In short, toss out Danny's testimony and you're still left with a man who was murdered, at least according to the medical examiner.

Yet, the judge failed to indicate that had the medical examiner not heard from the TPD in those days after Don's body was cremated, when they indicated that a homicide had occurred, there was no way he could have come to the conclusion he had.

"So I found a homicide," the judge declared. "I mean, I do find that . . . the homicide rises to the level of first-degree murder. Secondly, that it should be admissible as to finding that Mrs. Rogers was, in fact, a participant and involved in this particular matter." He then added how "the burden of proof" was "certainly not beyond a reasonable doubt as may be required or is required at the trial level."

Thus, coming as no surprise, the judge concluded he was "binding the matter over on . . . both counts" and bond would continue in the same manner as it had before the hearing.

Vonlee would stay put in jail, while Billie Jean, battling cancer, would be free on bond to wage war against a dreaded disease that had put Billie Jean, her lawyer said, "on her last leg. . . ."

Billie Jean was placed under house arrest with a GPS tether attached to her ankle.

By 5:31 P.M., with no indication as to how long it would take for both trials to begin (separately), court ended as Vonlee was led back to her holding cell. One burning question faced everyone as they filed out of the courtroom: would Billie Jean Rogers live long enough to face trial?

CHAPTER 54

THROUGHOUT THE SUMMER OF 2001 motions were filed and dates assigned as lawyers on both sides argued the legalities of each case. By August 1, 2001, Billie Jean's trial date had been set for October 29, a decision that set off a litany of court filings by the state and her attorneys.

As Vonlee sat in jail and thought about her future and how a first-degree murder conviction might land her in prison for the rest of her life, she considered that maybe it was time to play "let's make a deal." Why not? Vonlee had felt, all along, that she'd had nothing to do with Don's death—if anything, she had tried to stop her aunt from killing him. Yes, Vonlee knew, she had shared in the cover-up afterward, but she was not a murderer. And as she thought about her aunt, spoke to family members back home in Tennessee, Vonlee believed Billie Jean had set out from the moment she showed up at the Waffle House to manipulate her into helping to kill Don.

With Billie Jean's trial date set, Vonlee decided to enter into plea-bargaining negotiations.

"They want you to prove that you had nothing to do with the murder," Vonlee's attorney explained after speaking with the prosecutor's office. The thought was that the state had zilch against Billie Jean without Vonlee's testimony. Billie Jean was going to walk if Vonlee wasn't a state's witness testifying against her.

"How?" Vonlee wanted to know.

"Lie detector test."

Vonlee and her attorney, Richard Lustig, met with Don Zimmerman and a polygraph specialist at the John Nichols Law Enforcement Complex, where the examination was set to take place. The test was going to be based on what was an "official statement" Vonlee would subsequently make to the prosecutor's office, or the PO. This was common practice. After she gave a statement of the facts, the lie detector test would determine the "veracity," a report claimed, of Vonlee's involvement in the death of Don Rogers based on that statement she had given. The test would, effectively, tell the PO if Vonlee was going to be a good witness. Putting a liar on the stand, someone who had taken part in a murder, was not a good idea for any prosecution. It would backfire. Accusations would be tossed at Vonlee and she'd crack. But, if she was telling the truth and had nothing whatsoever to do with Don's murder, placing the onus on Billie Jean as the mastermind and sole offender, Vonlee would be a strong witness in the end. She would presumably make the state's case against Billie Jean Rogers.

The deal Richard Lustig brokered was for the first-degree murder charge to be dropped to manslaughter. Vonlee had reached a plea bargain with the PO that involved her spending "seven to fifteen years" (the actual number would be up to a judge) behind bars for manslaughter, providing she testified truthfully against Billie Jean after passing a lie detector test. For Vonlee, this seemed fair because she did feel as though she had taken part in the cover-up.

Before the actual lie detector test began on October 25, 2001, near 6:00 P.M., as Vonlee sat waiting to be interviewed, the polygraph examiner conducted a "pretest." This gave Vonlee an opportunity to talk about her story and tell it, for the most part, from beginning to end, focusing on those pertinent details affecting the test. This way, when the polygraphist conducted the actual lie detector test, he could ask simplified "yes" or "no" questions. No explanations by the person taking the test would be needed.

Vonlee explained during the pretest that Don had been drinking and passed out on the kitchen floor early that evening—and it should be noted that from the time of her arrest, she was always referred to as "Vonlee," "Titlow" or "he," never as a female, in any of the documents or interviews.

Without a prior plan, the report clarified, *Titlow and Mrs. Billie Rogers poured vodka down Rogers' throat and then Mrs. Rogers suffocated him with a pillow. Mrs. Rogers and Titlow then went to the casino.*

Thus, according to this pretest narrative, Vonlee claimed Billie Jean killed Don before they left the house, not when they returned, and that she played no part in the actual murder itself, but still left the house knowing that Billie Jean had smothered him.

When they returned from the casino later, the report of Vonlee's statement continued, *they called 911 and reported finding him dead. Titlow denied killing Rogers personally. Titlow denied that he planned the death. Titlow denied lying in his statement to the prosecutor.*

The polygraphist then "formulated and reviewed" the entire list of questions with Vonlee, going through each question before asking in an official manner: "Do you understand them?"

"I do."

Vonlee got settled in her seat. The polygraphist hooked her up to the machine and they took a few deep breaths together to get comfortable. Vonlee was not nervous, she later claimed, because all she had to do was tell the truth. She knew what she had done and not done.

Most important: she knew what Billie Jean had done and not done.

"Are you lying about what happened that night with Don?" the polygraphist asked Vonlee as the test began.

"No."

"Did you plan with Billie to kill Don when he was drunk?"

"No."

"Are you lying that Billie is the one that smothered him with that pillow?"

"No."

"Did you personally smother Don with that pillow?"

"No."

"Are you lying that you left when Billie smothered him?"

"No."

And that was it—five pointed questions and the test was over.

What would the results say about Vonlee after polygraph examiner Christopher Lanfear studied the graph and drew a conclusion as to the truthfulness of the answers? For Vonlee, the results would make or break her chances of striking a plea bargain.

CHAPTER 55

ONE COULD SAY THAT Vonlee's attorney, Richard Lustig, negotiated a sweet plea bargain on her behalf. Under that agreement, prosecutors arranged to reduce a first-degree murder charge—life in prison if convicted— to manslaughter if she passed the polygraph and testified against Billie Jean. As it turned out, when polygraphist Christopher Lanfear finished his review and report of the polygraph test he had given Vonlee, the only conclusion he could come to was "based on the analysis of the polygraph," Vonlee Nicole Titlow "is being truthful to the pertinent test questions."

Vonlee had passed the polygraph with flying colors. According to law enforcement and the PO, she was telling the truth about her role (or lack of role, actually) in the death of Donald Rogers. But what's more, Vonlee was saying that she had witnessed Billie Jean, her aunt, place a pillow over her husband's face and murder him.

It was no secret to anyone involved in either case that the PO wanted Billie Jean. This was clear in the way in which she was questioned before her arrest and how the prosecution was handled afterward. Part of Vonlee's plea deal included an agreement that she not challenge on appeal the prosecution's recommended sentencing range of that seven to fifteen years (even though sentencing guideline recommendations for manslaughter for a similar case were lower).

On Monday, October 29, 2001, after Billie Jean's trial date was pushed back a month to November 29, 2001, Vonlee sat in court at 9:37 A.M. to make it official. This proceeding, so routine and seemingly uneventful, would become one of the single most important elements within the entire legal portion of Vonlee's case as time moved forward.

APA John Skrzynski began the proceeding, stating for the record that Vonlee "is charged with one count of first-degree premeditated murder, and at this time, the People and the defendant have entered into a plea bargain and sentencing agreement."

That agreement and plea bargain, Skrzynski added, included that "the People, at this time, would move to add count II, manslaughter, and [the] defendant would agree to plead guilty to that count under these conditions." The rules for this deal were fundamentally simple: Vonlee "would agree to testify and would actually testify against the codefendant . . . Billie Rogers, during the course of her trial in accordance with a statement. . . ." That part was easy enough. Vonlee would have to sit and tell her story the way in which she'd been telling it from the moment she sat in Danny's truck and admitted to committing a crime in the first place. The second part of the deal, the APA went on to say, had Vonlee agreeing to a "sentence [of] a minimum of seven years to a maximum of fifteen years. And finally, that the defendant would agree and waive any kind of right to appeal on either the plea or the sentence."

The state asked for Vonlee's sentencing to be put off until "after her testimony in the trial of Billie Rogers." And perhaps most important to what would happen later, "the People would reserve the right, in the event the conditions that I set forth are not met by defendant . . . to withdraw the offer of manslaughter and would resume the prosecution of this case on a count of first-degree murder and proceed to trial at that time."

As deals go, this was your standard quid pro quo. Vonlee would give them the goods on Billie Jean, as promised, and she would catch a break.

It all seemed reasonable to Vonlee, considering that she felt responsible in some respects for taking part in Don's death, even if she wasn't the driving force and did not commit the actual crime.

As the short proceeding continued, Vonlee was asked a series of questions by her attorney, most of which placed her under a direct light of guilt. This was significant. Because once she admitted to her role in the crime on the stand, there was no turning back. It would be part of the record forever.

"Okay. You and I have gone over all of the evidence together over a long period of time, correct?" Lustig asked Vonlee.

"Correct," Vonlee answered.

"And you and I have discussed . . . that there are certain facts that could get you convicted of first-degree murder. Do you understand that?"

"Yes."

Lustig then explained how those "facts" included "two" particular items: "Number one, that you . . . received one hundred thousand dollars after the death of your uncle, correct?"

"Correct."

"And also, that during the course of the so-called homicide, you did feed alcohol into his system and you heard the medical examiners testify as to the effect that might have had. You understand that?"

"Yes."

Vonlee had just admitted under oath, in a court of law, that she had participated in the crime with her aunt.

"Okay. Now, although you didn't participate in what appears to be a *smothering*, you understand a jury could find you guilty of first-degree murder, second-degree murder, manslaughter, or nothing at all. You understand that?"

"Yes."

"When you plead guilty like this, you give it all up."

"I understand," Vonlee said, nodding her head in agreement.

Lustig said the only remaining issue was for the judge to accept her plea and Vonlee to testify against Billie Jean. After that, the judge "will give you a seven- to fifteen-year sentence, and there will be no appeal or anything like that. Do you understand?"

Vonlee said she clearly comprehended what was being asked of her and what she was agreeing to in a court of law.

"And now, finally, there's . . . regardless of the fact that I haven't been paid for a trial," Lustig explained, "I will proceed to trial without anything further. Do you understand that?"

"Yes."

"And it's not my intent here to abandon you at this particular time."

"Yes."

The judge questioned Vonlee about the same issues, making a point that in agreeing to this deal Vonlee was giving up all of her rights to remain silent. Then the judge wanted to know from Vonlee "what occurred that makes you think that you're guilty of manslaughter on August 12, 2000. What did you *do* that makes you think you're guilty?"

Vonlee explained that she had performed "an act in a reckless and dangerous manner, which put the victim in a position of great bodily harm and/or death."

Richard Lustig piped in and asked: "And what *did* you do? What was the act that you performed?"

"What I did, personally, was, I did pour a shot of vodka in his mouth and I did accept money afterward not to say anything about what had happened."

"Okay," the judge asked, "who was with you at the time?"

Vonlee stuttered a bit. Took a deep breath. Leaned into the microphone: "My aunt," she said. "Billie Rogers."

The judge hit his gavel and declared that "the court is satisfied there is sufficient factual basis for the plea. I find that its understanding, accurate and voluntary, and I do *accept* the plea. The matter will be set for sentencing on December 24, 2001. . . ."

As quickly as it had started, twenty minutes later, it was over. Vonlee Nicole Titlow had taken her plea deal and was now prepared to go head-to-head against her aunt in a court of law.

CHAPTER 56

NOTHING IN VONLEE'S LIFE was ever as it seemed. Things were constantly changing; some of the people involved were forever thinking of ways to alter the course of events—when the hard truth is, at least by some standards, much of life is predetermined by the choices we make.

In late November, just three days before Billie Jean was set to face trial, Vonlee was sitting, talking to a deputy corrections officer (CO) about her case, when that shameless dagger of fate slashed through what was her reality up until that moment.

"Innocent," Vonlee said of her part in the crime. "I might have embellished some things," she added, referring to what she had told Danny Chahine. She then explained that seven to fifteen years seemed like forever for someone who played hardly any role in an actual murder.

"I have a name for you," the CO told Vonlee. He gave Vonlee the name of his own lawyer. The CO explained that the guy might be able to hook Vonlee up with another lawyer, if she wanted one. He might even get her a better deal. The guy the deputy had in mind, he said, was top tucker. The best. The deputy added, "He's really good. I could ask someone to come in and talk to you, if you want."

Vonlee met with this new lawyer, Frederick Toca, a day later. Toca claimed later that Vonlee came across as an innocent woman with "very little time" left to withdraw her plea, for her codefendant was set for trial in a few days. "I passed a polygraph," Vonlee told Toca. "I am innocent!" Toca said she explained this to him "very, very strenuously . . . [and] indicated to me that [she] wasn't even in the room when the murder occurred."

According to Vonlee, Toca told her he could, in fact, find a better deal and that the proposed sentencing span—seven to fifteen—was not even within the guidelines of sentencing for the crime in which she had pleaded to, or the crime the PO believed she had actually participated in (manslaughter).

"When she first engaged me," Toca claimed later in court, "it was not to withdraw her plea. It was to see if the prosecutor would consider lowering the sentence . . . because . . . it was far outside of what her guideline range was."

For Toca, as he looked at Vonlee's case, he believed she had a strong argument for less time. Or, rather, that was what he told her.

"There was no disbelief in my mind," Toca said, "that the deal as she was being offered was not a good deal for a 'manslaughter' plea in a case where she was going to testify against a codefendant, in a case where she had *passed* a polygraph."

Vonlee told Toca she had no money. At the time she met Toca, Vonlee considered herself to be in a "vulnerable legal position and confused state of mind," she later explained in a civil case. She didn't know what was best for her legally and had "very little" understanding of "legal expertise."

That was okay, Toca suggested. All he wanted was a few things she could provide without having to come up with any cash.

"The agreement was in exchange for [all of my] jewelry valued at thirty thousand dollars," Vonlee said later, which was "agreed by both parties that the jewelry was worth this amount." Toca also asked her for, according to Vonlee, "the right to sell [my] story about how this crime was committed." In turn, Vonlee added, "[I] did give the jewelry over to [Toca and sign] away [my] literary rights to the facts. . . ."

Vonlee did all of this, she said, even though she never realized, at the time, Toca was breaking the "Rules of Professional Conduct," which, as a member of the Michigan Bar Association, he had sworn to uphold.

Without even calling to ask Lustig for Vonlee's file—after Vonlee had dumped Lustig as her lawyer—Toca approached the prosecutor's office with a new deal he had worked up. He felt Vonlee should not receive any more than three years for her part in the crime.

The bargaining chip here was the idea that without Vonlee the PO had no case against Billie Jean and would effectively have to drop those charges or risk losing at trial. They had a good, firm grip on the PO and were now squeezing the APA to try and get years slashed from the lower end of an already-in-place, already-sanctioned-by-a-judge plea bargain that Vonlee had signed off on herself and agreed to in open court.

In the eleventh hour like this, the proposition of the deal came across as ruthless and unethical.

The prosecutor's office said no way. Not a freakin' chance.

Vonlee threatened not to testify at her aunt's trial, thus breaking her agreement.

The prosecutor's office decided to withdraw the previous plea bargain Vonlee and Richard Lustig had negotiated—which it had the right to do before Billie Jean's trial had started because Vonlee was now "refusing to testify under the terms of the original deal."

A judge would have to, however, make the final decision.

CHAPTER 57

BILLIE JEAN'S TRIAL BEGAN on schedule, November 29, 2001, a Thursday, the entire session eaten up by jury selection. This day was a moment many thought would never come to pass. Billie Jean, frail and beaten down by the cancer, was clearly sick. But there she sat, in the hallway of the courthouse, ready and waiting for her day in court.

Billie Jean had reason to smile this morning, despite the circumstances of the threat of her remaining days on the planet being spent behind bars. At 9:23 A.M., on November 29, in the Sixth Judicial Circuit Court of Oakland County, before the Honorable Wendy Potts, who would oversee jury selection in Billie Jean's case, an unprecedented proceeding took place inside the courtroom.

APA John Skrzynski was there to represent the People, and Vonlee Titlow's new lawyer, Frederick Toca, stood on behalf of Vonlee, who looked as though she had been on whirlwind high the last few weeks. "Confident" didn't even begin to describe how Vonlee came across this morning. She was ready and willing, under the direction of Toca, to withdraw her previous plea and force the hand of the prosecutor's office, or so she believed.

Thus, after Vonlee said she was "convinced" that this man was going to get her off with minimal time served, the new team of Titlow and Toca was present inside Potts's courtroom. The duo was prepared to explain officially to the judge what Vonlee was doing, so Billie Jean's trial could commence without disruption. Vonlee would not be testifying against her aunt, which, everyone knew, was going to make a conviction on the state's part nearly impossible.

Skrzynski explained to the judge after Toca introduced himself that it was the state's understanding that Vonlee was going to withdraw her "previously tendered . . . conditional plea." Further, the APA added, "The defendant indicated through her attorney that she will *not* testify, except if her sentence can be two to fifteen, which is a violation of the agreement which we entered."

Not that he was seething, or visibly bitter, but Skrzynski was aggravated and impatient, considering he believed Vonlee was getting away with a lot more than she had done. Many on the side of law enforcement were convinced Vonlee had participated in the actual murder and had been far more responsible than she was letting on.

The APA asked the court to withdraw the deal it had offered. On top of that, APA Skrzynski stated, "We wish to proceed to trial [with Vonlee] immediately."

That's it. If Vonlee was going to take this to the next level, the prosecutor's office was ready for battle. The one case the PO had been certain of was Vonlee's. They had plenty of evidence against Vonlee to merit a conviction.

Vonlee sat looking on, seemingly stunned to hear those words, yet self-assured that her new attorney was advising her to do the right thing. It's striking how ignorant both Vonlee and Toca came across here: This was a slam dunk for the PO. Vonlee had admitted to her role in the crime—she had done so on the stand, on videotape, in court—and, additionally, the PO had that recording made by her boyfriend. By her own testimony during the hearing to accept the plea, Vonlee was a witness against herself.

Toca explained to the judge that he thought seven to fifteen was "outside of Ms. Vonlee Titlow's guidelines," without going into any more detail about what he meant, adding, "When I had an opportunity to speak to Mr. Skrzynski, he indicated that he would review that with his office. I spoke to him after that. He indicated they would not accept that. Based upon that, Your Honor, we are withdrawing."

The APA spoke up, rather candidly and with affirmation, saying, "No, no. The offer that was made on the phone by this man was three to fifteen or she would take the Fifth."

The judge called a bench conference. She was a bit taken aback by all of this, describing to the lawyers after they approached the bench how she didn't really know what the guidelines were in this situation.

Toca kept insisting the guidelines stipulated two to five years.

Skrzynski listened to Judge Potts and Toca go back and forth as Toca tried explaining that the guidelines were based on Vonlee having "no priors," and any charges she did have were "misdemeanors."

Potts looked at Skrzynski. She wanted to know what he thought. Did he have a response?

"Well," the witty assistant prosecutor said, "this is only her *first* murder."

Skrzynski continued to argue over Toca's bantering about the two to five by stating rather simply that, in the end, it didn't matter *what* the guidelines were, any lawyer knew that. What mattered was the *deal* to which Vonlee had agreed. And that was a minimum of seven years. *Period.* It was an agreement, in fact, that Vonlee Titlow, Skrzynski said, knew firsthand was "above" those so-called guidelines. "And she agreed that she would not only do that, but she would *waive* her appellate remedies . . . superseding the guidelines."

It seemed as though Toca did not study Vonlee's case at all.

Toca and the APA talked back and forth, the judge refereeing, each arguing about guidelines and what the probation department would determine the best guidelines should be, but the conversation turned tedious as Skrzynski pointed out that it was all for naught, seeing how Vonlee had agreed her deal was above the guidelines, whatever they were. That was all that mattered.

Toca accused the PO of proceeding with the deal "in bad faith" by knowing that, at best, it was a manslaughter case, to begin with.

Judge Potts ruled that if Vonlee didn't want to go with the seven to fifteen, the court would allow her to withdraw her plea bargain and the prosecutor's office was free to withdraw its deal and continue prosecuting its case any way it chose.

To be certain that Vonlee understood what was happening and the seriousness of what she was doing, the judge asked if she was clear that by "withdrawing" her plea of manslaughter, the "charge of first-degree murder" would likely "be reinstated . . . and the maximum penalty for her could be life in prison?"

"Yes, Your Honor," Vonlee said, indicating that she understood the ramifications of her actions.

"And do you do that freely and voluntarily?"

"Yes."

"You fully understand the consequences?"

"Yes."

The judge said she didn't have any additional questions. After a pause and a slight glance down at her notes, Judge Potts concluded, "All right, the trial will be January 14, [2002]."

Toca balked, saying that he had just been retained and there was a lot to go over. He would need more time. He might also have a scheduling conflict on that day. Then he explained how he felt the PO was "in a *rush* to try this. . . ."

"We're not in a rush, Your Honor," Skrzynski said.

The judge said two months was plenty enough time for Toca to get up to speed on the case and to prepare. And if the scheduling conflict on Toca's end was not a criminal matter, Toca should drop the other case and focus on Vonlee's trial. There would be no delay.

CHAPTER 58

WITH JURY SELECTION TAKING only one day, on Friday, November 30, 2001, at 8:48 A.M., *Michigan* vs. *Billie Jean Rogers* began on schedule inside Judge Wendy Potts's Oakland County Sixth Circuit Court, in downtown Pontiac. Potts, a well-respected judge, had served the Sixth Judicial Circuit since December 11, 1997, when she was appointed from a probate position by then-governor John Engler. A proud grandmother, Potts expected punctuality in her courtroom as a general rule. She hated when lawyers showed up late and rarely tolerated it without some sort of tongue-lashing or warning about it happening again. The one working model Potts liked to promote was that she and her staff functioned together as a team and drove equal portions along the road to justice. Potts once told an interviewer with *Motion* magazine that the "advice" she would most likely "give a new attorney about courtroom etiquette" is to "treat judge's staff with the same respect as the judge." Interestingly enough, more likely in jest, Judge Potts told the same magazine her favorite "law-related" television show was watching "reruns of my court TV programs."

On a more serious note, Potts said she looked up to her brother as a role model; he was a man who had undergone a liver transplant and planned to run a marathon after healing. She demanded preparedness and professionalism inside her courtroom at all times.

No excuses.

By ten minutes after nine that morning, Potts proved her reputation as a time-efficient judge who liked to keep things moving along. APA John Skrzynski, a slightly balding, blond-haired, middle-aged man, in good physical shape, approached the jury to begin his opening statement. Skrzynski was a prosecutor who had led the charge against the high-profile "Doctor Death," Jack Kevorkian.

Skrzynski knew his way around the law, no doubt about it. He started with a rather interesting theme, picking up on something Judge Potts had mentioned in her terse remarks to the jury before they got started: "a list of ingredients, or what we call elements" of a murder.

As the APA of Oakland County, a job he took more serious than probably anything else in his life besides family, Skrzynski said it was up to him to prove—beyond a reasonable doubt—these so-called elements. He acknowledged his appreciation for the jury and asked if they could focus throughout the trial on comparing those *elements* of murder with the *evidence* presented, before drawing their final conclusion. He then broke down each element.

Did Billie Jean *cause* the death of her husband?

A quick pause, look up from his notes. Then, if Billie Jean had caused that death, was there *intent* on her part to kill Don Rogers?

The third element was *premeditation,* Skrzynski insisted. Did the intent have premeditation supporting it?

And did that premeditation come before the "action took place"?

It had to, Skrzynski concluded.

The fourth element included a *deliberate* act taking place during the course of the murder: was Don's murder thought about beforehand?

"Premeditation" was a confusing word, the APA seemed to suggest by his comments. It did not mean that in the weeks and months before Don's murder, Billie Jean sat down and devised some diabolical plot to execute her husband or to make a drunken stupor of his look like a final bender. Premeditation could mean, quite actually, those crucial moments just before the crime was committed, mere seconds before.

"The fifth element," Skrzynski then announced, "is that the killing itself is *not justified . . . excused or mitigated.*"

He was referring to self-defense.

Skrzynski went through each element again, succinctly explaining the point he needed to make for each, before collectively asking jurors a rhetorical question, thus hoping to point to a mistake he believed Billie Jean had made, which subsequently led to her appearing to have something to hide: "How many of you ever lied to *get* into trouble? . . . Raise your hand." He waited a moment, and then repeated the question: "How many of you have ever lied to get into serious trouble?"

Billie Jean's attorney, Walter Piszczatowski, objected, saying he thought the question was actually more argument than opening statement.

Judge Potts called them both to the bench. She encouraged the APA to tell the jury what he was going to *prove* during the trial.

Skrzynski never said what that lie Billie Jean had told might entail.

After both attorneys resettled, Skrzynski gave the jury a narrative of what the state aimed to show Billie Jean

Rogers had done on the night her husband died. He explained how the evidence would ultimately "show that around four-thirty in the morning . . . the police received a call on 911. It was . . . Billie Rogers. And she was calling the police to tell them that she and her niece, Nicole Titlow, had come home from the casino and had found her husband, Don Rogers, dead on the floor."

He further stated that as police arrived on scene and took a look around, "they discovered Don Rogers lying dead on the floor of the kitchen—and [after looking] at Don's body," those same cops "thought it was unusual."

Skrzynski warned jurors they would see a photograph of Don lying on the floor, and it wouldn't be pleasant.

"He's dead. I want to prepare you for that. But this is what the police officers saw. It looks like he's asleep."

From there, the APA focused on the seemingly odd fact that Don's ankles had been crossed and it "looked almost like he had been watching TV or something." It was strange—everyone in law enforcement there at the scene had thought so. The scene appeared staged and gave the officers the impression that there was more to the death than what appeared to be a heart attack or some other natural way that death comes to people inside their homes.

With the thought in mind that something was wrong with the death scene, the cops "spoke to the two women that were there," Skrzynski explained to twelve members of the community that had not heard this story until that moment. "They spoke to Billie Rogers and to another woman that was with her, Nicole Titlow. Billie Rogers was fairly calm and Nicole Titlow was very emotional. Very, *very* upset. Didn't want to talk to the police."

The motive came up next as the APA digressed from the reactions of the ladies to how, as Don Rogers "lay there" dead on his kitchen floor, he "was actually a pretty wealthy man . . . [with] an estate . . . worth between one-point-five and one-point-eight million dollars." The APA further explained that the "account was in *his* name." Billie Jean Rogers, however, "had what's called a 'right of survivorship' in that money." He then took a pause before delivering what he hoped was a pithy punch line: "That means that if Don dies, *Billie* gets the money."

It sounded sinister the way Skrzynski had put it— maybe even evil. Here was one of the oldest motives for murder perhaps on record: a crime carried out by a woman hell-bent on killing the man she supposedly loved, and then happily riding off into the sunset with a bundle of his cash. The argument had a black-widow spin in the way it had been presented by the experienced prosecutor; he believed what he was selling.

The problem with this argument was that there was no supporting evidence to back any of it up besides some financial spreadsheets, a long and tortured bitterness between Don and his wife, and, finally, a choppy record-ing of Vonlee Titlow, the woman's niece, talking to her boyfriend, a convicted felon, about a possible conspiracy to commit murder.

Up against the bare facts, the argument felt weak and inconsequential.

The APA continued to march to the tune of the widow's thirst for, and possible addiction to, gambling and how she had amassed a fifty-thousand-dollar debt that she needed to pay off. This situation had potentially pushed her over the edge to murder the man whose money she had spent.

As a piece of evidence the APA promised, he men-tioned a floor plan of the Rogers household. He ex-plained where everything pertinent to the case was located: dining table, chairs, living area, couch, coffee table, a pair of shoes and glass of water. He said the glass of water on the coffee table in close proximity to that pair of women's shoes said something about the crime.

Billie Jean had admitted the water and shoes were hers—and that admission told a story. He relayed how the detective and officers on the scene, seeing the items, thought it was unusual for them to be there, seeing that Billie Jean and Vonlee had already said they had walked into the house through the garage. If that was the case, Skrzynski explained, one or both women would've had to walk *over* Don's body or step around it in order to make it into the living space to take off her shoes and drink from the glass of water. That alone, the APA presumed, was evidence of a nefarious crime the women had committed, solely because they obviously did not care about Don's dead body on the kitchen floor when they came home.

But what if Billie Jean simply said that it was routine for her to walk in and see Don passed out, walk over him, and then sit down to relax before committing to the nightly task of picking him up off the floor and dragging him up to his room?

Reasonable doubt?

Skrzynski hoped not.

By his opening, the APA appeared to be setting the stage with the elements of murder, and the peculiar nature of the "death scene," as noted by two cops, to all be evidence of a premeditated, well-thought-out plan to murder Don on that night.

Adding to his theme, the APA explained how the medical examiner first thought it was a heart attack but then changed his mind when those mitigating circumstances of an admission had come into play.

From that point, Skrzynski introduced Danny Chahine.

And then he zeroed in on Vonlee, Billie Jean's "niece," and how she had admitted to Danny that she was a man—and then the real "bombshell" of her revelation: Vonlee had taken part in a murder with her aunt, but she felt her aunt had done the deed herself.

Concluding, the APA said Billie Jean's "niece" would likely not testify, and that was her right. But if Vonlee Titlow chose to plead the Fifth, well, Skrzynski added, the jury could still be certain to hear from her via words from Vonlee's guilty lips to Danny's eager ears via a recording device Danny had hidden inside his truck.

CHAPTER 59

WALTER PISZCZATOWSKI WAS A well-respected attorney with sandy brown/blond hair, a trendy goatee (neatly groomed), along with a rather cheerful, easy-going demeanor—however serious he came across in a court of law. In that sense, Piszczatowski bore a striking resemblance to his rival, APA Skrzynski.

Billie Jean had chosen well in Piszczatowski for an attorney. He graduated from Wayne State University Law School in 1977 before joining the Wayne County Prosecutor's Office, where he stayed until 1983. From there, Piszczatowski became a member of the PO's Special Assignment Squad before moving on to become an assistant U.S. attorney (AUSA) in the Eastern District (Michigan), finally climbing into the chief of Special Prosecutions Unit's job. He left that post to go into private practice in 1988 and never looked back.

Piszczatowski was a serious player in the world of criminal defense in Oakland County, Michigan. He had been hired by a number of high-profile celebrities, whose cases commanded major media attention. Piszczatowski had represented Marshall Mathers (iconic rapper Eminem) on a concealed weapons charge in April 2001.

He had taken on cases for music industry heavyweights such as Marilyn Manson and Jack White, as well as Indiana Pacers basketball star David Harrison.

The way Piszczatowski viewed the position of anyone he defended was to allow the facts of the case to unfold before the jury in a fair and balanced manner, poking holes in the state's position, where he felt he could. Here, as Piszczatowski looked at the PO's case against Billie Jean, he had a client that didn't need to be defended, necessarily, more than she needed legal counsel to guide the jury toward the truth. Without Vonlee's testimony, the state was up against a brick wall, Piszczatowski knew. The PO had nothing that proved Billie Jean had murdered her husband. Yes, Billie Jean had spent a lot of her husband's savings and investment money after his death. She had accumulated a large gambling debt, which Don Rogers had been paying. But she had not just up and married the guy months or weeks before he died. She'd spent a lifetime with Don. Sure, Don might have been pissed at his wife, but that was not an uncommon problem between a man and his wife. If it was all you had to serve up as a prosecutor, it was certainly not enough grounds for the accused to have murdered the guy.

Beyond all of that, Billie Jean had been diagnosed with terminal cancer before Don's death. Why would she plot to kill the man when she herself was going to be dead within, supposedly, the year? Or maybe that was the PO's theory—that Billie Jean didn't care what happened to her? She could spend all the money she wanted and then check out. Was it morally wrong? Was it unfair to do that to a man you were supposed to love, honor and cherish?

Maybe so.

"Ladies and gentlemen, this case is about . . . being accused of a crime that you didn't commit," Piszczatowski stated, setting the tone immediately upon addressing the jury. "But thank goodness not everyone that's charged with a criminal offense is convicted of that criminal offense." This was an important point for Billie Jean's lawyer to make: just because she had been charged and faced trial, that alone did not mean Billie Jean Rogers was guilty of the crime.

Piszczatowski talked about the charges against his client being only—at this stage—a "piece of paper . . . in the court file." It was a charge. It wasn't fact. She wasn't guilty because she had been *charged*. A charge "is *not* evidence." The allegations on that piece of paper, he thundered, "bears no weight!" He said it had nothing "to do with the prosecution's case. It's no different than a civil complaint. If you're getting sued in civil court, there's a complaint that starts the proceedings. In criminal proceedings, it's what's called 'criminal information.'"

This was the point to Piszczatowski's argument. He encouraged jurors not to get caught up in what seemed to be a full court press to make sure someone goes down for the death of Don Rogers. Listen to the evidence. Realize the facts of the case as they unfold before you. Think things through. Put yourself in the position of Billie Jean. Ask yourself if there is any reasonable doubt whatsoever before dropping the blade on a guillotine that will "decide her fate."

Using that tone as a launching point, Piszczatowski ripped apart the PO, calling its prosecution of his client a "shoddy method" of seeking justice, adding how a "shoddy method of investigation" led to the arrest. Not good, solid police work. "There are three basic principles of law. Mr. Skrzynski alluded to one in his opening this morning, and that is that he has the burden of . . . proving each and every element in this case *beyond* a reasonable doubt."

Piszczatowski talked about a metaphoric "cloak" that his client sat in the courtroom and wore around her neck, one of which had "presumption of innocence" written on the front, and nobody serving on the jury should ever forget that fact, especially in a case such as the one they were about to hear. That cloak, he added, furthering his metaphor, should stay put until the PO stripped it off her "*with* evidence." He let the word— "evidence"—ring for a few beats before continuing, saying how if "they don't do their job, well, your job is to do one thing. Because *that's* how the judicial system works."

After introducing himself and his co-counsel, Piszcza-towski mentioned how the case should hinge on several important, unconditional essentials: "cold, hard facts, evidence, [no] sympathy or bias, the burden of proof" by the PO.

He asked jurors to wait and withhold judgment until the end, which sounded routine and rather mundane, but most juries, any smart lawyer knew, made up their minds by the halfway point. Piszczatowski did not want that to happen here.

The truth, Piszczatowski promised, would be "con-stant" in the case he would present. He said he would introduce a number of inconsistencies that would ulti-mately "cause you problems." Smartly, perhaps, he keyed on the point of there being "a number of questions . . . left open" and a "number of mysteries" that still needed to be solved. And if the jury had issues with "closing the loop," there was no other result except a vote for acquit-tal. The PO could not be "half right," and Billie Jean could not be found guilty based on the "poor quality of the evidence."

He called his client "a very reserved individual," who was "dignified" and "extremely accepting and loyal." She was "nonjudgmental," but also a "spendthrift," which might have made her not your typical housewife, but certainly did not make her a killer. He presented the notion of the PO wanting jurors to think that because Billie Jean had acted a "certain way" on the night her husband died, her behavior should constitute guilt.

Justice did not work that way. In a court of law, there needed to be proof, backed up by factual evidence; there should not be speculative assumptions based on a cop's opinion of a person and how she acted on a particular night.

Then he talked about Don, explaining how Billie Jean's husband was "an intensely private individual. Almost reclusive. He was a functional—some might say *barely* functional—alcoholic. But he was, indeed, an alcoholic—indeed a heavy drinker, who was in deteriorating health. . . ."

The "fact" that Don suffered weight loss came up next.

How weak Don had become in his last days.

How his "rectal bleeding" was a problem that signified an ending might be close.

And then several bare facts: how Billie Jean found her husband on the floor and called 911, along with her niece/nephew, and how the responding officers, upon first viewing the scene, had found it to be "normal" in their opinion, according to an early police report.

"Nothing unusual. No signs of trauma. No signs of any injury. No signs of any struggle. Those are the cold, hard facts." It wasn't until later that the case seemed to change: when a detective considered something might be off because Don's legs were crossed, and a glass of water was on a table, and Billie Jean's niece was acting weird, and then a man had gone to a cop friend to report something his girlfriend had said.

As soon as Piszczatowski hit on Vonlee, he focused on "the fact" that Vonlee was blasted drunk that night. Nothing she said should be taken as any serious truth, simply based on the idea that a drunk did not make a good witness.

Piszczatowski then spoke of how the medical examiner was going to walk into the courtroom and "rewrite history" with his "theories" about the way in which Don met his demise. The reason "they" would have to "rewrite history," Piszczatowski added, "was because there's nothing in evidence" backing up a murder charge.

Once the ME changed his cause of death on a man's death certificate—a man whose body had been cremated—Piszczatowski intoned, the floodgates opened and everyone jumped aboard a bandwagon of murder—which in turn made everything seem suspicious: the fallen-over chair, the shoes, the water. Plus, the slight bruise on Don's lip had now become a rug-burn type of injury they presumed under an assumption of guilt.

When he got to Danny Chahine, Piszczatowski held little back, saying at one point, "In spite of the fact that Danny Chahine was having sexual intercourse with Vonlee Titlow, he didn't know that she wasn't a woman. And there were a number of things that she said to him that are way out there. Way out there. She was not afraid to lie to him, when it suited her best interest. . . ."

All salient facts.

He then keyed in on Billie Jean's gambling and her "losses"—still not a motive for murder.

There was no "financial" reason, Piszczatowski said, because on the day Don Rogers died, Billie Jean already had everything she wanted: money, status, a nice home, cars and a nest egg.

What else did she need?

"She was living a very comfortable lifestyle."

"In the end, you're going to find that another person's life cannot be placed in jeopardy on the words of someone like Vonlee Titlow to Danny Chahine. Donald Rogers's death was clearly a tragedy. The only great tragedy would be brought by you, if you found Ms. Rogers guilty on the words of Vonlee Titlow."

Direct, competent, confident words, coming from a lawyer who obviously understood his way around a trial courtroom.

It was close to 10:00 A.M. when Billie Jean's lawyer finished.

The judge took a quick break.

CHAPTER 60

THE INITIAL COP ON the scene, Lynn Giorgi, was called as the state's first witness. Giorgi took the oath and subsequently told jurors exactly what had occurred as she answered that 911 call that brought her to Don Rogers's corpse lying on the kitchen floor of his home on August 12, 2000.

Giorgi said she arrived on the scene at the same time Pete Dungjen did. They entered the home together.

Wearing a gray sweater, her hair dyed brown, looking tired and unhappy, with a stoic look on her face, Billie Jean sat and stared at Giorgi.

The officer talked about how "calm" and orderly both Billie Jean and Vonlee were when she first arrived and walked into the kitchen to have a look at Don.

The state introduced those photos of Don they had warned jurors about. Don looked to be sleeping. He was on his back, legs crossed at the ankles. A chair was on its side near his head.

Next, Giorgi talked about learning that Don had some "problems due to alcohol" and that Billie Jean had thought he was passed out, but then she learned he wasn't breathing and realized he was likely dead.

"Did she indicate to you how much he drank?" APA Skrzynski asked.

"I believe she did, but I don't recall what it was. It was some large amount."

"A large amount? Okay. She indicated he was a chronic alcoholic?"

"Yes."

As they discussed the position of Don's body and how neither she nor Dungjen thought it to be at all odd, Giorgi said, "We saw no signs of trauma on the body." In fact, it wasn't until they began to speak with Vonlee and Billie Jean that both officers considered something was off. The first indicator was the position of Don's body as opposed to where the women walked into the house, that glass of water and the shoes in the great room, and how each of those clues told the officers they must have walked over Don's body and sat down.

The jury was shown a diagram of the house, Don's body marked.

Concerning where Don was lying, Giorgi explained during her testimony, as she and Dungjen thought about it, "It just seemed unlikely that you could fall from somewhere and end up with your legs—with your ankles perfectly crossed. . . ."

"It just seemed unlikely"—that phrase kind of rang like an out-of-tune bell inside the courtroom. Was this powerful evidence? Or was it a cop's "opinion" of what had transpired? How did they make the leap from legs crossed at ankles to murder?

Giorgi talked about the layers of suspicion and how they grew the more time she and Dungjen spent inside the house. Like how "strange" Vonlee began to act, for example. She noted that "loud, excitable and protective" were three ways in which she believed Vonlee was not conducting herself normally, as most people under similar circumstances generally would.

"[She] didn't like me asking [Billie] questions," Giorgi said.

Was this a drunk person protecting her aunt, or someone trying to hide a crime?

Giorgi didn't make it clear.

As they talked about Vonlee's demeanor, Piszczatowski objected, due to relevance.

It was sustained.

The way the questions and answers were framed suggested that the way in which the situation was handled by Vonlee and Billie Jean was out of the norm compared to other death scenes Giorgi had attended. This generated some concern within the two cops. They wondered why the women were acting in such a way. To give an example, Giorgi mentioned how neither woman wanted to write a statement about what had happened. This seemed suspicious and out of the norm for how a similar scene should unfold. Most people would do whatever the cops asked of them. Giorgi and Dungjen were quite taken aback, Giorgi explained, at the notion that the women basically did not want to comply with whatever the police suggested.

She said Billie Jean chain-smoked cigarettes and didn't say much, while Vonlee protected her aunt and spoke very aggressively and loudly.

Of course, when Giorgi talked about what Vonlee was saying, Piszczatowski smartly objected (hearsay) and the judge encouraged the PO to move on.

Within all of her testimony, Giorgi offered very little to bolster the PO's case. In fact, at the end of the APA's direct questioning, Giorgi noted that she had not written a report and had left that part of the call up to Dungjen. It was standard procedure to do this, she explained. But when Detective Don Zimmerman became actively involved, he then went to Giorgi and asked if she could, after the fact, write a report for him. But it wasn't until Zimmerman had what Giorgi described as "other information regarding this case."

"Did he suggest to you anything to write?"

"No."

It would have been a powerful statement, had the PO left it there. But APA Skrzynski then asked: "He just said, 'Anything that seemed out of place'?"

"We had a conversation," she explained. "He had asked me if I could remember that . . . call and I did."

Giorgi said it stood out because of Vonlee's off-the-wall, loud and boisterous behavior.

That was it—the APA was done. He passed the witness.

Piszczatowski began by asking Giorgi—who was, most in the courtroom knew, an important witness for Billie Jean—about a meeting she had been at where he and "the whole cast of characters" in the case were asked questions: a pretrial deposition. He wanted to know if most of the direct testimony she had just gone through with the PO was on par with that line of questioning earlier in the year during the deposition.

She said it was.

Billie Jean's defense attorney then pointed out that during her depositions in the case, Officer Giorgi had said the kitchen floor in Don's house was linoleum, which it wasn't, and that only when she went back and looked at photographs did she realize she had that fact wrong.

"Yes," she agreed.

Memory, Piszczatowski was pointing out without coming out and actually saying it, was a fragile, delicate and not pitch-perfect way of accurately depicting situations. Even simple, basic facts, like a floor. It was a subtle, yet noticeable jab at the officer.

He then focused on how Giorgi had once said she moved the chair in the kitchen "not more than . . . about one foot."

"That's my approximation, yes," she said.

They talked about Giorgi not finding any injuries— she agreed.

No signs of struggle—and she agreed to that also.

And nothing unusual about the body: "Other than, what you tell us now, the legs were crossed." Giorgi agreed "that was correct," too.

Next, Piszczatowski asked the cop about her training. How long she had been on the force at the time of the incident. How part of her training involved learning to write police reports, which was "an important part of your function as a police officer. . . ."

"Yes."

The purpose of the police report, Piszczatowski said in one leading question, was to "note anything that you might think might be unusual . . . and something that might be relevant if, in fact, an investigation continues. . . ."

"That you *think* might be pertinent," she clarified.

They moved on to the responding officer's "role" at the scene.

The way Piszczatowski went about pointing out all of these simple and relevant aspects of what first responders do every day was to let everyone know that as Giorgi surveyed the scene with Officer Dungjen, nothing seemed to be wrong—besides a dead man, a nontalkative wife, a drunk and loud niece. The scene was anything but a murder—it seemed more like what the women had claimed it to be: a tragedy.

Piszczatowski then brought in Dungjen's report as an exhibit.

Giorgi agreed that she had reviewed her colleague's

report after Detective Zimmerman came into the case and asked her to write one herself.

Then a significant question: Piszczatowski wanted to know if, prior to asking Vonlee to write a statement, "Did you give her any Miranda rights?"

"No."

"And that's because, based on your observations at the scene, you didn't think there was any *need* to do that?"

"That's correct."

From there, they discussed how Giorgi had been to several death scenes and all were "different." No two people responded to death in the same fashion. No two people cried, yelled or withdrew in the same manner; each scene, although very similar, was not the same.

Yes. Yes. And yes, she agreed.

"People are people, and every individual deals with death differently . . . ," Piszczatowski said.

Yes again.

Giorgi also agreed that Billie Jean smoked constantly while she was at the scene and that it was pretty common for people to do that.

Piszczatowski got the officer to agree that she had "approved" of Dungjen's report and unofficially signed off on it.

The bottom line with all of this, some of which came across by Piszczatowski as sarcastic and pushy (for good reason), was that for Giorgi, there wasn't anything at the death scene misaligned to the point of making an accusation of murder until after Zimmerman came and asked her to rethink it. Piszczatowski hammered the officer on a number of valid points, making sure jurors understood that Giorgi and Dungjen did not conduct an investigation while they were there, nor did they suspect anything to be that much out of the norm besides a few women acting different and a dead guy's legs crossed at the ankles.

As Piszczatowski wound down his cross-examination, he asked about Zimmerman going to Giorgi and asking about "writing a report, and that was sometime in November—that correct?" Almost three months after the day she had been at the death scene.

"Yes."

"Okay. And at that time, had you heard anything *new* about the case?"

"No."

"So no one had . . . It wasn't like the buzz of the Troy Police Department that a witness was engaging in sex with a transsexual?"

"No!"

"That wasn't around the department at *all?*" Piszczatowski asked as if he had a hard time believing her.

"No, it wasn't."

"Nobody had heard that fact?" Piszczatowski pressed.

"No—and I work in the same area as Detective Zimmerman and I had not"—she started to add before Piszczatowski cut her off.

"Okay," the defense attorney inserted.

But she finished, concluding, ". . . heard that."

"So that didn't happen?"

"Right."

"Okay. So he just came to you and said, 'Write a report'? Write [a] report about what you remember at this scene, correct?"

"Well, he asked me—we had a conversation. He asked me what types of things I thought were unusual and other things that weren't on the report, and he supplied me with a copy of Officer Dungjen's original report and I had reviewed that. And the few things that we had discussed, he said, yes, anything that you can recall, including those things, to please put in the report."

"Okay. Did you ask him why?"

"He had told me at the beginning of the conversation that there had been some other types of information that would lead them into an investigation—that it might not have been a natural death."

This was important testimony for Piszczatowski. Giorgi had written her report while *knowing* that the detectives in the unit had come to a conclusion that there might have been a homicide.

Casting a line, Piszczatowski then asked Giorgi if she knew, from Zimmerman, if the "position of the chair might be an issue" in his case.

"No," she said firmly.

"You weren't told that at all?"

"No, I wasn't told *anything*."

"Just that there was an investigation continuing into a possible unnatural death, right?"

"Yes. They had gotten some other information he did not disclose to me—that it may not have been a natural death and for me to include these other items."

Piszczatowski took a moment.

"Thanks," he said, feeling victorious. "I don't have any other questions of this witness."

CHAPTER 61

THROUGHOUT THAT FIRST DAY of the trial, Officer Giorgi testified, and withstood what turned out to be an inconsequential redirect and recross. The state next brought in Officer Pete Dungjen, who did not add or detract from anything Giorgi had testified to. Jurors would either believe these two cops had integrity and were speaking from a place of it, or would not believe them at all, tossing out their testimony altogether, feeling it was too vague to matter. The jurors could potentially side with Billie Jean and put the focus on a theme Giorgi herself had kept bringing up: not all death scenes are the same, and not all people react in a similar way when faced with the death of a "loved one."

By the end of the first day of testimony, forensic pathologist Dr. Ruben Ortiz-Reyes was in the hot seat answering questions posed by the APA—softballs. *All of them.* Ortiz-Reyes's direct testimony would set the stage for the state to argue that it was not so uncommon for a pathologist to change his opinion once he learned new information about a so-called natural death. The only major problem—one that Piszczatowski would no doubt seize upon when given the opportunity—was that the medical examiner's office never got a chance to conduct an actual autopsy after it changed its now-controversial opinion.

A pathologist testifying in a court of law can be a cumbersome prospect, tedious and completely dull, if not handled correctly by the attorney doing the questioning. Allowing doctors to meander on and on about their profession, skill, medical knowledge or education can alienate jurors and leave a sour taste in their consciousness, even sometimes bringing a certain heaviness to their eyes, beckoning a nap, as they try to withstand the arduous task of what might be unimportant nonsense. Best way for a lawyer to handle a talkative pathologist or medical doctor is to keep peppering him or her with direct, pointed questions, while knowing when to butt in and interrupt.

Luckily, Ortiz-Reyes was not your typical blabbering clinician, looking to boost his ego with a list of credentials, or a rundown of his accomplishments. He was terse at times, long at others, perhaps when he needed to be, and overall was a very confident and capable witness.

After being asked, he explained his craft of carving up bodies, taking fluid and tissue samples, weighing livers and hearts, sawing through skull and bone. He talked about his vast education experience and how qualified he was to be sitting in the courtroom. He was no novice; he had done some two thousand autopsies in his years behind the buzz saw. Contrary to an unquestionable, soon-to-be focus of the defense, Ortiz-Reyes explained, there were "hundreds of times" in which a medical examiner's office would not perform a complete autopsy, but "only perform [an] external examination in order to determine the fate of the death. . . ."

After some lengthy discussion between the judge and the APA, along with several questions by Piszczatowski to qualify the doctor as the expert he claimed himself to be, the court said it was going to go ahead and meet the requirements of Ortiz-Reyes being considered "an expert in forensic pathology."

He said he had testified in hundreds of cases, all over Michigan.

The judge agreed and the questioning by the APA picked back up.

Ortiz-Reyes talked about receiving Don's body at the morgue. It was a Saturday, he explained, so he did very little examining other than what needed to be done, establishing a "natural death" diagnosis, tabling the remainder until Monday, as they normally do on weekends, unless it's a law enforcement emergency of some sort.

When he did conduct the examination—Ortiz-Reyes said he never did a complete autopsy on Don—he came to the conclusion that Don had died of a heart attack, and his death was ordinary and there was nothing outwardly pointing to anything else but an older gentleman who had likely died of natural causes, facilitated by an unhealthy lifestyle. Furthermore, he had come to this conclusion because "most men in this country," specifically in Don's age range, "die of heart disease."

It was common. The ME's office saw it all the time.

But on that Monday after Don's death, a red flag popped up for Ortiz-Reyes and the team when the blood and urine analysis came back with those astonishing numbers, indicating an enormous amount of alcohol in Don's system at the time of his death. So this revelation made him change his "opinion" about the heart attack.

"In that death certificate, the first was alcoholic intoxication [as] the cause of death in this gentleman," Ortiz-Reyes told the APA, "and the number two was the arteriosclerotic cardiovascular disease, meaning heart attack."

This new information on Monday alerted the office that it might be prudent to conduct an actual autopsy.

But when they went to go get Don's body, it had already been checked out under that first death certificate. They had no idea then that Don had been cremated.

So Ortiz-Reyes amended the manner of death to now read "accidental." This, too, wasn't abnormal. Though not a common practice, it certainly happened from time to time.

Don had ingested an accidental overdose of booze, Ortiz-Reyes thought.

There was another surprise, Ortiz-Reyes explained, when the TPD called a "few days later" and said they had *more* information, which subsequently changed the status of Don's death yet again. It was at this time, he said, that the medical examiner, his boss, Dr. Dragovic, got involved, as is generally the protocol when a case proceeds as such.

"Every time there is a big surprise, he comes and takes over the case, because he is the chief medical examiner and he is in charge of the office. I also worked this case with him, but he is the one that takes over."

As they talked back and forth about Don's death, and the way in which the medical examiner's office handled it was not so uncharacteristic a series of events, Ortiz-Reyes mentioned that the amount of alcohol alone in Don's system was enough to cause concern. Then, when they learned about Don's drinking habits, they realized he could very well survive drinking that much—which meant maybe something else had killed him. The point was: The medical examiner was open to interpretation of death, as facts became available. And sometimes "small findings mean a lot," Ortiz-Reyes made clear.

Near the end of his direct testimony, Ortiz-Reyes talked about a "little abrasion" on Don's nose and lip— a few faint red marks that he did not notice the first and only time he looked at Don's actual physical body. It wasn't until he saw the marks in the photographs of

Don's body later on, after they had learned Don might have been the victim of a homicide, that "it was suggestive that something was put on the face of this gentleman."

Not that the marks could have been made as Don fell to the floor, or as he maybe stumbled into a wall while walking into the kitchen or by some other way people hurt themselves when drunk. For Ortiz-Reyes, these marks, coupled with everything else they had learned from law enforcement, possibly meant that someone had murdered Don by suffocation.

The APA asked what could have left those marks.

"Like some rough piece of something that's rough, like a pillow, but a *rough* pillow . . . and that [was] the reason he had that little scratch [on] there (meaning his nose)."

These were strong, accusatory words coming from an experienced pathologist. Ortiz-Reyes believed what he was saying. He was speaking from confidence.

The doctor called it a "fresh abrasion." He likened the scratch to a cushion of a seat marking up the surface of the skin if a person, wearing shorts, sat down wrong.

All of this led Ortiz-Reyes to change the manner of the death yet again: "After reviewing *all* of the additional information, I said the gentleman was smothered by putting something on the face, plus the alcohol, of course."

CHAPTER 62

PISZCZATOWSKI BEGAN WITH A question about the doctor's "initial external examination" of Don's corpse, pointing out for jurors how the ME "never performed an autopsy" on Don.

Ortiz-Reyes agreed, of course.

It was important for the lawyer to get that out there, clear and concise as possible.

No autopsy.

From there, Piszczatowski went over the exact series of events as Ortiz-Reyes had just described for the APA: body on Saturday, staff meeting on Monday, toxicology report changing opinions. The defense attorney highlighted how those opinions were changed again "without conducting an autopsy" when the TPD called.

"Yes," the doctor said.

They discussed the level of alcohol in Don's system. Then Piszczatowski read a statute written for the state of Michigan that explained when an autopsy should be conducted, but Ortiz-Reyes corrected him by saying the statute didn't specify "autopsy."

It specified "investigation."

There was a difference.

The statute also required, Piszczatowski explained, ignoring his own mistake, that the medical examiner is warranted by the state to issue a permit before a body can be cremated.

"Yes," Ortiz-Reyes said.

Piszczatowski then offered as an exhibit to the court the permit for cremation in Don's case, which the ME's office had given Billie Jean. But just then, as the lawyers started to argue this point, the judge allowed the jury to be cut loose for the day (it was late, anyway), so the attorneys could, in Judge Potts's words, "tidy up a few things."

Which they did in a matter of a few minutes.

Piszczatowski was now clear on how he could continue down the road of that supposed permit.

Yet, the day—and testimony for first week of the trial—was over.

CHAPTER 63

AFTER THE WEEKEND BREAK, on December 3, 2001, Dr. Ortiz-Reyes was back in the witness seat answering questions from Billie Jean's sharp, prepared lawyer once again.

Piszczatowski started off the new week on the alcohol levels and the testimony balanced uneasily on that fence of boredom. One can only beat a drum so long before the tune starts to get old and overstated. There was a fine line. Piszczatowski was close to crossing it.

Piszczatowski kept referring to the work of the ME's office as an "autopsy."

Ortiz-Reyes kept correcting him, saying they never conducted an autopsy. It was an "examination."

A point the defense was able to bring out was that Ortiz-Reyes and the ME's team signed off on Don's body for cremation on August 16, 2000, four days *after* his body had been brought in and several days *after* it had been released. To Piszczatowski, this was significant. It meant there had been plenty of time for the office to make its determinations about how Don had died and it allowed Don's body to be, essentially, destroyed.

Why?

Because they didn't think they'd ever need to look at it again.

For the next hour, Piszczatowski produced reports and toxicology tests and asked the doctor about his and the ME's office's findings—which routinely came back to the same cause of death: heart attack and/or acute alcohol poisoning. Then he began to pepper the doctor with simple questions that pointed to the idea that the ME's office had ample opportunity to conduct an actual autopsy, but Ortiz-Reyes, on that Saturday, chose not to do so.

All that the doctor could answer was "yes, yes, yes," over and over.

They talked about the lighting inside the morgue on that Saturday.

It was adequate.

They talked about how Ortiz-Reyes could "touch" the body.

Yes, he was that close to it during his examination.

They talked about the fact that Ortiz-Reyes could get "as close to the body" as he wanted.

Again, his answer was yes.

They talked about how Ortiz-Reyes could have done whatever he had wanted to Don's body at that time, including a full autopsy, and that it was his decision alone.

Of course, he could have, Ortiz-Reyes said.

They spoke of how Ortiz-Reyes had made notes about Don's eyes, specifically his "cornea" and how they weren't remarkable in any way.

Ortiz-Reyes said yes again. Unremarkable eyes, totally.

They talked about the fact that Ortiz-Reyes investigated the inside of Don's mouth.

He found nothing.

They talked about Don's neck being "unremarkable." Nothing there, either.

They talked about how Don's chest was—you guessed it—"unremarkable."

The point here for the defense was that Dr. Ortiz-Reyes had conducted a pretty damn thorough examination of this man on that Saturday and did not find anything whatsoever to indicate foul play.

"And would it be fair to say that the body . . . of Donald Rogers showed *no* evidence of bruising at that time?"

"I didn't say that," Ortiz-Reyes balked. "There were old bruises around the left eye socket."

"O-o-o-kay," Piszczatowski said, drawing the word out, kind of hinting to the fact that the doctor did not mention any abrasions on Don's nose. Those came later.

Piszczatowski could have questioned Ortiz-Reyes all day and perhaps had gotten him to admit that the office believed nothing out of the norm when this old man came in and it was believed he had died of a heart attack. The message for Piszczatowski was quite simple in that regard: reasonable doubt, reasonable doubt, reasonable doubt.

As Piszczatowski wound down his superb cross-examination, he had Ortiz-Reyes point out by the answers he gave that the office came to its "asphyxiation" determination slowly, over a period of time. And came to this conclusion only *after* the detectives pointed out what had been noted by a witness and then they relooked at the photos of Don's face and—*aha!*—saw that there were abrasions on his face to match what the witness had said.

Ortiz-Reyes even implied that it wasn't until they got a magnifying glass out and studied the photos that they saw the abrasions, adding how, yes, they can sometimes be that small. But the size doesn't change what the evidence suggested.

By the time they got to the end, Ortiz-Reyes was using the phrase "it is our opinion" a lot of the time when he answered. It was the opinion of the ME that this and that took place, based on all of the information the office had received during the entire investigation.

In his defense, Ortiz-Reyes held his ground fairly well, explaining that they always defer to several sources when making a determination of death by homicide. It's not something the office takes lightly or comes to easily, maybe like a heart attack. Just because some cop comes up with a theory, it doesn't mean the ME is going to back him, in other words. Ortiz-Reyes mentioned how it wasn't only the abrasions that swayed them, nor was it the new information by the TPD. It was, in fact, the totality of it all, plus what the ME himself found within the toxicology and the study of available documentation and photographs.

Accept it or not, that was how it happened.

Before long, they got on the subject of alcoholics and how people that drink a lot routinely fall down and bruise themselves. Piszczatowski made a point that maybe that was where Don's abrasions and bruises had originated.

"Alcoholics tend to fall all the time," Ortiz-Reyes agreed. "That's the reason they have old bruises, new bruises, black eyes. You can see all kinds of injuries in an alcoholic. . . ."

"And there's no absolutes—is that correct?"

"No."

"So you can't say they would or they wouldn't, but you're just saying that it's *more* likely?"

"Yes."

"And is it also whether someone gets injured, if you

will, when they fall, does it depend, for example, *where* they fall?"

"Yes."

The gist for Piszczatowski, which he then explained by bringing into the conversation some photographs, was that there was nothing within the photos of Don's home or Don's body that would or could indicate how "he fell or how he came to rest on the ground."

Ortiz-Reyes agreed there wasn't.

Piszczatowski asked if there was anything indicative in Ortiz-Reyes's opinion that the "manner and cause of death in this case, on those photos alone, was a homicide, as opposed to an accidental death or natural?"

"No."

Piszczatowski was on a roll. He then got Ortiz-Reyes to say that Don had no bruises to the back of his head, which one might expect after someone was pressing a pillow against his face, or from a man who took a fall on the floor.

They talked defensive wounds next. Don had none.

Then Piszczatowski pressed Ortiz-Reyes to admit that he had no idea whether Don was alive or dead before he came "to rest on the ground" inside the kitchen.

That was an important piece of this puzzle.

The three words Piszczatowski kept going back to as he wrapped things up were "acute alcohol intoxication." He said these words, over and over, to thrust into the jury's collective consciousness that Don was wasted and had enormous amounts of alcohol in his system, and he could have died any number of ways. The *least likely* way in all of this was asphyxiation by smothering with a pillow. If Don had been murdered in that manner, where was the evidence? Billie Jean's attorney suggested this, time and again.

"The information that the police gave you," Piszczatowski asked, "caused you to doubt—is that correct?"

"Yes."

"And so you *changed* your opinion. Is that correct?"

"That's correct."

"And could you agree that reasonable people, reasonable experts, reasonable doctors, could differ as to the cause of death in this case?"

Ortiz-Reyes gave a somewhat awkward answer, noting, "Anybody has the right of giving an opinion. It depends on what is their mood or what they think. You know, everybody can say whatever they want. . . ."

Piszczatowski got Ortiz-Reyes to admit he had "no scientific discovery" in this case that was inconsistent with the initial conclusion of death by acute alcohol intoxication or from heart attack.

Thus, as Ortiz-Reyes repeated many times, after all the information was in, it was his and the chief ME's "opinion" that Don had been murdered.

"And the evidence that the police gave you that changed your mind," Piszczatowski concluded, "was the statement of an individual that they had talked to, that said the death occurred by asphyxiation—is *that* correct?"

"Yes. That's correct."

Piszczatowski had nothing further.

CHAPTER 64

APA SKRZYNSKI BROUGHT IN Don Rogers's business partner, Donald Kather, after forty minutes of redirect and recross with Dr. Ortiz-Reyes had become very monotonous and nonproductive. The state was losing this case. The PO needed a strong witness, someone to elaborate for jurors the sort of personalized evidence showing why Billie Jean had a reason to place a pillow over her husband's head and smother him. The APA was two steps back from where he wanted to be at this point. Ortiz-Reyes had not really put into the record a cause of death for Don Rogers. One could speculate, sure, that Don had been smothered, but there was no actual forensic evidence besides an "opinion" of some photographs and an ME's office that kept changing its mind based on what law enforcement was telling them. And if there was no proof of one spouse having killed a spouse, well, how could a woman be found guilty of murdering her husband?

Donald Kather told jurors he and Don Rogers had known each other for close to four decades. They ran a machine shop in Troy that focused on car assembly tools. They had five employees, and about four thousand square feet of space. It wasn't much, but at one time it made money. Plenty of it. The past five years, however, Donald Kather explained, "We haven't been generating any profits."

This didn't mean they were broke. It meant the business was breaking even, keeping five families working and the doors open.

Donald then talked about the last time he saw his old buddy, Don Rogers. It was that Friday, August 11. They had gone to lunch together, as they normally did almost every day. And with that, and the fact that Kather saw Don Rogers every workday, came the next question, making it clear where the APA wanted to go with Don Kather's testimony.

"So, any other day of the week, had you noticed *any* kind of bruising or abrasions?"

Piszczatowski rolled his eyes. Billie Jean did the same. *Please.*

"No, I didn't," Kather said. It sounded dramatic. Like this piece of information was a bombshell.

"Nothing on his lips?" the APA asked.

"Nope."

"Or his nose?"

"No."

The APA showed Donald Kather a photograph. It was of Don Rogers's lip—postmortem. Then he implored Kather to explain to jurors if he had seen those same abrasions on Don Rogers's lip on that last day he saw Don for lunch, August 11.

"No," Kather said, "they were not evident to me."

Again, this exchange was meant to shock. Meant to hammer home a point that Don Rogers had sustained these injuries while being murdered.

The next thing Donald Kather brought to the courtroom was that Don Rogers was not an extravagant guy, buying himself toys and spending money irresponsibly.

He was frugal, in fact. His only luxurious expenditure, if it could even be called such, was going out to eat every day for lunch and having a nice dinner ocassionally.

Wearing a white sweater, sitting still and indifferent, a lack of concern on her face, Billie Jean listened intently, whispering to her attorneys when she felt something needed to be said.

Kather said he had known Billie Jean for almost twenty years. He had gone to Don and Billie Jean's first wedding in Vegas, but not their second ceremony.

Ending his direct questioning rather abruptly, without asking Kather to go into any lengthy discussions about Billie Jean and the relationship she had with Don, the APA said, "And the last time you saw [Don] was when he left at four P.M.?"

"Correct."

"Did you expect to see him Monday?"

"Certainly did."

"Were you surprised, sir?" Skrzynski asked.

"Yes."

"I have no further questions."

Kather offered nothing to the prosecution other than the notion that Don Rogers's face might not have had those small, minuscule abrasions, apparently seen only with a magnifying glass, when he ate lunch with him on the Friday afternoon of his death.

Some wondered why he had been called to give any testimony.

Piszczatowski started his cross-examination with the daily lunch Don Rogers and Donald Kather shared. The defense attorney called Don Rogers a "creature of habit," and Kather agreed with that assessment.

Since Don Rogers was such a creature of habit, as

Piszczatowski had put it, Billie Jean's lawyer wanted to know what Don Rogers had to drink every day at lunch.

"Two beers," Kather said. That was it.

Interestingly enough, it was rare for Don Rogers to order lunch, Kather told Piszczatowski. He generally just drank those two beers and never ate much. But it wasn't because Don wanted to enjoy the buzz a few beers coupled with an empty stomach produced. "I'm certain the reason was if he had breakfast, he didn't order lunch. . . ."

The other piece of Don's character his business partner was able to relate to jurors was Rogers being such a "private person." He rarely talked about personal matters with anyone. It was to the point where Don Kather once asked him if he had gone and married Billie Jean for a second time and Rogers told him, "It's none of your business."

Don Rogers "pretty much" went into the office every day and "watched TV." He stayed away from the day-to-day operations or running the business, Kather explained. He gave input from time to time, but it was Kather who ran the show there. And Don Rogers was cool with that.

Piszczatowski trekked from family to business and then into the last day Kather had seen Don Rogers. He asked him if he recalled noticing that Don had a black eye on that day, August 11.

"No," Kather said.

What about the day before? Piszczatowski wondered.

"No. I don't recall having seen him that whole week with any abrasions or anything on his face."

They went through each day of the week.

Kather said no to each.

Next, Piszczatowski asked Kather if he had noticed any changes in Don over the course of the weeks, months, "the last year, three years, say, two years" leading up to his death.

"I would say that Don had lost weight over the last five, eight years. When I knew him, he was much beefier and stronger. He became more frail. But at seventy-four . . . I think it's natural attrition or something. . . ." In terms of health, Kather added, it was only Don's weight he noticed. Not much else.

And then one final question by Piszczatowski gave Kather a reason to explain how Don Rogers had smoked unfiltered Camel cigarettes, which, along with his heavy drinking, probably contributed to what was very poor health.

After Piszczatowski was done with Donald Kather, jurors were left with an undeniable image of the deceased: an unhealthy guy in his seventies, drinking every day at lunch, not eating, smoking and losing weight.

In other words, Don Rogers had been a good candidate for a heart attack.

CHAPTER 65

THE SECRETARY FOR DON'S business answered questions next. Toni Brosseau spoke of a simple man who never swore around the office and never mentioned anything of a sexual nature. He pretty much kept to himself. Toni also said she was "shocked" to learn from Billie Jean that Don's niece, whom she referred to as "Nicole," was a man. She learned this in November, when Billie Jean showed up at the office to collect some of her late husband's things.

When asked about her boss's health issues, Toni spoke of Don Rogers's "rectal bleeding." She said it was Billie Jean who told her about it. After suggesting Don should go see a doctor about the condition, Billie Jean told Toni it was difficult to get him to go and she had basically given up on the prospect.

Quite surprising, after those few questions and answers, the APA said he was done, leaving many in the room to wonder once again why the witness had even been called. Toni had offered nothing to further the PO's case against Billie Jean. If anything, she said the Rogers couple had a fairly normal marriage, as far as she could tell.

* * *

Piszczatowski kept his cross simple. He set it up with questions so that Toni talked about Don being a private person. Yet, in speaking of what she did for Don throughout the workday, she also explained that she had "balanced" his checkbook. This led Piszczatowski to ask a fair question regarding Don ever complaining to her about the amount of money he had paid on his Visa bills. Piszczatowski knew it was going to be the PO's contention that part of the reason why Billie Jean wanted to rid herself of Don Rogers was the enormous debt she had amassed and how pissed off Don was because of it.

"Mr. Rogers kept his personal business to himself," Toni said.

"So he never really complained to you?"

"Not really."

They talked about Don's habits at work and she admitted that she'd found empty vodka bottles in the Dumpster and realized he was drinking. Seeing Don every day, however, she didn't notice a man who was deteriorating over the years from poor health and excessive drinking. But when she met Don's brother at his funeral, a guy older than Don, Toni then suddenly realized how bad Don Rogers looked and how far his health had spiraled downward.

"His brother is older, and his brother looked like Mr. Rogers did, you know, *fifteen* years ago."

From there they discussed how Don looked during the week before his death. Toni did not notice any marks or bruises on his face, she explained. And she would have, because he often gave her tasks to do that required him walking to her desk and handing her paperwork. This brought him up close to her.

"If he would have had any real injury to his face, I would have noticed it," she testified.

As they talked about Don's funeral and the arrangements, it sounded as though Billie Jean had engaged her late husband's secretary to help her out, ordering flowers, delaying things so his family could make it into town, calling the funeral home. The way Toni described her relationship with the widow during this period was akin to a wife and her husband's secretary working hard together to bury a man they both loved. There was no animosity from Billie Jean, Toni noticed. There was no anger from Billie Jean projected toward her dead husband. On top of that, after Don's death, Toni said she had taken on "more responsibility" at the machine shop and because of that Don Kather gave her a raise. Billie Jean was told about it, because she now had taken over for Don.

And guess what? She "was very nice about it."

At 2:47 P.M., the state called Dr. Ljubisa Juvan Dragovic, the chief medical examiner. This was an important witness for the APA—maybe the most important of the trial. Dragovic would either seal the deal on an acquittal by not explaining why the ME's office changed its mind on the death certificate, or he would bring jurors back into the state's fold and convince them Don Rogers had, in fact, been murdered.

After listing the doctor's credentials, the APA asked the ME if he could explain his actual position within the office.

"I work in the capacity of chief medical examiner, chief forensic pathologist for the County of Oakland."

Dragovic was the top dog; what he said was gospel, the final word on death, countywide. He had been "qualified" as an expert witness in hundreds of trial cases, he told the court. He was an associate professor at a local university. He had published scores of articles on pathology over the years. The guy's credibility, on paper, was rock solid.

As he testified, Dragovic said he had not gotten involved in Don Rogers's death on the day his body had been brought in. That was Ortiz-Reyes, a pathologist he oversaw. Dragovic had not deeply immersed himself in Don's case until the TPD had called to ask him to take another look because of some new information.

And "after reviewing it," he explained, "together with Dr. [Ortiz-Reyes], I decided that we had to proceed to reevaluate everything in conjunction with the activities that the Troy Police Department was carrying out."

The APA asked him to explain why the TPD had thought the case needed further examination and what had convinced Dragovic there might have been something going on besides natural death. This was the question of the trial, thus far. A lot rode on what the doctor would say.

He spoke of "suspicion that the death . . . was not an accidental death or natural death. That it was a—that it was foul play involved and they had some suspects and that they were progressing along the line, investigating all that information, and I encouraged them to continue doing that and I evaluated our end of things."

He was then asked what he found after evaluating the files.

"Significant discrepancies" was part of his answer. Most of what he found, Dragovic explained, he uncovered within the "Polaroid photographs" from the death scene and pathologist's initial examination. Once he realized that Don's body had been cremated, he knew that they could not have him exhumed, which they certainly would have done after a call from law enforcement, like that one he received from Troy.

Regarding his office giving a permit, or permission, for the body to be cremated, the way Dragovic framed the situation it made perfect sense: requests of all types came across his desk every day, he had to look at them, decide what to sign off on, what to talk to his staff about, and how to proceed, deciding if anything needed further examination or evaluation. With Don's case, it was simple. At the time, his pathologist had given a cause and manner of death. So, as his boss, he signed off on the cremation permit. This sort of thing was a normal course of any business day. There was nothing that led anyone to believe—at that time, "based on the information that existed"—that they should not okay the permit. The case had gone through the proper channels, via the system the county had in place, and was approved, the doctor told jurors. Most of this was done, he further stated, "by our clerical staff." It was only brought to the ME's specific attention or to his staff if there was a question. Many requests are done with an "automatic approval."

A rubber stamp.

Happened every day.

"So you would not have personally reviewed this case request for cremation?"

"No."

The system had approved Don's cremation, essentially—not an actual medical examiner. "Unless," he said, "there was a problem or issue that is brought to my attention, but not routinely. I saw that"—the issues summoned by the TPD—"only when I started looking into the file."

Those Polaroid photos.

Dragovic then talked about how after he began to look intensely into Don's death and studied the toxicology reports, the photos taken by the pathologist, the remainder of the file, that "it looked a little bit odd and a little bit different, and looking at everything together, things did not add up."

The more information he digested, the more he felt he needed to look deeper into it all.

The way the doctor painted the series of events leading up to what became a murder investigation indicated that he was doing his job the way in which he had been trained, the way in which he had done it in hundreds of cases before this. However, as he followed procedure and policy, "things began to make less and less sense," and so he raised a hand and "encouraged" everyone on his staff, including himself, "to dig more into this matter so that we can come to the bottom of it."

Jurors were clearly not bored or impatient with this testimony. The ME was putting the case into a broader sense of facts as they unfolded in real time within the ME's office. He was explaining, not in a defensive manner, but professionally, how everyone involved came to the conclusion that Don Rogers was murdered.

Had the tables turned for the PO? Had the APA finally won a round?

Piszczatowski, who vigorously scribbled notes and spoke with his co-counsel as Dragovic spoke (that is, when he was not objecting), did not seem at all worried or concerned about the ME's testimony—probably because Piszczatowski knew that at some point over the next day or so, he was going to get a crack at him.

CHAPTER 66

SKRZYNSKI AND DR. DRAGOVIC discussed the particulars of the early heart attack claim, the acute alcohol intoxication diagnosis and a final judgment that included asphyxiation by smothering. It took the remainder of the afternoon for the APA to get through it all. In the end, Dragovic had been a superb witness for the APA. He spoke of how important the crime scene photographs had been in his determination after he had immersed himself in the case and had "all" of the information in front of him.

"Position of the body" came up again, and it was something Billie Jean and her attorneys needed to knock down. They could ignore the significance of this seemingly irrelevant fact, but it would not prove sensible to do so.

"Comfortably resting," Dragovic noted, while staring at the photos of Don. This stood out to him, he told the APA. Don seemed to be "placed there on the hard tile floor." It didn't appear he had fallen. Or had passed out drunk. This was important, along with how Don's legs had been crossed at the ankles, Danny Chahine's accusations, the abrasions, along with several other minor factors, Dragovic said with authority, that "were more *conflicting* than matching."

It's funny how when an expert looks at a crime scene under a new light, or changes the focus of his observations, predictable appearances can have different meanings. That was what the good doctor meant here: it all added up for him, once he had answered a few unanswered questions about Don's death.

The *aha* moment, in other words, came late.

But it certainly came.

They discussed the position of Don's body for several more moments, before moving on to the crime scene and what truly made Dragovic take notice.

"Well, the scene was very *neat*," he told jurors, "for a person that is heavily intoxicated." He mentioned those crossed legs yet again. "That appearance to me was unreal and still is. This is unreal."

The chair had been tipped over, the doctor suggested, "in such a way that is—it just does not make any sense of this body falling out of this chair. . . ."

One could argue that his "opinion" was mere speculation, mere conjecture and not at all a fact in this case. The doctor was qualified, certainly, to make this judgment, but in the end, who could know how a chair fell when a drunk passed out and landed on the floor? Moreover, had anyone done any tests? Had a crime scene reconstruction lab conducted any tests? Or was this all based on Dragovic's personal and professional opinion and experience?

They talked about this chair for perhaps too long, which only drew more attention to it. Then the APA asked about manner and cause of death—the differences—and how science played into his final opinion.

"People don't die in a vacuum," Dragovic explained, which sounded rather strange just left out there hanging. "People die under circumstances, and those circumstances define the manner of death—the manner of death being how death comes upon a person. . . ."

Dragovic called his relationship with law enforcement a "two-way street," one in which he and the police often used to connect on cases.

It was "a process," he said after being asked.

Piszczatowski leaned over and whispered something to his co-counsel. The man nodded his head in agreement. Billie Jean looked on, clearly aggravated—and why shouldn't she be?—by the doctor's testimony.

The APA asked the doctor to break down, step-by-step, the fall Don allegedly took. Then:

The alcohol levels in Don's system.

The alcohol numbers of a person that consumed" a lot.

How "alcoholics" had higher numbers than social drinkers.

"Hypothesized" X-ray photos of Don and what they "might" have said.

How the fact that Don did not show any signs of major injury to the back of his skull likely meant he had not fallen.

"Pinpoint bleeds on the eyelids" and what they mean: asphyxiation—but not all the time.

Pinpoint bleeds were not present in every smothering case the doctor said he had seen. Plus, pinpoint bleeds are generally "the hallmark of manual, *ligature* strangulation. . . ."

The image here was that Don was passed out drunk. His killer(s) had placed him on the floor and then poured additional straight booze down his throat, which might have put him into an alcohol-induced coma, so he could not react when he was deprived of oxygen. If he had been conscious, this would have caused those little blood vessels in his eyes and eyelids to burst. It was a well-composed—

and perhaps rehearsed—argument, peddled fairly cleanly and somewhat persuasively by the doctor.

Dragovic was convinced, he said over and over, that asphyxia by smothering had killed Don. Nothing was going to sway him from this opinion. And for the next twenty minutes, they discussed it, piece by piece. Near the end of the doctor's direct testimony, the APA asked if the "terminal fall"—a strange way to phrase it—that Don took "could have caused" the "abrasions on the lip and nose"?

"No, sir," Dragovic said emphatically.

"Why not?"

"Because for a terminal fall, you'd have a solid bruise . . . covering the one place that your face, if you go on your face, there will be a plane and you can actually take a piece of glass, apply this to someone's face and reenact exactly how much of the surface got into contact on those exposed parts of the face, and it wouldn't be the form of these light scrapes." It was manifest, the doctor added, "in the form of *bruising*." He also noted how the skin above the lip was more sensitive to this type of injury.

That comment sparked another interrogation by the APA into the bruising and exactly where the doctor had found the bruises on Don's face.

Whenever it felt as though the APA was wrapping things up, he found another opening and asked the doctor about it. The testimony, by then, was getting technical and quite fatiguing; it seemed as though they were going over the same issues. The doctor's explanations became long and exhausting.

Dragovic brought up "burking" at one point. This is the act of smothering without leaving any markings on the body, whereby a killer would sit on the victim's chest, using his or her weight to hold him down, and then place his or her hands over the victim's mouth and nose, thus cutting off not only the victim's oxygen but the act itself of breathing by moving the chest up and down. It is said that burking leaves no trace of murder.

Dragovic called the murder of Don Rogers not "perfect burking," but "the closest one gets to burking."

And again, instead of leaving it there, which might have been more powerful, the APA asked, "So this [was] kind of burking?"

"Kind of burking, yes."

With that, Billie Jean shook her head, as did her attorneys.

Kind of burking?

Is this the same as, like, kind of *murder?*

No doubt Piszczatowski was thinking it either *was* or *wasn't.* Any gray area in between was where reasonable doubt lived.

Piszczatowski stared at the APA with an almost *are-you-freakin'-done-yet* look of annoyance.

By the end of this final conversation between the APA and doctor, Dragovic had actually agreed—without visiting the crime scene or examining the body, only by looking at it in photos, mind you—with the APA when he said that there was "nothing on Mr. Rogers's body or in the scene that you see that is inconsistent with your diagnosis of asphyxia by smothering. . . ."

Dragovic, jurors knew, had not once examined Don's body while it was at the morgue. Everything he had done he did after the fact. This was a bold statement by the APA and the doctor—one that would be most certainly challenged.

The APA's final question was even bolder; he wanted to know if there was "any doubt" in the doctor's mind about the "medical manner of death being homicide" in this case.

Dragovic said that there was not one "doubt" about it. Don was "smothered by someone else."

And that someone else was his wife, the APA implied before handing Dragovic over to what appeared to be a defense attorney chomping at the bit to get going on this witness.

CHAPTER 67

A GOOD CROSS-EXAMINATION SHOULD combine several key factors. Leonard E. Davies points this out in his wonderful book, *Anatomy of Cross-Examination*. For one, a winning cross should always be part of, or "integrated into," the entire "whole of the trial process." It should never stand out on its own. That type of solitary cross feels more like an attack; it's a trap that less experienced defense attorneys, as much as they don't want to, often fall into without realizing it. In addition, a cross is "more than questioning a witness and, with some luck, scoring . . . points." With each witness cross-examined, a pyramid of persuasion regarding the defense's complete position should be constructed, along with the fundamentals of "obtaining evidence for [the defense's] final argument." On top of that, questioning a witness after the prosecution has laid out its purpose for direct questioning should always include advancing "the client's chance of success," or it "serves no purpose." This approach sounds rather simple-minded. But many a defense attorney has done nothing more than try to embarrass a witness after he or she has realized there is nothing to be gleaned from the witness to support a client. There is "technique, style and strategy," Davies claims in his book, in every successful cross—and it was no secret to anyone who had paid attention over the past several days in that courtroom that defense attorney Walter Piszczatowski had all but mastered each.

As the second day of testimony wound down, Piszczatowski began with his cross-examination of Dragovic right where the APA had left off. Quite snappishly, Piszczatowski forcefully stated in his first question to the doctor, "No doubt in your mind—*right?*"

"No doubt in my mind, sir!" Dragovic cracked back, referring to Don being the victim of a homicide by smothering and how "certain" he was of that diagnosis.

"You are a *certain* kind of guy, are you not, Dr. Dragovic?" Piszczatowski asked, steepling his hands in front of himself, as if he was silently praying instead of intensely thinking where to take his cross next.

"Well, on matters that I"—Dragovic tried to say before Piszczatowski cut him off.

"On *all* matters, correct?"

"Yeah."

"When you know something, you *know* something? Correct?" Piszczatowski asked.

"There are limits to everything . . . ," Dragovic said before asking the court for a glass of water.

"Oh, allow me," Piszczatowski said, obliging the doctor's water request, as if to say, *"We are just getting started here, so settle in Big Boy."*

The softballs were gone.

After he took a sip from his white Styrofoam cup of water, Dragovic explained, having been asked to, that he had been called as an expert in hundreds of cases, as he had told the APA.

Piszczatowski dug into the subject of Dragovic having the correct numbers on the "inspections" of bodies he or the office had conducted. Because, "in this case,"

Billie Jean's lawyer said, "there was an inspection only. Is that correct?"

"That's correct, sir."

Finally, on this subject, Piszczatowski said what everyone was thinking: "And we've heard that ad nauseam, so I am going to get off of it—but it *was* an inspection?"

"Sure."

Piszczatowski provided a letter he had received from the ME's office after asking for the statistics, which stated how, according to the ME's own numbers, there had been only "one inspection for a homicide case" during the entire year of Don's death—and that was Don's. The point was that every other homicide that year had been diagnosed after a full, complete autopsy. It was the same for the year 2001. In 1999, there had been zero homicide cases "preceded by way of external inspection."

Dragovic said he had to agree, if that's what the letter stated.

This was significant information. In the spectrum—or totality—of this trial and how it ebbed and flowed, this was a major contention. One that, additionally, the PO had left out.

Keeping things moving along, Piszczatowski put up a photograph of Don's upper lip and lower nostrils on the overhead projector. He asked the doctor to point out any injuries to Don's upper lip, noting they were using a "high-tech machine" to display the photo.

Dragovic couldn't find any.

They talked about lighting: high-tech versus low-tech. Magnifying glass versus projector.

The "limitation" of the screen inside the courtroom.

The left side of the lip as opposed to the right side.

Don's lower nostril being "pinkish" or "reddish," but not truly "injured" in any other way.

How Dragovic "changed" the opinion of his pathologist.

As Dragovic broke into a lengthy discussion about a previous black eye Don had had and how they noticed it during the examination, the clock struck 4:54 P.M., which meant it was time to call it a day.

The judge gave the jury her stern warnings about keeping the testimony to themselves and not reading about the case and told everyone to be back promptly at 9:00 A.M.

CHAPTER 68

IT WAS THE THIRD day of testimony, December 4, 2001. The APA had gone on for so long the previous day, Piszczatowski had only a fifteen-minute block of time with Dragovic to work with. But the doctor was back on this cold, dry and overcast morning, and was seated in the witness chair by 9:10 A.M., once again ready to answer any questions the defense attorney had. It was slated to be a long morning, everyone was well aware of that.

Dragovic did not waver. In fact, as they got underway, his answers were long and detailed, coming across as extremely confident. They discussed the role of the special investigator for the ME's office and how, in this case, he had done an investigation at the scene and looked at the body.

"Looked at," Dragovic stated. "The investigation proceeded and, at some point in time, the case was deemed complete."

Piszczatowski asked about that Monday meeting they all had where Don's case came up. Dragovic went on to explain how the Monday meetings worked, giving jurors an understanding of how the operation was run.

Don's alcohol levels came next.

Then Piszczatowski brought up a valid point, asking the doctor if the ME's office had wanted to conduct an autopsy on that Monday, could they have gotten Don's body back from the funeral home?

"Absolutely," Dragovic answered.

Piszczatowski had Dragovic break down the hierarchy of the office and how much "help" Ortiz-Reyes and Dragovic had at their disposal at any time—giving the impression that they could have sent someone over to retrieve the body from the funeral home if there was any concern.

Then the lawyer and expert witness talked about how off-the-charts the toxicology report was when it came in. Those types of alcohol levels, even for a chronic drinker, were sky-high and sent up red flags throughout the office.

Dragovic said the toxicology report "asked for attention."

That was one way to put it.

"What were *you* thinking . . . What 'attention'—" Piszczatowski used air quotes to make his point heard— "did it need?"

"Well, whatever attention necessary by the person who was handling *that* case. . . ." It was Dr. Ortiz-Reyes, Dragovic went on to say without naming him, who was "handling that case." He "took note of it and proceeded with whatever course he deemed necessary to proceed."

This was all interesting testimony and seemed to suggest that the defense and PO were at an impasse here regarding their opinions. Neither was going to budge. The witness was seasoned on the stand; he knew his place well. If Piszczatowski felt he was going to crack him, he probably thought different at this juncture.

Piszczatowski wanted to know if Dragovic, being the ME in charge of the county, "at the point" Ortiz-Reyes indicated something was up with the toxicology report, "That you thought an autopsy should be conducted?"

"There might have been some discussion along those lines and some criticism from me, but . . . [it's] part of the overall communication in these cases."

They went back and forth: cause of death, manner of death, who made the call first, who backed it up. By the time they moved on, it was clear Dragovic oversaw the office and its procedures and policies, but he encouraged and watched closely as his medical examiners made their own decisions. And there was nothing inherently wrong with that process. Was it flawed? Maybe. But these were competent doctors, respected in their fields, looking to do the best job they could. There was no conspiracy here to help the TPD make a murder charge stick. The ME's office did what it thought was best for the public.

"And you would not allow someone to continue in their employment if you believed them to be incompetent?" Piszczatowski asked.

"That's—" Dragovic tried to say.

"Fair enough?"

". . . correct."

"And you have the interest of Oakland County at stake?" Piszczatowski said.

"That's correct."

"That's part of your job as the boss?"

"Well, it's a responsibility. It's *my* responsibility," Dragovic stated.

Piszczatowski brought up the TPD next, so far maybe the most contentious issue. Dragovic explained how a detective had "faxed" him a "request for further investigation. . . ."

It seemed as though Piszczatowski and Dragovic were going over the same old ground already covered. Nothing new came out of it. Then they got to the crime scene.

"And you indicated that in this case, it was . . . your opinion where you talk about [the crime scene] . . .

upon reviewing all that information [something] became obvious to you, correct?"

"Correct," Dragovic answered.

"[Some] discrepancies that emerged. The scene of death was altered, correct?"

"That is correct."

"Okay. And is it also correct that it was altered with the purpose to deceive the authorities, by disguising the death as a nonviolent one?"

"That is correct."

"Now, when you indicated yesterday that the . . . reason you believe that the scene was disguised, one of the reasons . . . was because of the position of the chair in relation to the body, correct?"

"Those are . . . not by one single detail."

"I understand, but . . ."

"By the composition of those details, yes, sir."

"That's why I said, but *one* of the reasons."

They talked about the "position of the chair in relation to the body" and how the chair was "tipped over."

Dragovic agreed. It was the chair "in relation to" the body that concerned him.

And the legs, of course, being crossed. "That too," Dragovic said.

Then, for the first time, a new piece of information emerged after Piszczatowski asked: "And what else in those photos, if you can tell me?"

"Absence of injury," Dragovic said.

"Absence of injury?"

"Yeah." Dragovic sounded more clear and certain than he ever had.

"But you cannot really see that from the photos. You're relying on Dr. Ortiz-Reyes for the absence of injury to the back of the head—is *that* correct?"

"Well, we did the assessment. We have some information about that and, sure enough, there is a body diagram where he documented all what he saw on the outside of the body."

"Yes. He and you relied on the fact that there was an absence of injury, based on the fact of the external examination done by Dr. Ortiz-Reyes, correct?"

"Sure."

They agreed the examination Ortiz-Reyes conducted did not show any sign of bruising.

Dragovic explained a "terminal fall," a phrase he had used during his direct. He described it as a "last fall." And Piszczatowski asked him if he was basing all of this by "assuming" that Don was sitting in a chair.

Dragovic said he never assumed anything. The available evidence had told him that.

"Okay. In cases of a terminal fall, did you not testify yesterday that in a case of terminal fall, you would expect to have injury?"

"Sure."

"Okay. And the words 'terminal fall,' are those words that are defined in medical . . . terms? Is that a recognized medical term?"

"A recognized term among medical examiners," Dragovic said. "Other doctors do not deal, necessarily, with terminal falls. Because they don't address that issue of death occurring suddenly and unexpectedly where a person actually falls down."

"Right."

"A result of losing control over his body or her body and striking the unyielding surface, and that unyielding surface providing the opportunity for someone to get injured."

They discussed terminal fall for far too long. Some call it splitting hairs. Others call it unnecessary bickering over nothing. To his credit, Piszczatowski wanted the doctor to explain if there were various explanations for a terminal fall. For instance, would a heart attack, which occurred first, be followed by a terminal fall? Would any precondition leading to that fall be part of the terminal aspect of it?

Dragovic accused Piszczatowski of adding some "seasoning" to the term.

One staggering fact brought out was that the amount of alcohol in Don's system was equivalent to "twenty-five drinks," maybe "even thirty," in a very short period of time, which led them to believe that someone had forced the alcohol down his throat. A man, in other words, could not consume that much alcohol on his own.

But Piszczatowski put some water on the fire by asking the doctor if he or his staff had gone around the house—at least inside the kitchen—and looked for empty bottles of alcohol or looked inside the refrigerator or freezer to see how much booze Don had hanging around. There was a fine line there: If the person did not drink, had no or little alcohol in the house, well, okay, the amount in his system was suspect. But since Don drank every night, from the moment he walked into the door until he passed out, according to testimony, and had half-gallon bottles of booze all over the house, didn't that have a bearing on the outcome of the opinion?

"I don't treat alcoholics," Dragovic finally said.

"Fair enough," Piszczatowski came back with, before looking down at his notes—this, mind you, as Dragovic finished another thought.

"So, you know, but how people drink and how people die in relation to their drinking habits is part of being able to put logically the things . . . ," he trailed off, losing the thought. Then Dragovic added: "And there is some common sense missing in this matter."

"Yeah—at least in *your* opinion? That's all you're giving us?"

Important point.

"My *firm* opinion, yes," Dragovic concluded.

They continued the exchange, with Dragovic explaining what constituted a "drink" in the eyes of the ME's office.

"Vodka will be in shots," he said. "Measured by shots, because that's what a drink is. . . ."

As they reached what would become the midway point of Piszczatowski's cross, the defense attorney brought up burking. This led the two of them into a long discussion about the so-called injuries Don had sustained, each party disagreeing with the other how severe the injuries were and where they were located.

After that, "There is no science that predicts how the body will come to a rest" when it falls off a chair? Dragovic asked after realizing what Piszczatowski was trying to get at.

Was there any science explaining that the body would or would not cross the legs when coming to rest after a fall?

Dragovic said no.

This sort of agree-to-disagree banter went on and on, all morning long.

CHAPTER 69

IT'S ONE THING TO get a witness on the stand and have him admit that an autopsy is, at best, a conventionally opinionated science, with some "exactness" involved, as Dragovic put it to Piszczatowski. Yet, it's quite another for both sides to disagree on just about every facet of a medical examiner's findings in a case. And that's what was going on here as Dragovic's cross-examination testimony wound down during the late-morning session of December 4, 2001.

A particular bone of contention was the idea that all heavy drinkers are created *unequally*. Piszczatowski would not allow the idea any rest.

"And you don't know for a certainty, to 'exactness,' because you can't do a test on a person to say, 'Mr. Rogers, why don't you drink to a .44 and let's see if you stay alive or you die?' We can't do that—that is inhumane, correct?"

"I would have never attempted to do that. But there were . . ."

"Okay," Piszczatowski said, having a difficult time getting Dragovic to answer simply with a "yes" or a "no."

Dragovic finished, anyway: ". . . some tests done and

volunteers who have been exposed to drinking over many years and some inferences had been made. Yes."

"And you don't know what his coordination was at a .44, is that correct?"

"I know that being significantly impaired—"

"No!" Piszczatowski said, cutting him off.

But as was his MO throughout, Dragovic continued, adding ". . . but to what degree, of course, you have to assess the person himself."

Piszczatowski dropped his head. Then: "And you don't know whether, based on your review of *all* the photos in this case, and whether based upon your experience and training in this case, that . . . it was common for Mr. Rogers to hold on to a banister that was located in that house. Do you know that fact? Or not?"

"A banister?"

"A banister, yes."

"I do not see a . . . banister in the photos."

Piszczatowski moved on. His point had been made.

Some point later, Dragovic said, without being prompted, "He did not fall, as a result of the appearance of his body, as a result of the constellation of things at the scene. . . . I do not know who placed Mr. Rogers's body there in that position. That I don't know. But I can tell you that I do *not* believe that he fell. There is no evidence whatsoever that he fell there."

Vonlee Titlow, a name that rarely come up in this trial so far, had said, in her statement, that Don passed out and fell that night. Dragovic, apparently, did not have that information at his disposal when he made his analysis.

"Now," Piszczatowski said, pressing forward, "is other than the things that you told us before, the discrepancies that emerged from the scene as being an altered one and the lack of the bruising, we went through all that stuff, were not going to do that . . ."

"We did?" Dragovic said with a smart tone.

"Is there anything about the lividity of Mr. Rogers that would indicate that he had been repositioned?"

"The lividity, as is there . . ."

Piszczatowski was now more than impatient. "If you can answer 'yes' or 'no,'" he said with as much restraint as he could manage, "I would appreciate that. Is there *anything* about the lividity of Mr. Rogers that would tell you whether he had been repositioned?"

"No."

They went back to the chair and its position on the floor as the courtroom seemingly took a collective sigh.

Then the crossed-legs argument once again and the alcohol levels.

Piszczatowski brought up a valid point when he asked the doctor if he could say with absolute certainty that the slight "injury" on Don's lip was not, in fact, a common cold sore.

Dragovic said he couldn't.

Maybe a cold sore that had healed? Piszczatowski mentioned.

"I suspect that it is, but I am not sure," Dragovic answered.

Piszczatowski put the photos of the injury on the overhead projector and had the doctor point to it, repeating what he now thought.

The doctor seemed to be all over the place. First it was an injury sustained when Don's "killer" placed a pillow over his face, a scrape of some type. Now it was an old cold sore.

Then Dragovic agreed that .44 was a level of alcohol in the blood that would be "sufficient" to cause death "in people that are not regularly exposed to alcohol," which led to a discussion about "regular drinkers" and the difference between those who drank responsibly.

After saying he considered himself a "regular" drinker

because he had a glass of wine each night after work, Dragovic brought up the notion of a "regular heavy drinker"—a category they both placed Don into. This was a person who "regularly consumes substantial amounts of alcohol."

"Now, asphyxia is a diagnosis of exclusion. Is that correct?" Piszczatowski asked, finally getting them out of the alcohol discussion.

"Yes."

"And you would agree that as a general principle, medical examiners have always, I think, said asphyxia is a diagnosis of exclusion. Would you agree with that statement?"

"Well, it is. It's a diagnosis of exclusion on physical grounds, examining the body itself, but it also incorporates the circumstances."

In other words, it had to be ruled out.

"And when you talk about a diagnosis of exclusion, one generally *excludes* competing causes of death as a medical examiner . . . by way of autopsy, correct?"

Piszczatowski looked down at his notes.

Dragovic added something: "That's a helpful tool to demonstrate that there is *nothing* in the body. Yes."

"And in this case, we didn't have that benefit, correct?" Piszczatowski pointed out.

"That's correct."

"And were you able to *exclude* any other cause—possible causes of death in this case, medically? And by 'medically,' I mean via the external examination viewing or via autopsy . . . ?"

"Well, we talked about that earlier, about forensic pathology—not being sterile signs without sense. We talked about forensic pathology taking into consideration *everything*. Sure enough, it would have been nicer to have the body examined and have all the details there and show that, hey, there is nothing there—because in asphyxia, you don't see anything *in* the body . . . [and] scientific principles are only applied with common sense. If they are applied without common sense, then medicine is no good for anything."

"So, in this case, though," Piszczatowski said, again looking for that "yes" or "no" answer Dragovic seemed unable to give, "we did *not* rule out any competing causes or possible competing causes of death via either the external examination or an autopsy?"

"We did," Dragovic said, surprisingly.

"Oh, 'we did'? Which ones?"

"As a matter of fact . . . all of them that prompted that report I issued in December of 2000, sir."

"You were able to rule out *other* competing causes? You were able to rule out *all* other competing causes of death?"

"Absolutely, to my satisfaction. Yes."

"To *your* satisfaction?"

The exchange was becoming heated and tense.

"Yes, sir."

"Because that's *all* you can give us?" Piszczatowski reminded the doctor, with the jurors looking on with intensity.

"I'm a person. Only one."

"I understand. And you were able to do that via looking at the *scene,* correct? The absence of a bruise on the head—correct?"

"The absence of injuries. Not only on the head, elsewhere on the body."

"Okay. And . . ."

"Particular injuries," Dragovic added. "Specific injuries."

"And the statements that you received from the police?" Piszczatowski noted.

Dragovic clarified that the statements he received from

the police had actually "prompted" him to "evaluate *everything*. I did not take statements from the police as something that is *without* question." He claimed that he needed to "satisfy" his "conscience first and that's why I went through the process of reviewing *everything*. And if it made sense, it made sense. If it didn't make sense, it *didn't* make sense."

"Personally, Dr. Dragovic, I'm just curious. How many times have you declared an unnatural cause of death, where you actually had the body, *without* performing an autopsy?"

Good question.

"On a number of occasions," Dragovic said, "when I had some adequate history, information about the circumstances. That's more or less routine in certain instances."

"But you reviewed autopsy finds in those cases, correct?"

"No, we're not talking about *autopsies*. You said without autopsy."

"Oh, okay. So, on a number of occasions, you have?"

"That's right."

"And did you have the body in *all* those cases that we talked about [during this trial]?"

"In some instances, yes. In other instances, it was not even a body."

"But that was why I asked the question. When you don't have a body, I understand that. But when you did have the body . . . how many times have you opined as to an unnatural cause of death, *without* autopsy?"

"It's a regular occurrence. If there are injuries occurring in a person . . ." Dragovic stopped himself. Then: "Did you want me to explain?"

"No," Piszczatowski said, and then he asked the doctor

if he had any research that could back up what he was saying.

"I probably have . . . yeah."

Piszczatowski asked him to get it.

"In the year 2001, there was one case of homicide that did not involve autopsy," Piszczatowski explained, going back to what he and the doctor had discussed the previous day. "Were you involved in that case? Do you know?"

"Yes, sir."

"Okay. Did you have the body in that case?"

"Yes."

"And in the year 2000, that would be *this* case. There were none in '99. There were none in '98. There was one in '97. Do you know if you had the body in *that* case?"

"We had the body, possibly. But—"

Piszczatowski put up his hand like a traffic cop for Dragovic to stop. "Thank you."

But Dragovic continued: "I might not have been involved. Sure, it's a routine. . . ."

"'Routine'?" Piszczatowski questioned.

"And I can explain that, too."

Piszczatowski asked the doctor how many autopsies in the year 2000 the ME's office performed.

"Probably about eight hundred fifty or so. I don't know. I'm guessing. Maybe nine hundred. Maybe."

"Okay," Piszczatowski said, clearly heading toward a conclusion of some sort. "And do you know many of those . . . involved . . . homicides?"

"Well, I'll have to check the statistics."

"Okay."

The doctor took a moment to look at the research provided by the APA.

"We are fairly low on homicides in Oakland County. It's not like when I worked in Wayne County, we had seven hundred homicides a year, you know. This is different."

"And is eight hundred fifty kind of a standard number?" Piszczatowski wondered. "I mean, is that about what you had? Is that an *average* number—seven hundred to eight hundred autopsies a year?"

"That's within the reasonable variation there, depending on caseload and things that happen."

"Okay. Thank you."

Piszczatowski looked at the judge, asked for a minute, and then quickly ran through a checklist he had in his hand, making sure he covered every base.

A moment later, the defense attorney stated, "Thank you, Your Honor. I don't have any other questions."

Though APA Skrzynski gave the doctor a chance to clarify anything he wanted to on redirect, which lasted about seven additional minutes, Piszczatowski's argument here was well-established by the questions he asked and answers Dragovic ultimately gave: The medical examiner's findings, at least in Don's case, were subjective—completely open to argument by other experts. There was no objective science in this particular case. And if a jury, Piszczatowski was no doubt hoping, could not come to an agreement on a cause and manner of death, well, how in the hell were they supposed to find the defendant guilty of the same crime?

CHAPTER 70

FOR THE REMAINDER OF day two, financial experts tried to lessen the widening gap in that kill-him-for-his-money motive the APA had been trying to prove. Amy Mouradian, a Bank One employee, and Randall Pangretic, a Merrill Lynch retirement advisor, looked at charts, graphs and financial documents presented by the state. The message was that Don had some money and Billie Jean spent it recklessly and generously before and after his death—mostly on stupid, worthless stuff, like clothes she didn't need, gambling, drinking, cigarettes, dinners, and cars. The downside here for Billie Jean—if there even was one—became that the documents showed she was the estate's main beneficiary when Don died. The upside, on the other hand, was that she had been spending her husband's money long before he was dead. She had set her own precedent. All this testimony did, in the end, was drizzle more reasonable doubt into an overflowing pool. Okay, so the woman liked to spend her husband's money on luxury items, liked to piss it away at the casino, she bought a few cars after he died, and she continued that behavior without seemingly having grieved for the loss.

Still, none of it proved Billie Jean was a killer.

* * *

After those two witnesses, Danny Chahine walked into
the courtroom. Danny was dressed nicely in dark slacks
and a dress shirt, his hair combed slickly back, a large
flashy watch and several expensive-looking rings
sparkling in the court's modest lighting. Billie Jean did
not know this man more than seeing him at the casino
and once in a while with Vonlee at the house. Danny was
there to talk about his conversations with Vonlee, a third
party in all of this.

At forty-one years old, Danny had learned many les-
sons. Yet, the most predominant piece of life education
on his mind as he began to talk about his background
was undoubtedly the notion that nothing was what it
seemed in this case. Everything had a gloss over it, some
type of sheen shielding the truth just underneath.

A jeweler from Lebanon, who was running his own
shop here in the United States, Danny explained how he
had met Billie Jean and Vonlee at the casino. But it was
many months later before he learned the big secret—
Vonlee was a man.

The APA got this out of the way quickly.

"But in [midsummer] 2000, you didn't think so?"

"No."

They talked about the "relationship" Danny and
Vonlee had "formed" throughout that summer.

For the most part, Danny said, they went out to the
casino, gambled and had nice, romantic dinners.

The APA had Danny talk through his issues with the
law: possession of cocaine, a case that was dismissed;
Danny lying to immigration about his citizenship status;
a second cocaine possession charge that stuck.

It was Vonlee—or "Nicole," as the APA referred to
her—that called Danny to tell him Don had died. A day
after she called, Danny went over to the house. He saw

Billie Jean on that evening. He said she wasn't crying and didn't seem to be upset. This was striking to him, because he would have been sad, had his spouse just died. He couldn't understand why Billie Jean wasn't torn up and crying over the death of her husband.

One thing Danny made clear was that Billie Jean and Vonlee were at the casino in those days after Don had died, and Danny thought this to be in bad taste. And two or three days after Don's death, Danny said, he wound up selling the widow a few thousand dollars' worth of jewelry. Another red flag to him, one indicating she wasn't acting "normal."

Within just a few minutes of them talking back and forth, the APA asked Danny the most important question he was called as a witness to answer. APA Skrzynski set it up by explaining how Danny and Vonlee had dinner at the casino one night. As Vonlee ordered a bottle of vino, she told Danny she had a secret and wanted desperately to share.

"Well, she started telling me that she wants to tell me the truth about everything," Danny began, adding that Vonlee had first made him "promise" he would not be upset and would not leave her after she divulged her so-called secret. "And I was like wondering what's going on. . . ." So he promised Vonlee he would not leave or be mad. "And she started telling me that she's not really a woman. She was a man. And I did not believe her, because of what I seen. It doesn't match of what she's talking about. . . . I did not believe she was man . . . and then she kept telling me what happened at the Rogers residence, how Rogers *really* died."

Danny said Vonlee was "very upset and very nervous" while she spoke to him during the dinner. She wasn't bragging or being sarcastic. She had obviously been carrying around a burden, and she needed to rid herself of its weight. As the wine flowed, she explained more about herself and what happened that night between Billie Jean and Don.

Piszczatowski objected, knowing the APA was walking a fine line here of hearsay and Danny working his feelings and thoughts into the testimony. They agreed that Danny could testify to what Vonlee had said, but that was it. He could not speculate about her feelings or his, or talk about what she *might* have thought or meant.

Danny explained that the "secret" was beginning to wear Vonlee down and she had to tell him for fear of destroying her life with booze and drugs. She was now drinking more than she had been since arriving in Michigan. She was worried about her aunt, too.

Danny continued to speak: "We continued to sit . . . and she said, 'Are you not upset or anything?' And I said, 'No. How could I be upset? I mean, you just told me you are a man, and you just told me you killed somebody. How could I be upset?'. . . ."

"Mr. Chahine," the APA said carefully, now treading in waters Danny had likely said he was a little uneasy about going into, "let me ask you this."

"Yes," Danny said, staring at him.

"Had you, like, actually been physically intimate with this person?"

"Yes."

"You kissed her?"

Danny took a breath. He leaned into the microphone, this after being told several times that they were having trouble hearing him: "I mean, you want me to feel bad now, because I . . . *kissed* a man?" Danny had an attitude all of a sudden, as if the APA was accusing him of regretting his entire relationship with Vonlee.

"I mean . . . no," the APA said, a bit embarrassed.

"I did kiss her. Yes. And I'm like . . . I'm not a homosexual and I do feel . . . It has never happened to me before. . . . There was nothing I could tell that she was a man. There's *nothing*. That's why I was very shocked."

It was not his fault for being duped, Danny seemed to say.

Danny talked about how he demanded Vonlee show him the goods to prove she was a man. He told the jury about going out to the car, having that conversation, and Vonlee not dropping her pants until the next time they got together.

After that, Danny explained how Vonlee eventually told him "about the way they did kill Don Rogers—and she was describing what they did."

The APA asked Danny to explain in detail.

"She said that they got there at eleven and she said he was laying down on the floor, passed out from drinking, and that the other thing that she said that Billie Rogers told his family that they got there at three. . . ."

So there was some discrepancy in the stories and Danny thought this might become a problem for them.

The APA asked Danny to slow down a bit. Danny, obviously nervous, composed himself and continued in his broken, accented English: "When they got there, they found him on the floor, and Billie Rogers said to [Vonlee] that they got to do it now, because it's a good time. . . . So she said they start pouring alcohol, vodka, in his mouth. The way they do it, one of them will hold his nose, he cannot breathe—he open his mouth. The other will throw vodka in his mouth and they did that so many times that actually [Vonlee] said to her, 'Why are you wasting this good vodka on him? Let's get some cheap vodka.' That's what [Vonlee said she] said. And he would not die. She said that he would not die. While . . . they were doing that [Don] was playing with [Vonlee's] boobs."

And it was now clear to jurors where the APA and,

likely, the TPD developed its narrative that the ME's office tried so hard to back up with the science.

Danny mentioned how Billie Jean had blurted out to Vonlee something about giving her twenty-five thousand to fifty thousand dollars, and how if Don woke up the next day and remembered what they had done (pouring that alcohol into his mouth), they'd be in big trouble.

"So they got to do it right now," Danny claimed, referring to how Billie Jean felt after she allegedly tried to kill her husband by pouring the booze down his throat. "He would not die. And she said, [Vonlee] could not kill him, could not put her hands . . . on his mouth and nose. Every time he gasped for air, she would let him breathe, because she couldn't do it. So her aunt gets so frustrated, she went and got a pillow. . . ."

What happened after that was obvious. According to the narrative Danny Chahine was putting out there for jurors, Billie Jean placed a pillow over her husband's face and smothered him.

The APA brought Danny back around to that moment in the car as he and Vonlee sat and talked, when Vonlee refused to show him her private parts to "prove" her manhood. The APA wanted to know what happened when she refused. Did Danny and Vonlee then leave the casino and go to his apartment that night or the next?

Danny said the following night they were at his apartment, again talking about the "murder" and Vonlee's penis.

"What happened?"

"And that's when I found out *exactly* that she was man."

"How?"

"By seeing."

"Her penis?" the APA asked, without any hint of irony.

"Yes."

"*His* penis?" the APA then corrected, after realizing the possible confusion of his earlier query.

Danny nodded in the affirmative, without speaking.

The APA wouldn't let it go. "You saw that?" he asked again.

"Yes!"

Danny talked about those videotapes Billie Jean had given him. He said he couldn't understand why she would want to throw them out.

However, in the grand scope of things, what did this part of his testimony mean? That the recent widow didn't want a memory of Don around the house? It was clear from most everyone that the husband and wife had despised each other. More than that, mostly all of the tapes were pornography.

Danny said he had called his friend, the cop in a nearby town, and asked him to relay the information about Don's "murder" to the TPD.

He then spoke of how he met with TPD detectives Tullock and Zimmerman at the TPD and talked through everything he knew.

He testified how the TPD had offered him nothing for his "testimony."

"Has anyone given you *anything* to do this?" the APA asked.

"No."

The APA took a look at his notes and indicated he was finished.

CHAPTER 71

IF WALT PISZCZATOWSKI WAS a knuckle-cracker, this would be the appropriate moment to stand, intertwine his fingers and then crack his knuckles out in front of himself before shaking his head and saying something along the lines of *"Okay, Mr. Chahine, let's talk about your story."* But Piszczatowski was, of course, a professional; he was a defense attorney who knew when to poke and prod a witness and when to allow him the space to bestow upon his client even more reasonable doubt than had already been presented.

Piszczatowski established right away that Danny had reviewed his statements in the case just a few days before testifying, which can be significant, given that the best testimony is spontaneous truth; the worst is scripted and practiced recollection. Obviously, Danny had spouted a combination of the two during his hasty direct examination.

After apologizing for ultimately delving into what was surely going to be "very personal matters," Billie Jean's lawyer started with Vonlee and Danny's relationship. The questions focused on Vonlee's ability to routinely posture herself as the "center of attention," whether she was with Danny, Billie Jean, the two together or just perusing the casino by herself. Vonlee Nicole Titlow was a woman who "liked being looked at," Piszczatowski suggested to Danny's reluctant agreement.

Danny testified that "every woman" he had dated previously "looked just like" Vonlee. He had been fooled completely by her appearance and the romance. He was totally taken in by the charm and lies.

Vonlee was also someone who "did most of the talking," Piszczatowski suggested to the witness.

Danny, in turn, believed Vonlee was quite "normal" in that regard.

When they first met, Piszczatowski asked, wasn't it Danny who "put the moves on" Vonlee, which Piszczatowski referred to as "sexual advances"? And when Danny put his hand on her leg one night inside his apartment, she "kind of pulled back"?

"Yes," Danny agreed.

They settled on the idea that Danny and Vonlee were "emotionally involved."

"And during that . . . *relationship,*" Piszczatowski asked as sincerely as he could, "you did engage in intercourse with her on a couple of occasions?"

"Well, I don't know what you call 'intercourse' . . . if you want to say 'sex'?"

"Okay."

"Yes," Danny said.

"So you engaged in *sex* with her?"

"Yes."

"Again, I apologize for getting personal, but on one of those occasions, or was it more than one, you had—it was oral sex, correct?"

"Yes."

"And the other . . . it was, well, I guess was considered more conventional sex, correct?"

"Yes."

"Other than oral sex?"

"Yes."

The goal Piszczatowski had in mind here was to convince jurors that Vonlee had lied to Danny about everything, even the most intimate aspects of their relationship. Danny was a guy who thought he was having sexual intercourse with a woman, but he was actually having anal sex with a man. And if she could lie about— or exaggerate—such intimate moments, was it so hard to believe she could do the same with the story she had told Danny about Don's death? Also, another point Piszczatowski wanted to make to the jury, with his ingenious, leading way of questioning this witness, was that Danny Chahine, because he had been duped so easily (and completely) by Vonlee, may have had an ax to grind with her and Billie Jean. Therefore, coming in to testify might just be his opportunity to get back at Vonlee for all that dishonesty.

Piszczatowski had Danny talk about the jewelry he had given Vonlee and how much it cost.

When they arrived at Billie Jean, Danny called her "private, reserved, polite and well-mannered."

Not the way your typical, budding black widow might be described.

Billie Jean liked to play the slot machines, Danny explained.

As they discussed Billie Jean, Danny spoke of a night when she chastised him and told him "all" he wanted out of her niece was to "just have babies . . . and kidnap them and take them to another country. Meanwhile, she knew that *she* was a *he*." The point being: Billie Jean had no standards when it came to taking Vonlee's lie to this level. The indication was that Vonlee and Billie Jean were together in a big charade.

A word Walt Piszczatowski kept going back to with regard to Vonlee was "deceive." He asked Danny how it felt to be "deceived" on the "most basic level," but Danny steered the defense attorney away, making it seem as though he "thought" it would have been Billie Jean who would "be more deceiving than" Vonlee. What had shocked Danny the most was that Vonlee had been the bigger liar between the two of them.

"Were you upset with [Vonlee] for having *deceived* you?"

"No."

"You were not *angry* with her for having deceived you?"

"No."

"Over seven weeks?"

"You see, I understand human beings who go through stuff like that," Danny explained. "She was a man. She's changed into a woman. Of course, she's going to lie about it. I mean, that's normal. . . . As long as she told me the truth [ultimately] that she *wasn't* a man—that she wasn't a woman."

This comment could be backed up by the videotape of Danny Chahine's conversations with the TPD. During the initial interview the TPD conducted with Danny, when he talked about Vonlee and what he believed had happened to Don, Danny was relaxed and even laughing at himself for being cuckolded by a man. There was no animosity in his voice at all. He wasn't angry, or even the slightest bit perturbed by the fact that a man had misled him into believing he was a woman. Danny was more dumbfounded and shocked than anything else. Not once did he raise his voice or speak unkindly about Vonlee.

One important issue Walt Piszczatowski brought up next, tossing more reasonable doubt on Danny and his story, was that when Danny testified during the preliminary hearing phase of the case, all he could recall about that dinner conversation—the first one, which had not been recorded—was that Vonlee only had admitted to him that she was a man. She had not mentioned anything about what happened to Don. Piszczatowski wanted to know why, now, at the trial phase, was Danny changing that testimony?

Or, rather, adding to it.

"This is what happened," Danny said. "Um . . ." He didn't know what else to add.

"And when you were testifying four months, five months ago [during the preliminary phase], you couldn't remember anything else that was said at that dinner table, except that she told you she was a male, correct?"

"See . . . ," Danny tried to say.

But Piszczatowski kept him focused: "If you could answer the question . . ."

"Yeah."

"Okay."

"Wait, wait," Danny pleaded. "I didn't answer yet."

"I thought you did."

"I'm just saying . . ."

"Okay."

". . . What happened before, you were asking me to just specifically answer your questions, and I kept asking, and I wanted to make sure if you asked me *before* dinner, I would say 'yes' or 'no.' Maybe *after* dinner, I have to say 'yes' or 'no' or 'I don't remember.' I wanted to be very exact with you."

"Okay," Piszczatowski said, trying to get Danny to stop talking, not quite understanding—same as everyone else—what he had just said.

Danny concluded that the timing mattered little: whether it was before, during or after dinner, he couldn't recall exactly when she told him about Don, but she did tell him on that night.

Piszczatowski was saying that was fine, but Danny had not mentioned this during the preliminary phase of the trial.

Perhaps brilliantly, Piszczatowski used the word

"memory" several times during his next set of questions, bringing attention to the idea that perhaps Danny Chahine's memory wasn't—and shouldn't be considered—science. Most importantly, Piszczatowski said at one point, anyone's memory is more accurate closer to an event, and that the preliminary hearing was merely months after the events Danny was describing today.

They stayed on this subject of the dinner for quite some time. It became tedious and repetitive. But Piszczatowski had a hard time letting it go, asking, "When you left the car that night, had you seen her, ah, *his* genitalia?"

"No. In the car, no."

"And so . . . you hadn't touched the genitalia?"

"I touched something in her, but I didn't feel anything. She—"

"All right," Piszczatowski said, holding up a hand for Danny to stop there.

But he finished, anyway: "She said you can touch, and I did touch, but I didn't feel nothing."

They discussed Vonlee's penis for about five additional minutes, Danny wanting to make it known—and perfectly clear—that he certainly hadn't touched Vonlee's penis.

Not then.

Not ever.

When they finally got off the subject of Vonlee's penis, Piszczatowski switched gears and talked about Don, asking Danny if he had ever met him.

Danny said no, but he knew what Don looked like from the photographs he had seen while at Billie Jean's house.

So Piszczatowski asked him to explain what he saw on those videotapes that Mrs. Rogers had given him.

Danny said they were supposed to be pornography

tapes, but there had been some family videos mixed in. And so it became clear that it wasn't as though Billie Jean had been ridding the house of all of her memories of Don. No, she believed she was getting rid of Don's dirty business.

As quick as they talked about porn, Piszczatowski switched it up again and asked Danny about the alleged "pillow" used in this case. He had told detectives he believed it was a "bedroom pillow." Why did he say that?

"I guess so," Danny said. "I could have said that."

"Right."

"I don't know exactly where this pillow came from," Danny then admitted. "I wasn't there."

"Exactly. And you have to rely on what [Vonlee] told you."

"Absolutely."

Piszczatowski circled back to his main argument: "Now, Miss [Vonlee] was very convincing in her deception of you—is that correct?"

"Yes."

As Piszczatowski began to wind things down, he reminded Danny that he was "convicted of a felony."

"Yes."

Sometime later, "Was it true that [Vonlee] told you that Don Rogers was worth ten million dollars?"

"Yes."

From there, Piszczatowski went through a list of about ten lies Vonlee had told Danny—all of which Danny had bought into. When he was finished proving that Danny was very susceptible to Vonlee's charm and believed all of her stories, he turned to look at his co-counsel, and then indicated he was done.

There was very little redirect and recross; it was unrevealing and mostly a waste of time. With that finished, the APA called the car salesman from the dealership where Billie Jean bought those cars for her and for

Vonlee. Over the course of about five minutes, the APA got the car salesman to explain how Vonlee and Billie Jean showed up not long after Don's death and purchased two cars.

Piszczatowski had no questions for him.

And the day was over.

CHAPTER 72

ON DECEMBER 6, 2001, during the morning session, Donald Tullock and Donald Zimmerman, along with Donald McGinnis, Don Rogers's lawyer, testified, bringing the total of Dons talked about to four—five, if Don Kather, Don Rogers's best friend and business partner, was referenced. None of these three witnesses offered much to move the state's case toward a conviction.

Most cops, for example, will testify about every aspect of an investigation: the interviews they conducted, the reports they filed, the leads, the dead ends, the persons of interest they developed and crossed off, forensic evidence collected from a scene, and so on. Here, in just twenty minutes of direct testimony, Detective Tullock discussed the scene as he came upon it, how Billie Jean and Vonlee acted that morning, and how "odd" Billie Jean's "demeanor" was throughout the time he was at the house.

Quickly, then, Tullock moved into meeting Danny Chahine and that entire thread of the case. He spoke briefly about the controversial medical examiner's involvement and how that all came about. By the time he finished, Tullock was explaining to jurors how the TPD transported Vonlee's car back from Chicago after her arrest. When all was said and done, some wondered what—if anything—his testimony had to do with shedding any guilty light on Billie Jean Rogers.

Detective Don Zimmerman's direct testimony lasted all of five minutes. He spoke of serving that search warrant on the Rogers house and collecting Billie Jean's checkbook and—big reveal—seeing that notation Billie Jean had allegedly made on the checkbook: *Vonlee—$100,000.*

After Piszczatowski questioned Zimmerman, and the state refused to redirect, the APA stood and rested his case.

Piszczatowski called his first witness, Robert Allegrina, the investigator for the ME's office.

Allegrina was maybe the most important witness for Billie Jean besides a celebrity pathologist the defense had lined up. The ME's investigator was an integral part of the multipronged approach Dragovic talked about when deciding on death by natural causes or homicide. The investigator was the first to make a judgment call on a body. Some considered the investigator's role as biased from the start—hence, if he was called to a scene, well, that in and of itself meant that someone there had found something out of whack.

Focus is the defense attorney's best friend when bringing in witnesses to support the defendant. Here, Piszczatowski kept the emphasis on Allegrina's *role* for the ME's office in this case and asked what he did when he first got to the Rogers house.

"Well, as a general rule, we observe the scene, photograph the body, document the evidence, talk to the family and witnesses, and make a determination to bring the body in or release it."

"All right. When you say 'make a determination to bring the body in or release it,' what does that mean?"

This was a simple, direct question, and yet so vital in this case.

"Well, if there's adequate information and the person was under a doctor's care, we could release it, pending the doctor signing the death certificate."

"And that when you say 'under a doctor's care,' that would be under the care of a personal physician?"

". . .. In this case, did you make some inquiry to determine whether you could release the body or whether you had to take the body to the morgue—to the medical examiner's office?"

"I talked to the wife and she advised that he had not seen a doctor, had [not] been to a doctor, so there was no reason, you know, we would have to bring the body in."

Allegrina agreed that the woman sitting in the front of the courtroom wearing a beige blouse—with a fatigued air about her, quietly processing everything going on around her—was the same woman he spoke to at the scene.

Further, Allegrina said he basically went to a scene, took Polaroid photos of the body, spoke to cops, spoke to family members, before making an evaluation.

Defense attorney Piszczatowski wanted to know why Allegrina used Polaroid instead of 35mm film or even digital. It seemed that 35mm or digital would be more accurate, more detailed, more easily transferred, and would fall in line with what a crime scene investigator would use by today's standards.

Allegrina said Polaroid was a personal preference.

After the APA objected because of Piszczatowski's use of leading questions, Billie Jean's lawyer asked the investigator about the conversations he'd had with the defendant on that morning at the house. Basically, all they talked about, Allegrina testified, was Don's rectal bleeding and his desire not to go see a doctor. Beyond that, they did not speak about much else. Allegrina said he noticed what he thought was feces and dried blood on the carpet; he understood Billie Jean to be talking about a husband who was severely ill, bleeding rectally and unwilling to do anything about it.

Equally important was the fact that Billie Jean, after Allegrina asked her at the scene, was "not opposed to an autopsy" on Don.

Piszczatowski passed his witness.

The APA asked three questions.

None of them mattered.

CHAPTER 73

AFTER A LENGTHY DISCUSSION (without the jury present) regarding the merits of the state's case, and if the judge should issue a "direct verdict" based on the lack of reasonable evidence presented so far, to which the judge basically laughed, Walt Piszczatowski called Scott Hadley, Billie Jean's future son-in-law, her daughter's fiancé.

Scott explained how he had helped his future mother-in-law with her finances after Don's death. He said he advised her not to buy the cars, but he did not intervene when she had made the decision. He didn't want to meddle in the woman's grief, no matter what way she chose to express it. There was also an issue of Billie Jean wanting one hundred thousand dollars, and then a quarter of a million, as wire transfers to help out her family in Tennessee.

Was it extreme? Was it irresponsible? Was it, perhaps, heartless in one manner, spending Don's hard-earned money like that so soon after he was dead, but also quite a morally acceptable gesture in another, showing how willing Billie Jean was to help out her less financially fortunate family?

The jury had the information and would take it either way.

Scott Hadley's direct and cross-examination testimony was rather terse and inconsequential in the scope of the trial as it had played out before he had taken the stand. Billie Jean spent Don's money at will. The continuous message was: big freakin' deal. So she was careless with cash. Maybe it was her way of dealing with the stress of her husband's death.

On cross-examination, the APA asked one question, and Scott said yes, he saw Vonlee at the wake/funeral and she wore an "extensive amount of jewelry on her hands."

Billie Jean's daughter, Vanette Vereeke, was next. She spoke of a day she would never forget, when she and her mother went to the University of Michigan Medical Center. There was a doctor who wanted to see her mom in person. Billie Jean had gone in for a battery of tests in the months before this day and things were not looking so good. She was tired all the time. She felt nauseous and dizzy. According to Vanette, her mother did not know she had cancer at this time. No one did.

In realizing that her mother did not like to "deal with things," as Vanette described the call, she had phoned the doctor herself to find out what was going on. Vanette feared her mother would blow the doctor off and not go, much like Don Rogers had done. Many adults live under the same rule when it pertains to their health: not knowing means there's nothing wrong.

"I told your mother that she has a tumor," the doctor explained to Vanette when she called him. Since he had her on the phone, the doctor said he wanted to relay some additional important information to Vanette, asking if she could, perhaps, tell her mother, seeing that

Billie Jean did not want any part of talking to the doctor. He needed Billie Jean to know this was no joke. She needed to take it seriously. "I need you to tell her this is severe," the doctor explained.

Billie Jean cried as she listened to her daughter testify about this moment. It was actually heartbreaking for her to understand the fear and sadness in her daughter's voice as she explained to the jury how and when she learned that her mother did not have long to live.

"I can't do that," Vanette testified she told the doctor on the day they spoke. "What if I bring her to you?"

"Yes," the doctor answered.

Vanette convinced her mother to go. They brought along Vanette's sister, Billie Jean's other daughter. When they arrived, her mother was exceptionally calm, Vanette explained. Here they were heading into a meeting with a doctor, who was obviously not going to be delivering good news, and her mother was walking and talking as if it were another day. This was the reason why Piszcza-towski had called Vanette: to explain by example how Billie Jean reacted to bad news—or, rather, some of the worst news a person could get.

Vanette and her sister, Billie Jean and the doctor, sat down. The doctor proceeded to describe how hard this was for him, but he did not want to paint his patient's health with any sort of broad brush. He needed to be completely up front. Billie Jean needed to know.

"Terminal," he said. "The tumor is on the liver and now it went around the portal vein and it's inoperable."

"How long?" Billie Jean asked. Again, not flinching a bit. No tears. No drama.

"Your chances of living a year are very minimal." (This meeting occurred, Vanette explained, within the past eight months.)

"Is there anything I can do?" Billie Jean wanted to know.

"I'm sorry, but there's really nothing you can do, Mrs. Rogers," the doctor said.

Billie Jean had been on a list to get a new liver. Yet, the doctor explained further, because the cancer had spread, she'd be taken off the list at this point. There was no sense.

"You can try an experimental drug, but there are no assurances in any way for that. But listen, go home and think about that. Don't make the decision now."

As Piszczatowski brought Vanette back into her testimony and away from that anecdote, they discussed her mother's spending habits. Vanette said she had gone shopping with her mother many times: "When she saw something she liked, she would just buy it. You know, she really didn't have a concept of money. . . ."

Money was "fun" to Billie Jean. Paper. Spending meant nothing to her.

Vanette also characterized her mother during those days immediately following Don's death as being in a somewhat "dazed" state. She was never one to cry outwardly, anyway, or become overly emotional around people. Just wasn't in her. Billie Jean had grown up in Tennessee under very poor conditions, maybe below the poverty/welfare line. Because of that, she had been hardened. It took more than a death to knock her down. Vanette made an analogy of when her brother, Billie Jean's son, got into that near-fatal car accident and how her mother was calm and cool, working her way through it all. If she hadn't fallen apart when her son was knocking on death's door, how could she be expected to break down when Don died?

"My brother got in a severe car accident," Vanette explained in her articulate and sincere manner of providing the facts as she understood them. "He almost died. He had a closed head injury and we had to fly out

to California and he was really bad." She described the
scene in the hospital after they arrived: tubes "going
down his throat." She said she and her "sister . . . were
basket cases. But my mom was, you know, pretty calm
and trying to keep us calm and reserved."

Her mother never cried, Vanette added.

Jurors listened intently. Was this why she had reacted
the way she did when Don died? It was simply her nature
to be the nurturer.

When the APA took his turn at Vanette, he once again
asked about Vonlee and any jewelry she might have been
wearing during the funeral/wake.

Was this all the PO had up its sleeve? The fact that
Vonlee wore lots of rings and bracelets and Billie Jean
had likely bought them? After all, her "boyfriend," Danny,
was a jeweler.

The day was over early. The trial took a break on
Friday, and then continued on the following Monday,
December 10, 2001, with Walt Piszczatowski noting he
would be concluding his case by the end of the day.

CHAPTER 74

TWO NONESSENTIAL WITNESSES SET up an expert who was as close to a knockout blow as Billie Jean's attorney could dredge up. In the courtroom, standing, raising his right hand, reciting the oath to tell the truth and nothing but, was Dr. Michael Baden, who, at the time, had a hit television series on HBO, *Autopsy*. Who better to present Billie Jean's side of that seemingly all-important medical examiner evidence than a well-known, well-respected, familiar face like Baden? Tall, slightly overweight—"Baden loves his Peking duck," a friend recalled—with a reassuring, grandfatherly air about him, Dr. Michael Baden, who became a celebrity pathologist during the OJ Simpson case after joining the "dream team," was going to scalp the PO and the medical examiner's findings. He would totally dismantle their argument from stem to stern.

Baden went through his massive list of credentials, extensive and noteworthy. At the time when he sat in the witness stand, Baden was employed as the chief forensic pathologist, the medical examiner for the New York State Police. As part of his dedication to science and the career path of his choosing, Baden was a popular hired gun, if you will, open to interpreting autopsies for defense attorneys and prosecutors, testifying on behalf of a defendant he believed in or a prosecutor that needed his expertise injected into a case. He made a serious living doing this side work. Baden had been in the game for forty years. He'd published articles and written several books, both commercial and educational. The guy was a walking/talking encyclopedia of forensic pathology knowledge, and he had traveled the world exhuming and studying corpses. More than that, he'd been to over one thousand crime scenes and had conducted, by his estimation, over twenty thousand autopsies. If there was a more experienced pathologist in the world who could better understand the Oakland County medical examiner's work in this case, he or she had yet to come forward.

Baden, under the direction of Piszczatowski, had looked at Don Rogers's death, specifically all of the documents and photographs. After Baden spent about five minutes explaining what he had looked at in the case—every report, Dragovic's findings, the photos, etc.—Piszczatowski cut to the chase: "Now, based on your review of these materials, were you able to form an opinion as to the cause of death of Donald Rogers in this case?"

Baden said yes.

Piszczatowski asked him to proceed.

"My conclusion after reviewing everything is that I agree with [Dr. Ortiz-Reyes's] initial diagnosis"—an ideal way to present his findings—"that the cause of death is acute alcoholism. Too much alcohol."

Baden wasn't going out on a limb by himself and saying he'd drawn some wild conclusion: he was agreeing with the pathologist who examined Don's body for the ME's office.

Piszczatowski presented a "blowup" of the original death certificate on the overhead projector, another brilliant move. There, for everyone to see in black and white, written in the space allotted for cause of death: *acute alcohol intoxication*.

What became a factor that might not have seemed important earlier, or ever, stood out as Baden explained that when the ME's office changed the original death certificate, no one changed the date, nor had they made a note of when they had changed their collective mind that Don's death was now by asphyxiation. So again, although the ME's office might not have been acting nefariously when changing its diagnosis, this ostensible, minor error of not changing the date—or at least noting it—gave the impression they were. And with juries, both Baden and Piszczatowski knew from experience, impressions are *everything*.

Piszczatowski asked Baden to recite a list of medical problems Don had suffered from. These were well-documented findings: heart disease and polyps in the colon, which led to rectal bleeding. Don was a heavy smoker and a heavy drinker. His veins were clogged up with plaque, and his blood flow was not quite as slow as peanut butter being forced through a pipe, but one gets the picture. You look at all that, Baden said, and you could pick any number of ways in which this man might have died. He was a walking dead man.

The big reveal, in Baden's professional opinion, came into view after he had gone "over in detail the medical examiner's explanation for the change to smothering," and, subsequently, when he "went over in detail Dr. Dragovic's *opinions* in the preliminary hearing as to the change to smothering." It was then, Baden told jurors, "I must respectfully disagree that I think there isn't the type of evidence available to permit a diagnosis of a change to smothering."

Baden had an uncanny way of verbalizing difficult medical matters in easily palatable language. Moreover, he wasn't coming out and blasting the doctor, a colleague, claiming he was incompetent. Instead, Baden was saying he respectfully disagreed with the man and then presented evidence to support that argument.

"Smothering," Baden added, "is a diagnosis that may leave no evidence of injury at all. One can have smothering without any changes in the body or there *may* be changes in the body." Baden had looked into hundreds of smothering cases throughout his career. He knew the particulars involved in this type of homicide. One might even call him an expert in this area. "And it's a diagnosis of *exclusion*. You have to *exclude* other more pressing causes of death, and here we have a very *impressive* cause of death—that is, acute alcoholism. . . ."

Further, Baden went on to note, people who drank a lot "have and, eventually, for whatever reason, the alcohol they consume can cause death. And without an internal examination to further evaluate whatever abnormalities may be present, I just think that the cause of death as established initially is valid. . . . and that there isn't sufficient change to make the change on the basis of all the evidence that's present in the files."

Casting even more bad light on the ME's finding, without much effort, Baden explained how the ME's office had done an "inspection report" and also filled out an "autopsy document."

"It was listed 'autopsy,' but an autopsy *wasn't* done. It was an inspection, an internal inspection."

As they went through the reports issued by Oakland County, Baden spoke of a "lethal amount of alcohol" in Don's system at the time of his death.

He spoke of the need for a "full autopsy" here, but that it had not been done.

He spoke of a seventy-four-year-old man who had diverticulitis and a host of other ailments who had, without a doubt, died from one of them.

He recalled how "people who drink a lot tend to bruise" more than others.

He maintained there just wasn't enough "evidence" to change the death verdict to asphyxiation, and Baden himself would have never done such a thing.

Baden testified to a whole litany of eye-opening observations:

Most deaths are "unnatural," and that, in and of itself, is no reason to raise a red flag.

"Most—ninety-five, ninety-six, ninety-four percent—of deaths in this country nowadays, those deaths are certified *without* an autopsy . . . [and] autopsies are becoming rarer and rarer. . . ."

The initial medical examiner (Ortiz-Reyes) had enough information to make the call to issue a death certificate.

All of these events were "not at all uncommon."

Baden was effectively saying the ME's office did the right thing, came to the right conclusion, followed the book, but then they suddenly changed their minds.

A valid point Baden made was that Don weighed about 140 pounds. The amount of alcohol in his 140-pound body (.44) was "significant and extremely high" for his weight. Baden further stated that for the chronic alcoholic, the more he drinks the later in life, the less he is able to handle the amount of alcohol he used to be able to consume.

"I think the problem with chronic alcoholism . . . it doesn't make you better. It makes you worse, because as you drink and damage the liver (the target organ of alcohol) . . . it causes cirrhosis and other damage to the liver. The liver, which is the main organ for getting rid of alcohol, becomes damaged, so that the older alcoholic often can handle it less well than when he or she was younger."

They spent the next ten minutes breaking down the alcohol argument at its most basic level. Baden had his facts and figures ready and fully prepared. As they did this, the idea that "alcoholism" was a potential killer kept coming up within all that Baden talked about. Then he switched to cardiovascular disease and it was clear that without an autopsy, how was one to draw *any* conclusion?

The topic of Don's body possibly being repositioned came up next. Baden said he'd studied all of the photos and there was no way, based on what he had available for evidence, he could come to the same conclusion.

"I don't see any evidence that this was a tampered scene," Baden told jurors. "Alcoholics can die just lying down and going to sleep. The legs being crossed at the ankles was not in any way remarkable."

What's more, at one time, Baden had done hundreds of autopsies on skid row drunks dying in New York City. He knew what to look for, as far as death by alcohol went.

In fact, as they concluded twenty minutes later, there was very little Dr. Baden could agree with regarding Dragovic's findings in this case. For all anybody knew, Baden said at one point, with "all of the rectal bleeding" reported, Don Rogers "could have died of colon cancer." It was possible—and "another consideration that an *autopsy* would have resolved."

As far as those so-called bruises on Don's face and nose, supposedly left by a pillow, all "alcoholics leave" scars and fresh wounds from bruising themselves. There was just no way to tell if those minor scrapes on Don could have come from a pillow. Baden stopped himself just short of saying how ridiculous it was even to claim they had been made by a pillow. For all intents and purposes, Baden said near the end of his direct, those scrapes, especially, could have been discolorations in the photo negatives. There was no indication that they were actually scrapes in the surface of the skin.

Concluding, Baden said, if he had to guess, he'd say no, those were not scrapes, they were old wounds.

"I don't think it's sufficient to indicate foul play."

What can an APA do after a show like Baden had just put on? Go after his ethics was about all. The APA began by hammering Baden on his "consulting" jobs, asking him repeatedly if he spent most of his time these days consulting on other cases, as opposed to conducting autopsies.

Baden said (twice) he split his time equally between autopsies, writing and consulting.

The APA asked where.

Baden said all over the world.

The cross-examination was, at best, a last-ditch effort; at worst, it came out as desperation.

Predictably, the APA went after Baden's "fees."

Baden agreed that he got three hundred fifty dollars an hour, and five thousand dollars a day while on the road. In this case, it amounted to about twelve thousand dollars, paid for by Billie Jean Rogers.

From there, the APA asked about Baden's contention that .44 might have been lethal.

Baden agreed when the APA asked that not everyone with that level dies from it.

As they discussed the alcohol levels for what felt like a nauseating umpteenth time, it appeared the cross-exam was going nowhere. A lot of Baden's answers consisted of a simple "yes" or a simple "no." Zero elaboration.

APA Skrzynski asked questions about the amount of alcohol in a person's system for the next twenty minutes; then he tossed in an OJ Simpson question (if Baden had testified in that case). As the state attorney finished, it was clear the PO had nothing left. If anything, Baden's cross-exam bolstered Billie Jean's case in the sense that the APA made a bigger deal than necessary about the amount of alcohol in Don's system, casting even more light onto it, which meant more doubt about the murder charge.

By 1:56 P.M., after lunch, the judge indicated all of the testimony had been heard. Closings followed a day later.

And then, quite unceremoniously, to no one's surprise, Billie Jean Rogers was found not guilty.

It had all happened so quickly. The closing arguments. The verdict. The good-byes.

And then the breakdown of Billie Jean's health: She faded fast. Heading toward Christmas that year, after it was announced that Vonlee would face trial within just a few months, Billie Jean secluded herself inside her home. No one saw her. Not many spoke to her. She'd beaten a murder rap—which was no easy task under any circumstance—but she still had a death sentence hanging over her.

PART 4

I now inhabit a life I don't deserve, but we all walk this earth feeling we are frauds. The trick is to be grateful and hope the caper doesn't end any time soon.

David Carr, *The Night of the Gun*

CHAPTER 75

ON DECEMBER 19, 2001, Vonlee's new lawyer, Frederick Toca, along with Vonlee by his side, appeared before Judge Wendy Potts and the APA to set a date for Vonlee's trial. Toca needed to ask for more time. He said he had not yet had a chance to order the transcripts from Billie Jean's trial and with the New Year approaching, the holiday season slowing things down, he wanted additional time to study all of the documents and consult with his client.

Judge Potts was not going to stand for any delays. Her court had always been run with an iron fist as it pertained to schedules. She said all of the witnesses had just testified in Billie Jean's case and their testimony was "fresh in their minds" and she did not want to disrupt that momentum.

It was a valid point.

From the state's point of view, Vonlee's trial was going to be a facsimile of Billie Jean's in the manner of witnesses and how they would appear—the most important among them being Danny Chahine.

After they hashed it out, Judge Potts said March 4, 2002.

No delays!

Gavel.

CHAPTER 76

BY FEBRUARY 6, 2002, fewer than thirty days before the scheduled start of Vonlee's trial, Frederick Toca filed a motion that would once again change the course of his client's life.

Fred Toca was now withdrawing from the case—a case that he had claimed to his client he could win for her.

Citing a "breakdown of communication" between him and Vonlee, and "also some other issues," Toca said he'd like the court to allow him to step aside.

Potts was a bit perturbed by this eleventh-hour revelation.

As he explained further, Toca said he was out of funds. They needed six thousand dollars to buy the Billie Jean Rogers trial transcripts and "certain financial arrangements have been made. Unfortunately, her family indicates that they may not be able to come through. . . ."

Vonlee looked angry. She stared at him.

"And, of course, that gives us four days until trial, and I think Ms. Titlow will tell you, quite frankly, that you know certain representations have been made by other family members of hers, that this was taken care of. It has *not* been taken care of."

Was Toca now saying that Vonlee's family had been partly responsible for paying him to finance her defense? Was the guy blaming Vonlee's family for the position he now found himself in?

"Are you going to come through and have you retained Mr. Toca?" Judge Potts asked Vonlee, who was standing before the court. "Have you paid any money to Mr. Toca?"

"Just some jewelry, that's all," Vonlee said.

"No money?" Potts asked, seemingly confused that zero dollars had exchanged hands.

"There was an agreement on, supposedly, on a *book* deal," Vonlee said before looking over at Toca.

"But that's—" Toca began to say before Vonlee cut him off.

"That's how I retained his service," Vonlee said.

"On a *what*?" Potts asked. She sounded perplexed by this.

"Your Honor, there was initially, per the first attorney in this case," Toca said—a statement no one else connected to the case would later agree with—"a book deal on this table that fell through as well."

"Oh!"

"But, Your Honor," Toca continued, "this has *nothing* to do with my retention. I mean, this has to do with trying to retain experts. Trying to get transcripts, et cetera, et cetera."

Toca claimed that the "book deal" portion of his defense, which was paid by Vonlee in her signing over rights to her story, only covered Toca's time and efforts, not his expenses. That money was supposed to, he said, come from Vonlee's family.

"Who is going to represent you in this case?" Potts asked Vonlee.

"I don't have anyone if he don't," Vonlee said.

"Okay. You would need a court-appointed attorney?"

"Yes," Vonlee answered.

Neither Toca nor his co-counsel was on the state's official court-appointed attorney list. So the state could not allow them to continue and pay them those monies they needed for expenses, if this was even an option Vonlee desired.

Potts asked Vonlee again if she wished to retain Toca or she wanted a court-appointed lawyer.

Vonlee said, "I just want it over with. Whatever is best."

Potts said she would get to work right away finding Vonlee a competent, court-appointed attorney that might be able to keep the trial on schedule.

CHAPTER 77

HE DIDN'T KNOW IT on that cold day in February 2002, as Judge Potts went to work locating an attorney to fill Toca's shoes, but forty-five-year-old—"feeling thirty-two"—William Cataldo was about to become involved in the legal mess that had become Vonlee Titlow's case. There had been so much misperception over what had happened between Toca and Vonlee, so much animosity between the two—with Vonlee telling people she was going to see Toca in civil court one day to prove he had destroyed any chance she had left to defend herself properly—the case was a complicated challenge for any defense attorney.

Cataldo, who was often called Bill, was a wispy, wiry man, with long, stringy, concrete gray hair, flowing inconspicuously around a shiny bald spot. He kept a salt-and-pepper mustache, wore small and round Ben Franklin glasses, and generally donned tailored suits. Cataldo had been a radio producer on his way toward entering the world of law. He'd overseen countless shows on ABC Radio in Detroit, finally producing a law series that sparked an interest in the profession. By 1984, Cataldo had given up on radio as his sole career and had graduated law school. His passion became trial work.

"Law was like my fourth career," Cataldo told this author. "I graduated and still didn't practice law for years while I continued to produce the radio program."

Oakland County did not have a public defender's office, same as many counties across the United States—a particular office, per se, where all of the cases in which defendants could not afford legal counsel were referred. Oakland had a court-appointed public defender list of lawyers it went to when in need of pro bono counsel. By the time Cataldo found his way into practicing law full-time, he had made friends with judges, lawyers and others involved in the business of criminal law. He knew the landscape and layout of a courtroom fairly well, and had become familiar with all the local players.

"Besides one house closing and two divorces, I have never touched civil law—all the cases I've done since 1984 have been criminal," Cataldo explained.

Criminal law fit Cataldo's character: fast-paced, thrill-driven, drama-based and edgy. He liked to be around the action. He took careful preparation to avoid the nonsense and bullshit that many lawyers participated in.

Judge Potts thought of Cataldo immediately when Vonlee was in need of an attorney after what had happened between her and Toca. Cataldo was on Potts's list of lawyers she was familiar with and liked to see practicing in her courtroom.

"I had done several high-profile cases in front of her, so she was comfortable with my skill set," he said.

One of the main factors for Potts, as the judge in this case, according to Cataldo, was she did not want to "adjourn the trial date." Potts needed the trial to proceed, even with this legal hiccup. And, lo and behold, the trial was set to begin when she had scheduled it in March. She believed Bill Cataldo could fill those vacant shoes and make it happen. What's more, she knew that handing Cataldo over to Vonlee, Vonlee was getting the best representation she could for the money she was willing to spend.

"We were six weeks out from the time of my appointment and I assured her that I could turn aside my other cases and focus on this."

A travesty, Cataldo thought as he sat down to look through the documents, study the trial transcripts from Billie Jean's case (for which the state could now provide at its own cost), shaking his head in disgust, learning about what had happened between Vonlee and Toca. As he flipped through pages, looking at it all in its entirety, he also considered that Vonlee's case at trial was unwinnable. She had already admitted her involvement in Don's murder in a court of law and could be heard on tape confessing, essentially, to the crime. It didn't matter what she said, the lawyer knew. Didn't matter that her role was minimized and she might have not even participated in the actual murder. Didn't matter what kind of witness Danny Chahine made, or what history with the law he had. All jurors would hear, Cataldo was entirely confident, was Vonlee describing how she and her aunt carried out this crime.

Vonlee had seven to fifteen years on the table and was now staring down the barrel of what could be anywhere between twenty years to life.

Incredible, Cataldo told himself. He wondered how someone could be so incompetent to have screwed that deal up for her. The attorney thought it was ignorance that had led to Vonlee's decision to remove Richard Lustig, and the deal he had brokered, and go with Toca.

What bowled Bill over the most was that his colleague and friend, a man he knew very well, Richard Lustig, Vonlee's initial attorney, was able to go into the PO and negotiate that deal of seven to fifteen during a time when the PO's administration had what Cataldo said was a "no plea" policy in place. That feat alone was nothing short of a legal miracle. Lustig had performed magic in that regard. The idea that a plea deal had been set between them, considering the evidence in Vonlee's case the state had against her, proved Richard Lustig had done the best work of his career, as far as Cataldo was concerned.

"Richard was able to have a deal struck," Cataldo explained, "that included a *first-degree* murder charge—think about that!—pled down to a much lesser offense, with a cap of *fifteen* years, reducing the charge to, basically, manslaughter."

Anyone practicing in Oakland County, he went on to note, "knew that those deals don't ever come along."

It revolved around Vonlee's testimony against Billie Jean. The PO knew they could never get a conviction without Vonlee, and the verdict in Billie Jean's case had proven that.

"Vonlee wasn't even in the fucking room at the time of this murder," Cataldo said. "They realized that."

But that was months ago. Now Vonlee, because of a decision she and Toca had made, was facing murder one. There was no chance of any deal. Billie Jean's case was over. There was no bait to make the switch. No longer any carrot on the end of the stick to dangle in the PO's face. And the PO, coming from a loss, now wanted blood.

Vonlee was screwed.

"I made that request, of course, as a formality," Cataldo said of a possible plea bargain, "but I was laughed at, just as I am laughing now thinking about it."

As he sat and looked over everything, trying to find a strategy to defend Vonlee, what amazed Cataldo was that he couldn't understand why the PO had tried Billie Jean's case first.

"They should have tried Vonlee before Billie Rogers,

made a deal with her, and then had her testify *against* Billie."

Cataldo was certain they would have obtained a conviction if they did that.

One major factor for Cataldo was the idea that the Detroit metro area has always been "starved for glitterati," and with Dr. Michael Baden riding the wave of his HBO series and the notoriety of the OJ Simpson case at the time, there was not a chance of winning against Billie Jean and that spectacle her defense put on. In Bill Cataldo's opinion, the PO knew it, going in.

"You bring Baden in and you put him opposite Dr. Dragovic, who can be exaggeratedly arrogant, an attitude not consistent with establishing an effective relationship with a jury and inconsistent with the local social structure out here . . . and Baden is a star. Remember, they had *no* evidence, and Dragovic was now coming in and saying it was a homicide—all with a little scratch on Mr. Rogers's nose and a *theory?*"

The PO's failure, Cataldo observed, was in the notion that they likely knew how the crime happened, how Billie Jean had allegedly killed her husband, based on what Vonlee had said and that she passed a polygraph, backing up her story, but they had no evidence to support their theories. And so going into the ring with that, "this is what happens," Cataldo added. "Baden comes in and says this guy was so drunk, with heart disease and lung disease and liver issues, yada, yada, yada, this *very well* could have been natural causes."

Slam dunk.

When he looked at Vonlee's role, however, Cataldo saw a few things he could not get around: these were fatal flaws—no matter what he did, or what expert he brought in, or how he portrayed Vonlee.

"All I could do," Cataldo explained, "was ask for a reduction when the time came. There's not going to be a *not* guilty. Won't happen. The biggest thing here was that audiotape."

There was just no way he could quash the significance of the admission on that tape Danny Chahine had made. It was going to ring inside the courtroom. It would be all the jury needed to hear. Moreover, he could not talk about Billie Jean's verdict or what had happened with Vonlee and her botched plea deal. None of it would be allowed in court.

"She explains it all on that tape," Cataldo commented. "Complete confession, premeditation, *first*-degree murder!"

This was impossible to ignore as a defense attorney.

Another major obstacle he faced, which he knew from experience, was that a defense attorney cannot mess with the jury. You cannot try to confuse or misdirect them. You cannot lie to them. You cannot make them feel stupid. You cannot try to say, *"Hey, this tape here . . . it's not what you think it is. . . . It means nothing."* That strategy would backfire.

"Here, going in, my only chance was, I needed to make the jury feel that, okay, Vonlee participated, but at *what* level? They needed to ask themselves that question. . . ."

If Bill Cataldo could get the jury to the point where they were asking that question during deliberations, he had a shot at a lesser charge, less time in prison for his client—that reduction he spoke of. Maybe even a manslaughter conviction.

On a personal level, Cataldo viewed Vonlee as someone he liked and someone he did not think was a vicious killer or dangerous in any way. However, she was a narcissist, in his view, which became another complication he needed to put a shine on for the jury. She couldn't present herself in court as the selfish-all-her-life, not-ever-wanting-to-work, looking-for-a-sugar-daddy, flashy-paid-escort transsexual she was—this would weigh heavily on their verdict. One juror gets it in his or her mind that

Vonlee is a sexual deviant or a money-hungry transsexual looking to fund her operation through the murder of her long-lost aunt's wealthy husband—as the newspaper headline writers had tagged her—and it was over.

Cataldo also believed Vonlee had "turned a blind eye to the obvious." Sure, she could have been wasted; she could have not known entirely what was going on inside that kitchen on that night because she had drunk too much. However, as Cataldo saw the truth through the documents and evidence, "She had *chosen* not to participate."

The point being, she had a choice. And if she had a choice not to, then she probably knew what was going on at some point and had a choice to turn her aunt in or stop the crime.

"She's never worked, and she's always looking for the glitter—always looking for the easy way."

These were all facts, whether Vonlee agreed or not, the jury might get into its collective mind-set. And once lodged there, it would be impossible for Cataldo to extract.

As a situation, Cataldo concluded, when Toca walked into her life and, combined with Vonlee's inherent narcissism, told her, *"You didn't do it,"* it was something, the lawyer contended, Vonlee *wanted* to hear.

"It's not that she's incapable of thinking logically, okay," Cataldo explained about that moment when Vonlee and Toca decided to withdraw the plea. "But that she is *not* going to think logically if there is an easy way out of it all. So, when he comes in and promises two or three years, of course, she's going to jump at it. Why? Because. It's. What. She. Wants. To. Hear. *Period*. Therefore, Vonlee was the perfect foil for what Toca was attempting to do.

"Did Vonlee know something was going on in that kitchen and it was wrong?" Cataldo asked rhetorically.

"Probably," he said, answering his own question.

"Was she a little bit wasted from all the booze?"

"Probably."

The reality of Vonlee Titlow, though, was that she never "looked that far into anything," he explained in his perfectly eloquent way of analyzing his client. "She knew it was wrong, yes, but let's look at this: her whole life has been 'Who gives a shit! I'm going to do it because it feels good. . . .'"

Vonlee's failure on that night was in not processing the information and her reality properly in those moments with Billie Jean in that kitchen. Either impaired by alcohol, ignorance or both, she wasn't able to judge for herself what exactly was happening before her. If she had just stopped to think about it, Vonlee was smart enough to know that her aunt was drawing her into a web that included the two of them allegedly getting rid of Don and sharing in the responsibility equally. But she never, as Cataldo determined, thought that far in advance about what was going on at any time in her life.

So how could Bill Cataldo possibly work some magic and get Vonlee off on a crime she admitted committing?

CHAPTER 78

ALL SHE KEPT HEARING from guards was "You're going to be somebody's bitch. You get up there to the state prison and you'll be raped repeatedly, beaten, and sold for sex and cigarettes."

Vonlee was more fearful than she had ever been in her life. The things she was hearing while waiting to go to trial painted a future in hell. She thought, *If there is anything I can do to keep from going to prison, I need to do it.*

There was a part of Vonlee, however, that had been satisfied with not testifying against Billie Jean. "It would have been a betrayal, in my grandmother's eyes," Vonlee explained.

She did not mind betraying anyone else in her family, even her own mother; but when it came to her grandmother, Vonlee was loyal to a fault. Beyond that, Billie Jean had convinced the grandmother that Vonlee was making it all up because she was so drunk. It was all a fabrication. And now, Billie Jean had the support of a verdict of not guilty—"See, even the jury believed me!"—to back up her argument.

Regarding the plea deal she had made after admitting her role in the crime, Vonlee claimed Toca had never explained to her that her prior admission was basically going to curtail any chance for a verdict of not guilty.

"When I looked at this later on," Vonlee reflected, "it was clear to me that a plea deal was not a good end to the story if we're talking movie and book deal. Toca wanted drama for his ending."

According to what Vonlee claimed, in selling the idea of a new plea to her, Frederick Toca had said, "Look, I know Richard Lustig and spoke to him. He told me if he was younger and had more energy, he would have taken your case to trial himself."

"In fact," Vonlee explained, "Toca told me one day he had just come from lunch with Mr. Lustig, and he said Lustig was 'so glad' that he (Toca) was now representing me. . . ."

Lustig later provided a document to the court stating he had never spoken to Toca, and Toca had never asked for any of the documents from Vonlee's case "until five weeks *after* the plea had been withdrawn."

Vonlee also made the accusation that when Toca withdrew from her case, he told her that the book deal and film had fallen through.

"I was so shocked when the judge allowed him to withdraw."

After Billie Jean's verdict, Vonlee wondered, "How could they possibly say I aided and abetted her if she was found *not* guilty?" Vonlee had never been charged with the "actual" crime, she said. "I was always charged with helping Billie."

There had been a part of Vonlee, she admitted, "that was . . . Well, I was hoping Billie would be found guilty. I felt like she needed to pay for what she did."

Vonlee had been in jail, waiting her turn in court, going on a year.

"And Billie had spent all of a few hours behind bars," Vonlee said. "Was that fair? I am the one in jail, and she is the one that killed Don! I'm the one that had a conscience. I'm the one that went crying to my boyfriend and told him I couldn't live with this. She's the one that lied. I'm the one that passed the polygraph. I'm the one that tried to do the right thing."

It was Vonlee's counselor at the jail that called her in on that evening, sat Vonlee down, and then told her: "Your aunt has been found not guilty."

Vonlee dropped her head. How was she supposed to react to it?

"Bittersweet" was the way Vonlee later put it. "Part of me felt that maybe I'll be found not guilty because she was. And part of me felt like, 'Wow, is this woman working with the Devil or what?'"

In Bill Cataldo, Vonlee found a "very nice guy."

When they first sat down, Cataldo said, "Just unbelievable. You had a deal for seven to fifteen and you withdrew it." He shook his head in disbelief. All the air had been sucked out of the room with that one comment. But looking back was not going to change the future. Vonlee was facing the fight of her life and Cataldo was in charge. They needed a plan.

"I know" was all Vonlee could say.

"I feel especially bad, because if I lose and you get more time . . . well, let's just talk about the case. You know, what [Toca] did, that wasn't aboveboard. I just need to look at all this, go through everything and see where we stand."

Vonlee said she'd help, obviously, in any way she could.

What became a focal point right away in their discussions was the idea of Vonlee testifying. Was there any way around her sitting and explaining to the jury her version of the events that had led to Don's death? Could she do it? Was she emotionally prepared?

"Nothing is ever cut-and-dry," Cataldo told her. "Look, it's going to be tough."

"I know," Vonlee said. "I'll think about it."

CHAPTER 79

WHEN THE FIRST DAY of her trial arrived, Vonlee sat in the courtroom goosed up on so many psychotropic medications, she later said, the numbness actually helped her deal with the anxiety and fear associated with what was the possible outcome she faced. The feeling inside the room was one in which everyone seemed to know the ending was not going to be what was expected. Concurrently there was a dismal feeling that it would not end happily for the defendant.

Vonlee did not look like the female she had in the past. She was a bit heavier, with her hair dyed blond, short and curly, and her more manly features showing prominence on her face and plump body. She looked like a transsexual, which, Bill Cataldo knew, was not going to help.

People judge by appearances. By looks. By what they *think* a person might want out of life. Jurors, of course, were no different.

The trial's date had been pushed back, but on March 11, 2002, things got under way with a daylong voir dire as a jury of fourteen was chosen. Following that, Judge Wendy Potts asked everyone to return the next morning,

March 12, for opening statements and the state's first witness.

Regarding his rival in the courtroom, Bill Cataldo viewed APA John Skrzynski as a skilled competitor and reliable colleague.

"He is thoughtful, professional, personal and a *very* good trial lawyer," Cataldo later said. "He doesn't play games and does not engage in trickery. If anything, I would like to think I have modeled [part of my career] on him. We both have this certain bravado when it comes to trials. We love providing complete discovery, then going to trial, mano a mano. . . ."

Both lawyers agreed that "winning feels better when talent and facts" usurp "cheating." Playing by the rules and coming out on top always felt better than the alternative.

Before entering into the world of law, quite interestingly, APA Skrzynski toured nationally with various rock acts as a horn player. Colleagues and friends said he did not involve himself in office politics and was a loyal soldier to those assigned to supervise him.

"He has a humility and understanding for the defense attorney plight that comes with having to ask for leniency," Cataldo explained. "He takes no pleasure in saying no. He treats all in our field with respect, including defendants. Some in our position love to point fingers and derogate those charged with crimes. He doesn't stoop to it. Neither do I. Respect isn't [just] a buzzword for John. He listens to all sides before forming opinions and is evenhanded in an environment that rewards pathological ideology."

Still, running alongside the charming, complimentary verbiage he spouted for his archfoe, Cataldo also claimed that there was a fair amount of "aggression" between the two men when they practiced in a court of law, on opposite sides. And yet, this was how lawyers, Cataldo added, at least the passionate ones, played the game.

The following morning, first thing, two words dominated the APA's opening: "aiding" and "abetting." This was the state's focus.

Vonlee helped her aunt kill her uncle.

"Now," APA Skrzynski said, "the law says that if you intentionally help another person commit a crime—even though you yourself are not the person that actually commits the crime—if you intentionally help someone else commit the crime, you are as *guilty* as if you had committed the crime yourself."

Was there anything left that the APA needed to say?

Vonlee looked on, terribly lost in an abyss of gloom and doom. When it was put that way by the APA, she felt, there was no chance for her to come out of this unscathed.

Of course, the APA didn't stop there. He banged on and on, carefully uttering that same narrative he had utilized throughout Billie Jean's trial, or one could say the "dress rehearsal" for this event. He hammered the same points home: the money, the cars, the casino, Danny Chahine.

"She helped her aunt kill her uncle to get money for a sex change operation—and, in fact, she *got* the money."

Thunderous.

Direct.

Condensed.

The APA was on his game here. And it was obvious that Skrzynski did not want to lose this case, too. As he worked his way through what was a brilliant opening statement, pointing out the law repeatedly, he won over the jury.

Then, upping the ante for himself (perhaps when he didn't need to), Skrzynski spoke of how Vonlee was on trial for a vicious, premeditated, planned-out murder with her aunt; she was here today to face that *and* the charges of aiding and abetting.

Skrzynski worked in the recorded conversation with Danny Chahine near the end. And just like that, the icing was sugary and sweet, capping off the charges she faced.

If there was one fault in APA Skrzynski's opening, it was that he went on for maybe just a bit too long, went over some pieces of evidence twice. In culinary terms, he seemed to be putting too many eggs into the pudding. Yet, finally, as he concluded, the APA asked for jurors to consider a few simple facts: "And when I come back at the end of the trial, after you've heard all the evidence, I'm going to ask you to render the verdict . . . of first-degree premeditated murder and that will be the verdict that you'll want to return."

From manslaughter to first-degree murder was all Vonlee could think as she stared at jurors. She couldn't get it out of her head, no matter how many meds she had taken. Rewinding the clock would be something she might make a deal with the Devil to achieve. Such a contrast in reality: her life for Don's life.

What could Bill Cataldo do? He had to pull out something substantial here. But where should he begin? As a defense attorney, one had to be careful with overpromising and then not delivering.

Cataldo stood, looked down at his notes one last time, and then conveyed his first line, a rather stark, terse piece of factual insinuation: "The state of Michigan, through Mr. Skrzynski, has improperly aimed their case of Vonlee Nicole Titlow."

Don't reach for the stars. Try to grasp onto a small piece of the pie and feed it to jurors. They might bite. Make them feel as though the state was stepping over a line and overcharging Vonlee.

Cataldo focused the early portion of his opening on the cause of death, or, rather, the lack of evidence. If he could prove, same as Billie Jean's lawyer had, that Don died naturally, then there was no murder to charge his client with.

Another strategy, one that Vonlee totally got on board for, was Vonlee taking responsibility for what she had done. She was entirely willing to do that, which that first plea bargain had proven, though Cataldo could not mention it.

"At best, or at worst, what Vonlee did was stupid. What Vonlee did was inappropriate. But there are appropriate charges that would hold her responsible for what she did. But those appropriate charges are *not* the state's worst-possible charges, first-degree murder."

As he continued, Cataldo talked about how the APA had focused his argument on the allegations Danny Chahine had made that, of course, *supported* the state's case. The APA did not reference everything else said between Danny and Vonlee, which would *refute* the idea that Vonlee was a murderer. Rather, these other conversational exchanges revealed that Vonlee had simply behaved in a stupid and ignorant fashion. Moreover, Vonlee would not be denying her involvement in what Billie Jean was doing. But once she realized her aunt actually wanted to hurt Don, Vonlee backed off and told her to stop. Only she then walked away—her mistake—and unknowingly left Billie Jean to finish the job.

"You're going to learn that Billie Rogers was married [several] times. That she had liver cancer. That she knew Vonlee Harry Titlow, who is actually now Vonlee Nicole Titlow—that she's a freak. That she's a drunk. That she's a person easily manipulated. She attempted to use her to do what she wanted to have done, and that was what she had to accomplish herself, the death of Don Rogers, so that she could collect the money."

Blame Billie Jean Rogers.

Could it possibly work?

CHAPTER 80

AS FOR THE STATE'S witnesses on day one, for the most part APA Skrzynski kept to the same script he had during Billie Jean's trial: The first responders came in and set the scene. Then Danny Chahine took to the stand to speak his truth. There were no surprises here. The direct testimony mimicked what they had said the previous year during Billie Jean's case. The APA walked each witness through his or her story, step-by-step, this time piling the culpability for the death of Don Rogers on Vonlee's shoulders, instead of her aunt's.

After a day off on Thursday, March 14, 2002, Bill Cataldo went to work on Danny Chahine. By far, Danny was the state's most incriminating witness against Vonlee. He held the cards deciding her fate. Cataldo knew this. Vonlee knew this. The APA knew this. Danny? Maybe not so much.

Cataldo kept on point with what was a familiar narrative: Danny's business, criminal history, problems with citizenship and lying to INS, his accent and English being a second language, the "pornographic tapes" Billie Jean had given him, and Billie Jean and Don's relationship. One important factor Cataldo was able to bring out during his cross-examination was that by Danny bringing forward the information he had about Vonlee, and then participating with police in recording her, would it ultimately "look good" for him in the eyes of the government when they checked to see if he was a "good citizen" before deciding whether to give him permanent citizen status?

Danny did not agree with this idea.

Cataldo moved on.

Later, Cataldo explained that part of what he wanted to accomplish with Danny involved "embarrassing him" on the stand. With his client, Vonlee, in the predicament she faced—an uphill battle, and Danny the one stopping her at the top of that hill—it was one of the only approaches the defense attorney could take, really, in order to try and cast as bad a light as possible on the state's most powerful witness.

This began when Cataldo asked Danny about a hotel room the TPD had bought and paid for on the night Danny recorded Vonlee. Vonlee's lawyer wanted to know if Danny had asked for the room because of "safety concerns," as he had once said during a preliminary hearing.

After argument and an objection, Danny answered: "Yes."

Further along, Cataldo was able to bring out the fact that the TPD had offered the room at the casino because Danny might be "emotionally exhausted" after recording his girlfriend with a wire. But through his expert way of questioning, the lawyer pushed forward the contention that Danny had bartered for the hotel room as a potential payment for what he had done—a trade that neither Danny nor the TPD had ever admitted or would agree to.

Then it was on to the sex Danny had with Vonlee. This

was an area where Cataldo could show, perhaps by the most intimate of examples, how naïve and ignorant Danny Chahine was at the time—not to mention how easily fooled he was by Vonlee's lies.

"The first time there was intimate contact, it was a matter of her giving you oral sex?" Cataldo asked, gradually leading into the raw, truly embarrassing material.

"Yes, sir."

"At that time she was *not* naked?"

"Top," Danny said, confusing just about everyone in the courtroom.

So Cataldo clarified, "She was top*less*? So you could see her breasts, but you *didn't* see her vaginal area or the groin area?"

"No, sir."

"And this was at your apartment?"

"My house," Danny answered.

"And then there came a time when you engaged in greater physical, intimate contact with her?"

"Yes, sir."

"And . . . this time it included an insertion . . ." Cataldo asked, looking up from his notes, waiting for Danny to answer.

Quite a way to put it: *"an insertion."*

"Yes, sir."

Cataldo finished: ". . . of your penis into what you *thought* was her vagina?"

"Yes, sir."

"And this was done in some sort of Greek style—doggie style—from behind?"

"Yes, sir."

"This was done at your house?"

"Yes, sir."

"And you're indicating that you *didn't* know the difference between a vagina and an anus at that time?"

"I didn't indicate that."

"Did you believe you were having *vaginal* sex or *anal* sex?"

"I thought I was having vaginal sex."

"Okay. And so at that time, you *didn't* know the difference?"

"When we're engaged in sex, no, I didn't know."

"I would assume for her to participate in this act she had to be naked?" the lawyer wanted to clarify.

"Yes, sir."

"And so she was naked. You were naked." He paused here, which brought a great deal of attention to his anticipated next statement: "And you *still* didn't notice a penis?"

"No, sir."

"You didn't notice an erection?"

"No, sir."

"You did no reaching around or touching down there yourself?"

"No, sir."

"While you were having intercourse with her?"

"No, sir."

"And that would have happened on a couple of occasions, correct?"

"Yes."

"Now, I understand from your direct testimony that [Vonlee] had made some statements to you . . . that there was some sort of medical condition that made her embarrassed to show her vagina?"

"Yes, sir."

"But she had, or was at least on these two occasions without pants—without underwear—in front of you?"

"Yes, sir."

Feeling confident in pointing out the most embarrassing moments of Danny's life by showing how Danny had been misled by Vonlee on more than one occasion, the defense attorney moved on. He asked about the jewelry Danny had given his girlfriend.

Still, had the damage to Danny's credibility as a witness, if the jury chose to see it that way, been accomplished?

If there was one point Danny made that helped the state, it was when he testified that he had never seen Vonlee wasted. This was important for the state's contention that Vonlee knew exactly what she was doing when she did it. If her boyfriend had never seen her "tipsy," as Cataldo put it, how could the jury believe she was drunk on the night Don died? Or drunk when she tattled to Danny about what she and Billie Jean had done?

For the next hour, Danny and Cataldo split hairs on common, well-worn subjects and facts related to the case. The one new piece of information that came out was that Danny had said during one pretrial hearing that he thought Vonlee had told him she held Don down while her aunt smothered him with a pillow. This was not an image Cataldo wanted the jury to have. Thus, he was able to get Danny to retract that statement by now claiming he had said so much over the course of the case that he couldn't possibly recall everything.

But a bell had been rung, nonetheless.

Cataldo pressed Danny on the subject of the money Billie Jean had promised to pay Vonlee for her help, focusing on what Danny had actually heard Vonlee say. And maybe he pressed Danny too hard here, because no defense attorney wanted the answer Danny subsequently gave.

"So," Cataldo asked, "what you're saying is while Billie's got the pillow, she's negotiating with [Vonlee]? If you want the money, I'll make it higher, and if you want the fifty [thousand], you're going to have to do more?"

"Well, it's probably hard to believe, but they were negotiating while they were killing the man," Danny said.

The APA cracked a slight smile out of the corner of his mouth, noting to himself, possibly, that the image Danny Chahine had just provided the court consisted of a passed-out husband on the floor, unable to defend himself, while the two moneygrubbing women in his life were trying to decide the best way to kill him and split his money.

CHAPTER 81

VONLEE WAS GROWING IMPATIENT while waiting to hear her fate. On second thought, maybe "scared" was more accurate. She sat in court, watching, listening, wondering, unable to stop herself from holding on to a slight glimmer of hope that one juror would see she had made a terrible mistake in not stopping her aunt from hurting her uncle, which was her fear at the time, and also not turning Billie Jean in when she had the chance. Vonlee was willing to pay for her mistakes with years behind bars. She had no trouble taking responsibility. She wanted to stand up and shout this to the jury.

But decades in a male prison? No. That wouldn't be fair.

Vonlee could not fathom the possibility of twenty years or more in state prison, especially considering her transgender situation.

"What I had learned by then," Vonlee said later, "was that the abuse from guards was going to be far worse than what I feared by my fellow inmates. And I had seen some of that abuse firsthand by then already."

There can be nothing worse—except death, perhaps—

than living in fear, especially when your oppressor is your keeper.

Don Tullock, Dr. Dragovic and two more witnesses sat in the witness chair next for the state and went over the same testimony they had during Billie Jean's trial. Only, here it meant a hell of a lot more because of the tape recording and transcript from that conversation Vonlee had with Danny, which seemed to back up what these witnesses were saying.

Friday, March 15, 2002, consisted of much the same, with Don Zimmerman and other familiar players casting a wider guilty net upon Vonlee, who began to believe that her only chance at this stage was to get up there and tell her own story.

"What do you think?" Cataldo asked Vonlee during a break that afternoon. For the attorney, there was no hesitation, no question, no doubt, what his client needed to do.

"Looks like I might have to," Vonlee said.

"I think so."

By the end of that day, the state had rested its case and Bill Cataldo called his first witness, the ME office's investigator. Cataldo wanted to point out through the investigator that this professional really did not see much out of the norm. The Rogers house was not even determined to be a crime scene until much later, when the investigator was asked about his Polaroid photographs by the TPD and the medical examiner. Cataldo was trying to make it clear that the ME office's investigation, as well as the TPD's, was flawed from the get-go. There was nothing here that indicated a homicide until sometime later, when Danny came forward and the TPD decided it was going to dig into Billie Jean's life and look at it all differently.

The midmorning session proved to be interesting when Cataldo brought in his own medical examiner to claim, for the most part, exactly what Dr. Baden had testified to during Billie Jean Rogers's trial. There was no murder, so how could there be murder charges?

And then, at 11:49 A.M., Bill Cataldo looked at his client. "You ready?"

Vonlee nodded.

Settled into the witness chair after taking the oath, Vonlee looked nervous and on edge. Cataldo told his client to "take a deep breath."

In and out.

Breathe.

Vonlee explained that she was eighteen when she changed her name to Vonlee Nicole Titlow from Harry Vonlee Titlow.

"Are you a female?" Cataldo asked.

"No."

"You are a . . . ?"

"I'm a transsexual."

Vonlee was having trouble breathing. A panic attack was slowly creeping up on her, because Cataldo repeatedly told her to "breathe deeply . . . relax a little bit."

After Vonlee took a sip of water, a few deep breaths and found her bearings, she and Cataldo talked about where she was born, when she realized she was a "female," school, her time in Nashville, Denver, Chicago, her employment, the escort business, exotic dancing, meeting Danny at the casino, gambling, drinking, as well as her days leading up to living with Billie Jean and Don. They stayed on the topic of Vonlee's escort service for quite some time. Vonlee was unafraid to be open and honest about how much money she made and how long she had been in business. She testified that moving to the Troy/Detroit area put a welcomed damper on it all.

When they arrived at the topic of Billie Jean, Vonlee had a look of melancholy about her that she had not shown throughout the trial thus far. She cared for her aunt; there could be no argument there. It was clear to those who knew Billie Jean was in the throes of cancer and was facing her last days. Vonlee felt this. While growing up in Tennessee, and even after she moved to Nashville and Denver, Vonlee had not heard much from her aunt. It wasn't until they connected at the Waffle House, and Billie Jean convinced Vonlee to follow her to North Carolina and then to Michigan, that their relationship began in earnest. From there, they were inseparable. Aunt Billie Jean needed a friend, Vonlee said, and she provided that companionship.

Vonlee talked about how her aunt would "give" her money to gamble. Vonlee didn't have much. Her aunt wanted Vonlee by her side at the casino, so she'd provide Vonlee with funds to have a good time.

"I would have to beg her to leave the casino," Vonlee said.

Cataldo asked Vonlee about something she said on the recording to Danny regarding Billie Jean being sick. He wanted to know how sick her aunt actually was.

"She had a liver problem from years of drinking," Vonlee testified.

Cataldo asked Vonlee about how "sexually aggressive" Don was toward her when Billie Jean wasn't around. Through this line of questioning, Vonlee talked about how much Don drank on a regular basis, claiming that he was wasted all the time and passed out often, and kept his vodka in the freezer—a place where cops and the ME's investigator never checked, Cataldo had gotten this on the record.

Vonlee next spoke of how Billie Jean witnessed Don grabbing her breasts one night and her aunt snapped, screaming at him that she now "had something on him" if he ever tried to divorce her.

According to Billie Jean, Vonlee explained, "she had the perfect marriage—that he didn't mind how much money she spent or how much time she spent away from home" at the casino.

Vonlee said Don drank about "half a gallon" of vodka every day.

Cataldo then got into some of what Danny had testified to and asked Vonlee to explain, beginning with, "So they did fight over her gambling?"

"Yes, they did."

"Were you involved in the argument?"

"No. I called Danny to come and get me."

"Why did you do that?"

"Because I . . . just didn't want to be around it."

"Danny testified that you told him that during the time [Don] was allegedly being smothered, that he was playing with your breasts?"

"That is not—" Vonlee started to say.

"Did Don touch your breasts that evening?"

Finishing, Vonlee added, ". . . That is not true. No, he did not."

"Did you say to Danny Chahine . . . 'At least [Don] died happy'?"

"No, I did not."

"Did you tell Danny Chahine that [Don] had touched your breasts?"

"I told him . . . about the incident [of Don] getting in bed with me. . . ." Vonlee later explained that Danny must have mixed up the two occasions: when Billie Jean and Vonlee were with Don in the kitchen, and that night when Billie Jean was away and Don came on to her. Danny had taken one story and merged with the other and told the cops that Don was trying to touch her breasts while they were trying to pour vodka down his throat. This seemed to be backed up by the simple fact that both Billie Jean and Vonlee, separately, had said Don was completely passed out during that time in the kitchen, and the toxicology results would indicate as much.

There was another discrepancy in Danny's testimony.

"Did you ever tell Danny Chahine that you were a transsexual?"

"Yes, I did."

"When did you tell him that?"

"I told him the first week I met him."

Danny would sometimes pay for Vonlee's gambling, she said. He was very aggressive when they first met, she told jurors. Within a week of knowing him, he had taken her back to his home, broke out a bottle of expensive wine, and then put his hand on her knee while they sat on the couch. He began massaging her thigh, indicating he wanted to do something. Vonlee said she told him no and he brought her home on that night.

Cataldo asked Vonlee to talk about the sex. He knew this was vitally important to bring up again, based entirely on what he knew Vonlee was about to say.

CHAPTER 82

BILL CATALDO UNDERSTOOD HE could take the scandalous tale of a straight man supposedly *unknowingly* having sex with a transsexual only so far without coming across as a defense attorney simply looking to embarrass a witness even further than he had been already. There was a fine line in there somewhere and the attorney had teetered on walking over it when he had cross-examined Danny Chahine. What would probing deeper into that same salacious content do for Vonlee's defense?

Vonlee deserved the opportunity to tell her side of the sexual story, Cataldo believed. Regardless of what anyone else thought, providing an opportunity for his client to do just that was the job he had signed up for.

"When you were having sex, were the lights on?" he asked.

"Yes," Vonlee answered.

"[Danny] said he didn't *see* that you were a male. He didn't *see* an erection. Were you hiding it from him?"

"No."

Cataldo mentioned how the APA had shown some rather racy photographs of Vonlee wearing skimpy lingerie. He wanted to know if she had ever dressed "that way" for Danny.

"I would wear lingerie underneath my clothing," she said.

"Lingerie that hid a penis?" the attorney queried.

"I was . . ." Vonlee started to say, but then stopped herself. Rethinking, she continued, "When we had sex, I was *completely* nude."

"Were you erect?"

"I would say semi."

"Was it obvious that you had male equipment?"

"Yeah."

A few questions later: "Did you place your penis between your legs and walk around like that so, like, he wouldn't see it?"

"No. But I just didn't . . . flaunt it, either. I mean . . . I don't hide it. I don't use it, I guess [you] could say."

"Were you *ever* drunk in front of Danny?"

"Yes."

"How often?"

"Every time I would go to the casino."

It was apparent from Vonlee's testimony that she and Danny disagreed on several different levels. Their stories were polar opposites in some places. Cataldo thought this was significant because it explained the possibility that Danny Chahine had an ax to grind and was sharpening it every time he said something about the relationship. It was plausible that he was taking various parts of a narrative Vonlee had given him and was twisting and turning each component to fit a story that painted Vonlee in a guilty light. This way, he could get back at her for deceiving him.

When they landed on August 12, 2000, Vonlee told her story of the vodka and cranberry breakfast she had at Danny's on Friday, August 11, before heading off to the Rogers household that morning, and then drinking all day with Billie Jean.

Don came home at 4:00 P.M., or thereabout, Vonlee told jurors.

She spoke of a plan the three of them had to go to the racetrack and how it had been curtailed by Don's becoming too drunk—which made Billie Jean mad. Not angry, but a "here-we-go-again" annoyed.

Then she spoke of how they all ate dinner together and . . .

Don was sitting at the kitchen table after dinner and drinking himself into oblivion, which was something, Vonlee explained, he often did.

Don passed out and Vonlee heard "a chair flip over" and a loud thud (*"plop"*) as Don hit the floor.

Vonlee pointed it out to her aunt, who didn't seem to care much.

"He wouldn't respond," Vonlee said after describing how she walked into the kitchen to check up on Don. "I was pretty inebriated."

Billie Jean then said she'd get him up and put him to bed; this was after Vonlee had tried and failed to wake Don by herself.

Vonlee told how Don's legs were "crossed," just like they were in the Polaroid photos.

She talked about checking to see how Don was doing and believed he was totally out of it, unconscious from too much booze. However, she had no idea if he was breathing at that moment. She assumed he was because she felt over his mouth and breath was coming out later on.

"What happened when Billie came into the kitchen?" Cataldo asked.

"She told me to hold his mouth and hold his nose and that would wake him up. And I told her no, that I was *not* going to do that. I was not going to do that because I was afraid I would hurt him."

"What did she do *after* you told her?"

"After that, she said, 'Well, you hold his mouth and I'll hold his nose.' And I did. . . . My judgment was very poor and I shouldn't have, but I put my hand over his mouth . . . [while] keeping my fingers apart. . . . He was breathing. And I kept letting go. . . . I told her, 'I'm not doing that. I can't do it. I just *can't* do that.'"

"Did you ever put your hand over his mouth so it was clasped?" the attorney asked, making sure the jury knew that Vonlee had never cut off his airway completely.

"Never. I never held his mouth to where he couldn't breathe. I would *never* hurt anybody. *Ever.*"

From this "fact" forward, Vonlee placed the entire onus of what happened next upon her aunt, telling jurors that Billie Jean poured the booze down her husband's throat and up his nose and "it came out and went on the floor." Vonlee admitted she had "poured just a little" bit of the alcohol into Don's mouth, but then she stopped when she realized it was wrong.

They argued a bit, Vonlee said. She told her aunt to leave Don alone before she hurt him. Her aunt, she claimed, got mad and yelled at her.

Vonlee then took the bottle of vodka Billie Jean had been using and poured herself a glass of straight booze. As Vonlee did that, her aunt "walked away from him. . . ."

Not once during this period of time did Vonlee ever think that Billie Jean was trying to kill her husband. She thought her aunt was messing with Don.

"Playing with him."

Then Vonlee said she walked into the bathroom to freshen up and finish her drink. It was about 9:00 or 9:30 P.M., she thought.

She spent "five minutes" in the bathroom, teasing her hair, "peeing" and applying some lipstick. She thought they were still going out to the casino—only now without Don. She believed Billie Jean would, at some point, get

Don up to his room, or Don would wake up himself after sleeping off part of his bender and then make his way up there himself.

Cataldo asked Vonlee to describe for the jury what happened next.

"I came out of the bathroom . . . and I seen her squatted down. . . . I was going to go upstairs, because I thought that's where she would be. . . . And when I seen her, I walked over toward her and I said, 'What are you doing?' I saw she had a pillow on his face. . . ."

The rest of Vonlee's narrative was, basically, mechanics, various pieces of the puzzle: Which way was Billie Jean facing, and which way was Vonlee standing? Was Billie Jean on her knees or not on her knees? Vonlee said as soon as she realized what was happening, she asked Billie Jean "what the fuck" she was doing as she realized her aunt was smothering Don.

Cataldo wanted to know if at any time prior to that moment, had Vonlee ever asked Billie Jean for money to get a sex change operation?

"No."

As for Danny testifying that Vonlee said she "helped pin [Don] down" on the floor while Billie Jean smothered him, Vonlee said that statement was nonsense.

"Don Rogers was passed out! I mean, he was . . . No one was holding him down. He was passed out. He was . . . *unconscious.*"

They spent another hour or more discussing what happened next, and how Danny Chahine had gotten the story all mixed up, and how Vonlee felt guilty to this day for not stopping Billie Jean. It was the reason why she had told Danny what happened; she had felt responsible in some way. None of it was planned. None of it was thought out beforehand and talked about. (At least not by herself, Vonlee said.) None of it seemed real at the time it was happening. And none of it was done with any nefarious nature on her part.

Vonlee said she got sucked into it and lied for Billie Jean because it was easier and less humiliating. After she lied, she started drinking more and more. The guilt was weighing on her soul, and the secrets she held were bubbling up inside. She started taking Xanax and other pills to quiet the demons inside her head. The images of Billie Jean and that pillow were nightmarish and overwhelming. She knew her aunt might have killed him. But she didn't do anything about it, and that was the mistake Vonlee believed she needed to pay for.

As her attorney's direct questioning seemed to be drawing to a close, he asked Vonlee to talk about the dinner she had with Danny when she first told him what had happened. She had explained everything one night, and then Danny hooked up with the police and she told him again on a second night. Cataldo was asking about that first time she told Danny, which had not been recorded.

After she told Danny what happened with Don and Billie Jean, Danny did something she had not expected.

"I mean," Vonlee testified, "Danny . . . gave me [a] ring and he said I could keep the ring on one condition."

"If you marry me," Danny demanded. He was smiling. Vonlee claimed he had a sparkle in his eye. He was serious, Vonlee believed.

"Marry you?" Vonlee said in turn. She was puzzled.

"You've made a decision, right?" Danny asked. They had jokingly talked about marriage before this night. Vonlee had written it off as nothing more than conversation.

"No!" she said during that unrecorded dinner. "Danny, you know that I can't marry you legally."

"Why?" Danny asked. "I'm a citizen."

"Because I'm a male, Danny."

"What do you mean?"

"Well, you know that I have a penis just like you do. And I cannot legally marry you."

Danny became "very upset," Vonlee testified.

Cataldo wanted her to clarify.

"I don't know if he was upset because I wasn't going to marry him or [because] he [finally] realized I [had] a penis."

What's more, on the night Vonlee first explained to Danny what happened to Don, she "went home with him" and "we slept together." They had consensual sex. Vonlee recalled specifically walking around in his bedroom with the lights on; her penis was hanging out there, flopping around for Danny to see.

"He *had* to have seen it," Vonlee said.

Closing out her direct testimony, Vonlee told jurors Billie Jean bought her a car, yes. But she never gave her that one hundred thousand dollars her aunt had written inside her checkbook next to Vonlee's name.

Cataldo wondered if Vonlee had been given any money at all.

She said seventy thousand dollars.

Cataldo posed a powerful question that jurors would certainly be asking themselves at some point: if Vonlee hadn't done anything wrong, as far as participating in "killing" Don, why had Vonlee taken that money?

"Well, I was drinking. She gave it to me. I wanted to get away. I didn't want to go home to Tennessee. I knew they would know I was upset, and I figured it was a way I could just start a new life, and I just figured, just take it and . . . I don't know, I just *took* it." She looked down at a crumpled-up tissue in her hands. Then: "Because she *gave* it to me."

Her defense attorney asked where the lion's share of all that money had gone.

Vonlee claimed she gave most of it away, some to an

AIDS organization, some to friends; she spent a lot of it on her drinking and drugging habits, which had become worse as each day passed and she lived with what she had done to Don.

Finally, Cataldo prompted Vonlee to explain why she told Danny—which would be clear on the recording jurors would have available—that "drinking drove me to kill somebody"? That was the one quote she had to explain. It was perhaps the most unfavorable and liable comment Vonlee had said to Danny, and it was clear on the recording.

"Drinking drove me to kill somebody."

How were jurors supposed to overlook what seemed to be such a bold admission—a confession?

Vonlee thought about that comment. It was true. She had said it. "I felt that [God] was, you know, showing me that it was my fault. If I had stopped drinking . . . If I hadn't have been drinking that night, I could have stopped her. I could have known that she was serious. I was just blaming myself. I felt like it was *my* fault. If [only] I hadn't been drinking—because I had made a promise to God that I *would* stop."

CHAPTER 83

VONLEE HAD ADMITTED TO taking part in a murder and also covering it up. Whether she was feeling guilty about it, sick over it, had drunk herself into denial and forgetfulness, it was all beside the point. For the APA, this was all about the law.

Skrzynski wasted little time getting into what he thought was the most important aspect of his cross. His first question: "Miss Titlow, you have male genitalia, right?"

"Yes."

From there, the APA brought in the escort business Vonlee had owned and operated, asking a series of questions regarding "soliciting men for sex."

"You never solicited undercover police officers?" the APA asked.

"No, I did not."

"And you were never arrested by the police for that?"

"Yes, I was."

"You never solicited an undercover police officer to give him sex?"

"No, I did not."

"But you were arrested?"

"Yes, I was."

This was a contradiction in facts. When such exchanges were left unexplained, just floating out there, the jury would assume the worst. A good trial attorney, Skrzynski, being at the top of his game here, knew that assumption and speculative questioning could be as powerful as an admission. He moved on from that line of questioning and focused on the idea of Vonlee "posing for pictures."

She denied that they were dirty pictures for public consumption—the photos were for her personal use only.

The postulation here by the state was that Vonlee had "made erotic pictures and sold them over the Internet."

She disagreed with the state on this point.

Skrzynski speculated how hard it was to believe that Vonlee made upward of twenty-five thousand dollars a month as an escort service owner/operator, and she and her girls had *not* slept with any of the guys.

She wouldn't budge on this point. (Though she later told the author they had indeed provided sex in some form for pay.)

The APA moved on to an idea that was central to any motivation Vonlee might have had for killing Don.

"At the time that this happens in August of 2000, you're not interested in the sex change operation, are you?"

"It wasn't on my mind, no."

"And that certainly was not a motive that you might have had to kill someone, was it?"

"No, it was not."

"All right. So that idea of a sex change operation was a media invention you said?"

"Yes, it was."

Bill Cataldo listened carefully and found no opening in which to interject and slow the pace down. With every question Skrzynski posed, Vonlee came across worse; the hole was getting deeper. Vonlee seemed to be a money-hungry transsexual, an escort service madam, a drunk, wild chick, who lived life in the fast lane, willing to go along with her aunt because she would ultimately benefit financially from the death. Skrzynski took a good hour questioning Vonlee on everything from how slippery the floor in the kitchen was to how she screamed at Zimmerman and Tullock, to those first responders arriving at the scene, to how Billie Jean had maybe once said to her niece that she should hire a "friend" for twenty-five thousand dollars to kill Don (a suggestion that Vonlee thought was nothing more than her aunt talking about the cost of a new floor).

After all of that, the APA put into question the "fact," according to Vonlee, that she had told Danny on the first day she met him she was a transsexual. The state wasn't buying it.

Then it was on to the ring Danny had given her and how she couldn't accept it because she "had a penis."

Skrzynski wanted to know if she had ever told Zimmerman and Tullock that "there were ways of hiding it (her penis) so that no one will ever know."

Vonlee denied ever saying such a thing.

The APA kept pressing. One question after the next. Hardballs, all of them, from the subject of her penis to how many drinks she had on the day Don died. Vonlee withstood the barrage fairly well and came across as sincere and, perhaps, a bit naïve.

It was perfectly clear from the APA's point of view that the state did not believe much of what Vonlee was saying. Her story didn't have holes—it had craters! She might have been more involved in the entire murder than she was trying to sell to jurors.

On and on, this went, well into the afternoon. Vonlee was asked about certain parts of her story, backward and forward. One would guess the APA was trying to trip her up. Skrzynski said a lot of "Now, wait a minute . . ." and "Is that right?" These phrases gave jurors the impression he did not believe her side.

Not once during this blistering cross-examination, though, did Vonlee lose it, or come across as if she was flat-out lying. She tried to answer every question as best she could, even those she knew would hurt her.

Vonlee said a number of times, "I had no idea she was trying to hurt him," as they discussed the actual moment when Don was passed out and Billie Jean and Vonlee were down on their knees, messing around with him.

In the end, Vonlee stuck to her story that she believed, at first, it "was all a joke" and that Billie Jean had done this before. But when she came out of that bathroom and saw her aunt with the pillow, she realized Billie Jean had a plan to kill Don and she was initiating it. And Vonlee's crime, or involvement, began right there, in that moment, when she helped her aunt toss the pillow and empty bottle of booze, went to the casino, came home, and called 911 and told the cops a story.

As they sparred back and forth about the details of that night, Skrzynski brought out one major contention through his brilliant cross-examination: Why hadn't Vonlee told Danny she went into the bathroom and came out and saw Billie Jean with the pillow? Skrzynski referred to the omission as a "big detail" to have left out of her recorded conversation with Danny—one that she was perhaps tacking on now to cover for herself.

"I really didn't want to discuss it with him," Vonlee said.

Skrzynski's allegation was a well-placed one. If jurors thought Vonlee had added this "detail" later, she was guilty.

The money came up again as Skrzynski wound down. The APA insinuated that Vonlee took the money because she earned it by keeping her mouth shut about the crime they had committed *together*.

Vonlee disagreed.

Skrzynski detoured back into Danny and when he realized Vonlee was a man. He was having a hard time accepting that Vonlee had told Danny when she first met him.

"So"—the APA asked, pacing a bit back and forth in front of Vonlee—"as of the time of Don's death . . . you're telling the jury that Danny already knew that you were a man?"

"If he didn't know, I don't know how he didn't. But he seemed very surprised when I relayed to him that I had a penis. I mean, there is a possibility he may not have known. I don't know."

Skrzynski saw one final opening: "There is?" he asked, surprised by Vonlee's answer. "So then he's telling us the truth when he says he doesn't know then, right?"

"If he doesn't know, I don't understand how in the world he *couldn't* know."

"I mean. Isn't the whole idea of you getting dressed up as a woman . . . to convince people that you are, in fact, a woman? Isn't that what's the whole idea of this?"

"No, it is not," Vonlee said. She felt insulted by the statement. (Skrzynski obviously had no clue what it was like to live inside the body of a man as a woman, and Vonlee considered the APA was being insensitive.)

"That's not why you have hormone shots so you can have breasts? That's not why you do that?"

"No! It's not."

"That's not why you dress in low-cut gowns and miniskirts? You don't want people to believe that you're a woman? That's *not* why you do that?"

"That's not the only reason."

Skrzynski kept at it, tossing salt.

Finally, Vonlee said, "I do that for myself. Because that's the way I feel."

"And your goal is to make people *feel* that you're a woman, too, right?" Skrzynski said, not letting up.

"My goal is for me to be comfortable, and I'm comfortable in dresses and heels and makeup and my hair done. That's . . . the way I *choose* to live. I mean, it's not to fool anybody. . . . I've always felt that way."

Skrzynski went through a series of questions centered on how dressing up as a woman was meant to "deceive people," and that's what Vonlee was good at—deception.

Vonlee said no, no, no. The APA had it all wrong.

"People think that I am a female," she said defiantly.

Skrzynski stopped. "Thank you," he said.

CHAPTER 84

ON TUESDAY, MARCH 19, John Skrzynski and Bill Cataldo offered closing arguments. There was nothing new here—or, rather, nothing that hadn't already been said ten times backward and forward. Each side argued calmly and with merit for his case. Vonlee was facing a mountain of evidence. Many courtroom watchers believed it would be an easy win for the state. Yet, as Billie Jean Rogers's trial had proven, surprises did happen within the confines of a high-profile murder trial.

As Vonlee sat and listened, she harkened back to a day when Billie Jean was "Aunt Billie," the fun aunt, the aunt every kid screams for when she comes through the door at Christmas, the aunt every parent worries about.

But here was Vonlee facing a murder charge at the hand of that same beloved, adored person. How life could throw daggers, with one seemingly always landing in the center of the heart.

As the trial drew toward an ending, her hero-worship sentiments held a nostalgic bitterness and sadness for Vonlee. As she sat and listened to Judge Potts give the jury instructions after each side concluded its closing,

Vonlee had mixed feelings about her aunt. She wanted to hate her, but she couldn't. Still, had this all been some sort of a dream? Had Vonlee fallen into a black hole? She recalled this period when the judge was instructing jurors as being a moment when she felt as though she was living someone else's life. It was that seven to fifteen years—there it was buzzing in Vonlee's head as the day's proceedings closed out.

Seven to fifteen.

It sounded so doable.

So fair.

On the following morning, March 20, the jury sent a note to Judge Potts. Within that note, it was obvious that each juror had taken his and her responsibility seriously. The jury wanted "pictures" of the "crime scene, forensics of the body, transcripts of the tape" that Danny Chahine had made. They also wanted a transcription of Vonlee's testimony.

Then a rather telling question—one that made Bill Cataldo smile: "Does someone's inaction, nonaction, to stop or prevent a crime resulting in death amount to fulfillment of condition three, second-degree murder, knowingly creating a high risk of death, knowing that death would be the likely result of his actions?"

The judge explained that she had provided the jury with everything each needed within her instructions, concluding: "It is up to you to decide an answer."

Later that same day, Judge Potts indicated she was bringing in the jury because "they have reached a verdict."

After everyone got settled and the foreperson stood, Judge Potts asked Vonlee to do the same.

With a worried gaze flushed over her, a look of utter instability, as though about to collapse, Vonlee stood. The wait was over. The jury was about to deliver her fate.

"We find the defendant guilty of the lesser offense of second-degree murder."

Bill Cataldo had pulled it off. "He had a full recorded confession," Cataldo said of the APA, "and I *still* beat him."

Judge Potts put off the sentencing until April. She wanted to take a look at everything, sit back, think it through, and then do the right thing.

Cataldo believed all along that Vonlee had been "used by Billie Jean." He considered the notion that the jury understood Vonlee had stopped. "She didn't commit the ultimate act. She was consistent." Her story never wavered. "Remember, she volunteered that statement to Danny Chahine. It wasn't coerced. It wasn't an interview in where the police are using leading questions to get information out of her. And she *passed* a polygraph."

Every one of those points, the defense attorney added, led the jury to believe that first-degree murder was not the right choice.

This alone was cause for a celebration.

CHAPTER 85

A "CRUSHING BLOW" WAS how Vonlee described hearing "guilty," regardless of the lesser count. She wanted a verdict of not guilty, obviously. Or maybe a manslaughter conviction with time served. But that wasn't to be. Harry Vonlee "Nicole" Titlow was now a convicted murderer. And always would be.

"I feel that I was found guilty of murder for not stopping Billie Jean," Vonlee said later. Vonlee especially did not appreciate the way Judge Potts answered the jury's question. She believed the jury was headed toward manslaughter and would have voted for the lesser offense, had their question been answered properly by the judge.

"Everything changed at that point," Vonlee said, talking about the moment they asked the second-degree murder question and Judge Potts told them to decide among themselves what the answer should be.

There was something inside Vonlee that kept telling her maybe Judge Potts would go easy on her. Perhaps she'd see that Vonlee was not a murderer, in fact, but rather someone who had taken responsibility for her small part in a larger crime committed by someone else.

Thank God I didn't get first-degree, Vonlee gratefully

thought as she went back to her cell and had a moment to take in what the course of her life had just delivered to her. She was ecstatic that it was simply over. Nothing was worse, she admitted, than all the waiting and wondering.

As the days passed and she focused on the upcoming sentencing, another feeling arose. Vonlee was obviously going through what was a series of emotions after a decision had changed her life.

"None of this was fair," Vonlee now believed. "My aunt did this and I am the one paying for what *she* did? I did not kill anybody. I did not kill *anybody*. Billie Jean did."

Falling back on her Christian roots, Vonlee started attending church services inside the jail. Her faith had played a large role in her journey and where she ended up, Vonlee believed. There were times, she claimed, when she'd lie on the bed in her cell and "speak in tongues" and not know how in the world she was doing it. She'd never spoken in tongues before. It was something that just started one night after church services and she went with it.

On her knees, praying, Vonlee became terrified by the notion that she had "let God down." She had broken prayer promises to God and was now paying for that deceit.

Seven to fifteen was what I should have taken, Lord, I know, she prayed one night. *I realize now it was a blessing that I had been given.* Vonlee could see that God had given her a chance and she squandered it. A divine gift had been handed to her and she had rejected it.

"I felt that the Devil had sent Mr. Toca in as one of His minions," Vonlee said later. "I mean, I'm not a religious fanatic or anything, but he . . . he was the Devil. He came to me with an evil intent. And the entire motive for me to follow him was money, fame and fortune. It was something both of us were motivated by."

As April came to pass, Vonlee was called back into court to receive Judge Potts's sentence. By now, she had left revenge in the wake of her emotional roller coaster and came around the curve of acceptance. Vonlee's focus after sentencing, however, was going to be getting Frederick Toca disbarred for what she believed he had done to her. Beyond all the appeals that would be filed, Vonlee was on the hunt for an appellate lawyer that could take a look at what Toca had done. Vonlee spoke to Bill Cataldo and others about her plan; there wasn't a lawyer in town she could find who actually disagreed with her on this matter.

CHAPTER 86

AFTER THE LAWYERS FINISHED haggling over an issue concerning sentencing guidelines, on that crisp Michigan day of final judgment, April 17, 2002, Honorable Wendy Potts indicated she was ready to proceed.

The APA offered Fiona Baldwin (pseudonym), Don's other daughter, on behalf of the family to stand up and say a few things for the victim. After all, despite his character defects, his supposed bad habits and the gulf between Billie Jean and her husband, Donald Rogers was a victim of murder. He deserved to be heard. In all of the sensationalistic grandeur associated with Vonlee's trial, perhaps like most murder victims, Don had been cast aside like just one more sidebar conversation. It was his time now to be heard through someone who loved him.

Fiona walked up and stood before Judge Potts, Vonlee to her right. She said her name, adding, "Don was my dad."

To most, Don was a business owner, maybe even a drunk, a man who kept to himself and had issues with his wife, seemingly since the day they had met and over the course of their two marriages. But here Fiona had put into perspective with one sentence what mattered.

"Don was my dad."

Fiona spoke of returning from a vacation back in August 2000. She and her family had gone to an amusement park, with "roller coasters and fright rides." Unknowingly, she walked through the door to face what was going to be a real-life "thrill ride" that would overtake every waking moment afterward and not ever let up.

It was the voice of her sister on her answering machine that Fiona would never forget, a message that would "change" life "for all of us," she said, her voice cracking as she spoke.

"Dad died . . . ," that message began.

The remainder was a blur of words. What else was there to say?

Dad was gone.

As she spoke to the judge, Fiona Baldwin's comments were blunt and brutally honest: "The day before the funeral, the story changed about where Nicole, the person who stands before the court today, and Billie (now her known accomplice) were when my dad died." Fiona said she "kept asking" herself the same question: "How can anyone not remember where he or she [was] at the time of a loved one's death?"

She was referring to that story Billie Jean had told at the wake—how Billie Jean had said to anyone who asked that it was 11:00 P.M. when she returned home to find Don dead, but had told the cops 3:00 A.M.

For Fiona, however, as she began to unravel the truth, in her opinion (Billie Jean was lying), the "answer soon became very clear. Nicole and Billie had killed my father. They killed him for money. Money that Billie had coerced my dad to give her in his will."

She continued, saying how Vonlee wanted the "money

for a sex change operation" and Billie Jean had promised to give it to her.

"But Billie is still without punishment of any kind."

Not Vonlee, though: "She sits before the court on her active, free willing and knowing participation in the murder of my father."

Toss the book at her was Fiona's message. This was the opportunity to make Vonlee pay for the both of them. The judge could honor Don and avenge his murder on this day, at this moment. Judge Potts held that power in her hands.

Fiona said, "Billie would be behind bars for life without parole, had [Vonlee] testified against" her, and that alone constituted additional punishment for Vonlee.

As for Fiona's life and how she'd managed, she told the court she had to "delete several painful and horrible memories, repercussions from" her mind "in order to function as a normal adult. . . ."

Fiona broke down crying before asking for a box of tissues.

The APA brought her some.

After taking a moment to collect herself, she talked about "balance" in life. She spoke of how her two "sons threw up every night before a [court] hearing" and "throw up whenever I tell them what a horrible day I had at court."

Fiona said she could "not put into words the loss" she felt. She mentioned how she'd had to call her local police department "several times, believing I was being followed or watched." She was "paranoid that Billie or one of her family is stalking" her, and how "every time I go into a store, I look around for Billie . . . or one of her family."

She was living inside a nightmare, still after all this time.

It never let up.

Potts interrupted and asked Fiona if she lived in Michigan.

"Yes," Fiona answered, outside of Troy, adding how she drove around town, "reading people's license plates . . . and always paid attention to who's behind me."

It was all so "horrible," the life she was now being forced to live. She was deathly "afraid" the kids would be kidnapped and "taken away" from her.

"I'm horrified to think of the things they did to [my father]," she told the court. "It's disgusting. It was clearly planned out. Death was their goal. They achieved it."

Fiona called Danny Chahine a "saint." Had it not been for Danny, they both would have gotten away with murder.

She next told a story about Vonlee "walking by" Fiona and her family in the courthouse corridor, handcuffed, being led by sheriffs, "apologizing" for everything that had happened. All Fiona saw there was a "good actor."

Fiona was "baffled" by the fact that Vonlee had been found guilty of second-degree murder, because she believed this case was the epitome of first-degree murder, nothing less. Vonlee's sentence should be "life without parole," Fiona said, feeling that "Nicole and Billie actively, knowingly, willing and readily, murdered my dad."

On that note, she said, her father was "very angry with them," and Fiona knew this because "he lives inside of me."

Fiona Baldwin was upset and hurt; she would never get over the death of her father. The court, at least, had the opportunity to lessen that emotional burden by making sure it punished the one murderer it could.

Harry Titlow.

The APA encouraged the judge to "adopt" the probation department's guidelines, which amounted to numbers Vonlee and Bill Cataldo did not want to hear.

With that said, the APA went off on a little tangent and reiterated the entire case again before stopping himself to make the recommendation that the department's guidelines should be followed.

Defense attorney Bill Cataldo said he agreed with one thing everybody had said: "There was a lot of gambling in this case."

Cataldo went on to talk about how Vonlee had made a "mistake." She hadn't accepted the deal offered by the People up front. "And my understanding is it was going to be reduced to manslaughter with a ten-year sentence. Mr. Lustig, a very fine lawyer, was able to work the prosecutor, renegotiate down to seven years, seven to fifteen. Then Ms. Titlow received some advice and made a decision that was different."

He said he hoped Vonlee would not be made the "scapegoat in the whole case."

She passed a polygraph, Cataldo reminded the court.

She did "nothing whatsoever to participate" in the actual murder.

She should "receive some penance for what she did."

Cataldo said the PO was "blinded by their policy" of not giving anyone a "break."

When Bill Cataldo finished, Judge Potts asked Vonlee if she would like to speak on her own behalf. Vonlee and Cataldo had talked about this. They decided Vonlee needed to man up (pun intended, perhaps). She had to take responsibility, and admit her faults and failures, before asking for the court's forgiveness and leniency.

"I'd like to express how very sorry I am for my part in Donald's death and express to his children . . . I am sorry that they had to suffer through all of this . . . ," Vonlee began.

She continued by stating how "sorry" she was "that my

aunt Billie was not made to answer for her actions that resulted in Donald's death. I honestly don't know how she can live with herself to this day. I can only pray that you can see she took advantage of me, because of who I am, and used my alcoholism to try to get me to help her murder Don."

From there, Vonlee expressed gratitude for those who had helped her along the way: the lawyers, the court and everyone else that had steered her in the right direction.

In the end, she extended once again her sorrow for Don's loss, admitting that "it should have never happened."

Judge Potts said she wanted "to be very clear" that Vonlee's plea agreement and her withdrawal of it had "absolutely nothing to do with . . . today."

This announcement gave Cataldo and Vonlee a moment of pause to reflect; they both felt the proverbial "uh-oh," simply based on the tone the judge used. Potts was passionate and serious.

"Another thing I'm doing," Potts added, "I am *not* making you a scapegoat."

Attorney and client looked at each other.

Potts said she was "taking the case on its own."

With all due respect, Potts then went on a bit of a rant: "The report says . . . you have no prior felony record. . . . You started using alcohol at an early age. . . . It's well-known that you are undergoing a sex change, were not comfortable with the sex that you were born with and wanted to make a change. Obviously, you have an identity problem, a drinking problem, and you come to the court and I am sympathetic to your issues. . . ."

Because the jury decided that Vonlee was guilty of the "second most serious offense," the judge was imposing a sentence that reflected that verdict, she explained.

Potts was "clear" the crime had been committed "for greed . . . and the actions after death did not show remorse from any of the people participating. . . ." It was the cars and jewelry and gambling and "going out to dinners" that spoke of a certain coldness to the judge. Those luxuries showed a tremendous lack of care for the deceased. It seemed Don was dead and nobody gave a damn—with the exception of his daughters and family members and friends and business colleagues.

After a few more words regarding court matters, Judge Potts cleared her throat and gave Vonlee Nicole Titlow "twenty to forty years" in prison, with credit for 462 days she had already served. If the verdict had been a crushing blow, this sentence was the drop of a guillotine on that hopeful head, lapping it clean off.

The sentence took Vonlee's breath away. She was devastated. The low end was thirteen more years than she had been offered initially; the high end twenty-five more than she would have ever served.

Twenty to forty.

And that was it. Court ended. Vonlee was handcuffed and taken away as she sobbed quietly and felt a twisting in her stomach.

Twenty to forty.

She thought it, again and again.

Vonlee was closing in on thirty-five years—which meant the possibility of parole in twenty, putting Vonlee at fifty-five years old, which felt like a lifetime.

CHAPTER 87

JUSTICE CAN SOMETIMES BE a slow-going, agitating movement of civic gears, like perhaps a waterwheel keeping time by the running of a whispering mountain stream that sometimes runs dry, cramming up the components. *[Justice is the] first virtue of societal institutions, as truth is of systems of thought,* John Rawls wrote in his sprawling book, his magnum opus, *A Theory of Justice.* *[J]ustice denies that the loss of freedom for some,* Rawls goes on to say in an enlightening manner, *is made right by a greater good shared by others.*

It is a critical statement and yet quite factual within the crux of the role justice plays in society: human nature at its absolute narcissistic core. We judge, therefore, not to be judged, but to continue feeling good about ourselves.

[A]nalogously, an injustice is tolerable only when it is necessary to avoid an even greater injustice, Rawls concludes.

To obtain true impartiality within the boundaries of a court of law, without the critical biases of witnesses and the seemingly uncritical bias surrounding the burden of proof, can take years. And for some, well, the truth never comes to light. For the inmate who believes he or she has been wrongly convicted—or, in the case of Vonlee Titlow, sentenced—those years can become an eternity. The soul can be torn apart by the time Lady Justice arrives with her scales in check. Thus, for Vonlee, the scorecard read, *Justice: 1, Vonlee: 0.*

Still, there was no way Vonlee Titlow was going to take the twenty-to-forty sentence lying down—or, rather, sitting back in her steel bunk on a smelly inch-thick mattress chalking off the days and months and years with stick figures on a concrete wall. This sort of tossing in the white towel wasn't Vonlee's style. Perhaps it once was—whereby she would rather walk away from adversity than face it. Sure, Vonlee might have made her own bed, but she believed that the involvement of Frederick Toca had disrupted her destiny and she could not allow that to end by her bearing the brunt of it all.

Billie Jean Rogers was free; Vonlee sat in prison.

"Unfair," Vonlee kept telling anyone who would listen.

In May 2002, nearly a month after Vonlee had been sentenced, Billie Jean lost her battle with cancer and died. If there was anyone that believed Billie Jean had not suffered, or the emotional and physical demands of her case did not contribute to her years being shorter on the planet, those people had never read about the sustained torturous toll that stress takes on the body and mind, not to mention the human spirit.

When Vonlee heard about her aunt's death, she cried. She was sad and upset. Death was not part of her plan for her aunt Billie Jean. She loved Billie Jean, despite all they had been through and all she would endure in the years to come.

According to Vonlee, for some in the family back home in Tennessee, Billie Jean had an inherent "evilness" about her that only those close enough to her could see, feel and understand.

And so the seesaw of emotions and feelings for her

aunt continued: One minute, Vonlee loved the woman, said how much she adored her and that Billie Jean knew not what she did, but took what she felt was the easiest road. In the next moment, there was Billie Jean filling the role as tyrant, a seductress whose mainstay in life was money and gambling and drinking and deception.

By the end of 2002, Vonlee had made good on her promise and filed a civil suit against the man who she claimed had steered her wrong at a vulnerable stage of her case. Affidavits and depositions were being taken in *Vonlee Titlow* vs. *Frederick Toca and* [the guard who had introduced Vonlee to Toca].

They spent years battling out the malpractice suit Vonlee had brought against Toca.

The bench trial was heard in the Circuit Court for the County of Oakland, the Honorable Steven Andrews presiding. Vonlee represented herself. Toca had the law offices of Cyril C. Hall in Pontiac, Michigan, there on his behalf.

Finally, after all was said and done, years had passed and Judge Andrews, taking his time to decide on an outcome, submitted his thirteen-page decision on October 29, 2004.

Vonlee alleged malpractice, malfeasance, breach of contract and failure to uphold fiduciary responsibility in light of what Toca had done. These were hefty accusations against the lawyer. Vonlee was saying that because of Toca, she had been given a harsher sentence and effectively forced into trial. Vonlee had even alleged, Andrews wrote in his decision: *[It is]default judgment against [the guard], which the Court granted based on [the guard's] failure to appear or otherwise defend.*

Andrews outlined the entire case, making a point that Vonlee had passed a polygraph. He said Vonlee accused Toca of convincing her to "withdraw" her plea: *Plaintiff maintains that Defendant Toca said that if he did not think they . . . could win, he would not be there, and that they (his firm) did not take cases unless they thought they could win them.*

Bottom line concerning Toca, Andrews opined: *[He] denies that he advised Plaintiff to withdraw the manslaughter plea. . . .*

He said.

She said.

In the end, Andrews agreed that this was a "troubling case." However, he went on to write, *[The] Plaintiff claimed innocence and was unhappy with the 7-15 sentence for the manslaughter charge. . . . These were the factors that the Plaintiff elected to withdraw the plea and go to trial. The bottom line is that [the] Plaintiff chose to proceed this way and must accept the result of that choice.*

Judge Andrews finally concluded, *[A] judgment of No Cause Action be entered in Plaintiff's claims.*

Justice: 2.

Vonlee Titlow: 0.

Though, it still wasn't over for Vonlee Titlow.

CHAPTER 88

IT WAS ALMOST TEN years before any real action in Vonlee's case would come up again. In 2012, there was a man one afternoon scanning SCOTUSBLOG, reading stories and getting up to speed on what was happening in the nation's highest court. SCOTUS is an acronym for the Supreme Court of the United States.

The big, *big* leagues.

"Hey," the man said to a coworker, Valerie Newman, "you aware of this?" He motioned for her to come over and have a look.

Newman nestled up to the computer screen. "What?" she asked.

"Check it out."

Valerie Newman had been an attorney with the State Appellate Defender's Office (SADO) in Michigan for close to twenty years on the day she first heard about Vonlee's case when that colleague and friend pointed it out on SCOTUSBLOG. By then, Newman had argued hundreds of cases before appellate courts in Michigan, and one very high-profile case in the United States Supreme Court. As she read the post, she knew nothing about the details of Vonlee's case. What caught her attention was the legal issue at the center of it all, which was identical to an issue in a case she had argued before the U.S. Supreme Court.

"I thought that given my experience before the court on that same issue, the client, since she was unrepresented according to the court's docket sheet, might be interested in my representation," she said later.

Between her sentence in 2002 and 2012, a decade later, Vonlee had been in and out of every appeals court the state of Michigan offered. The Sixth U.S. District Court of Appeals had recently ruled that the original sentence of seven to fifteen Vonlee had plea-bargained for with Richard Lustig "should be reoffered"—or that Vonlee should be released from prison with time served.

This didn't mean Vonlee was getting out of prison anytime soon; she still had one more hurdle to jump: the United States Supreme Court. Michigan solicitor general John Bursch was not going to take the Sixth Circuit Court's new decision without a fight. He now argued that the Sixth Circuit Court's decision was "wrong" and vowed to prove it at the highest level.

As Val Newman read about Vonlee's plight, a series of compelling facts emerged. In the interim (since Vonlee's conviction and subsequent appeals), Vonlee's second attorney, Frederick Toca, had been disbarred over two separate matters, each dating back to 2005. In the first matter: *[A] panel found that Toca's conviction of one felony and three misdemeanors, all relating to forgery of license documents and driving while [his] license [was] suspended, constituted misconduct,* wrote the State of Michigan Attorney Discipline Board. The second matter was even more egregious: *[Toca had] filed false evidence with trial and appellate courts in a personal injury matter,* the board concluded. The state of Michigan had disbarred Toca on January 27, 2010, revoking his license to practice law; this occurred after he had been suspended from practicing back in 2005.

Still, while Toca was punished for his behavior as a lawyer and stripped of his ability to practice law any longer, the appeals courts in Vonlee's case apparently did not see a correlation at all between Toca's prior behaviors and Vonlee's case. One revelation did not have anything to do with the other.

While working for the largest appellate office in the state of Michigan, Newman took a keen interest in Vonlee's story. She began to do a bit of research about Vonlee on her own. She was confounded by the notion that Vonlee essentially had lost all of her appeals, except that final one in the Sixth District, which had been subsequently accepted by the Supreme Court, which grants very few petitions submitted. In the years following her conviction, Vonlee had accused Toca of this charge: *ineffective assistance of counsel for allowing him to withdraw the original guilty plea.* But both the trial court and the Michigan Court of Appeals rejected Vonlee's assertion. And when she petitioned the Michigan Supreme Court to hear her case, it flat-out refused to do anything. From there, Vonlee was determined to see it through; and so she petitioned for "federal habeas corpus relief," and it wasn't until that Sixth Circuit Court stepped in that something finally did happen in Vonlee's favor.

What struck Newman immediately was how the district court determined: *[Vonlee had] failed to meet the standard for overturning a state-court conviction under the Antiterrorism and Effective Death Penalty Act (AEDPA).* The Sixth Circuit Court then turned around: *[It] reversed the lower court's decision and ordered the state to reoffer [Vonlee's] original plea agreement.*

Vonlee's case had all the earmarks of a legal hornet's

nest someone had stuck his or her hand into long ago. It was a mess.

Although nothing had come of it, the decision by the Sixth Circuit Court seemed promising. It was a step in the right direction. And although the scorecard for Vonlee heading into this decision was 5 to 0, the Sixth Circuit Court reversing its decision—*[Vonlee's] second attorney was ineffective for failing to investigate his claims further, failing to obtain documents from the first attorney, and failing to convince [Vonlee] to take the plea bargain*—had now made it, in effect, 5 to 1.

Newman was concerned about the obvious ineffectiveness of counsel in Vonlee's case during the plea bargaining way back when. Newman had argued a pivotal case in front of the U.S. Supreme Court surrounding the same issue. On October 31, 2011, she stood before the Supreme Court justices as counsel in *Lafler* v. *Cooper*. On March 21, 2012, the Supreme Court ruled in her client's favor by a close 5–4 decision. The University of Michigan Law website wrote: *The* New York Times *cited the case as "being the most important right-to-counsel case since* Gideon v. Wainwright, *while legal rights groups and scholars alike cite it as one of the most important cases of that Supreme Court term."*

In Newman's *Lafler* v. *Cooper* case, the Supreme Court's argument was "brutal," Newman later explained. Its decision, effectively, said that a defendant has the right to effective counsel in the plea-bargaining stage of the criminal process. This turned out to be a statement, Newman added, "That they had never made before explicitly." Thus, that case, by itself, "extended the right of effective assistance of counsel into the plea-bargaining stage"—which was where Vonlee's case came into play.

"Ninety-seven percent of cases are settled by plea bargaining," Newman said. "So my opinion was that if you don't protect defendants in the plea-bargaining stages, you are leaving ninety-seven percent of cases out of the rubric of the right to effective assistance of counsel."

In *Lafler* v. *Cooper*, Justice Antonin Scalia said in his opinion the Supreme Court would be "constitutionalizing plea bargaining" if it ruled in favor of Newman's client.

The *New York Times* billed the arguments as "faulty-lawyer cases," reporter Adam Liptak wrote in his article. According to Liptak, the cases Newman argued *concern[ed] what should be done when criminal defendants pass up favorable plea bargains based on unprofessional work by their lawyers.*

Valerie Newman and Vonlee Titlow were the perfect match.

After she read through the blog and did some additional research, Newman wrote down Vonlee's new attorney's name and number and decided to call her. Newman was willing to argue Vonlee's case for her in front of the U.S. Supreme Court.

"I did call her prior appellate attorney, too," Newman explained later. "I did so because Vonlee had filed a response *pro per* in the Supreme Court, so I wanted to know who had represented her up to that point. It was a courtesy on my part to check in and double-check to verify that she was no longer representing Vonlee and see if she had any objection to my stepping in. I would never try to take a case away from someone."

By that time, Vonlee Titlow had spent a decade and some change in prison. She didn't know it then, but there was one of the state's—hell, the country's!—most aggressive, able, competent, experienced and smartest appellate attorneys, with a winning track record in the U.S. Supreme Court already, looking at the possibility of arguing her case at the highest level in the nation.

CHAPTER 89

VALERIE NEWMAN HAD ACTUALLY chosen environmental law as her major in law school. Arguing appeals in the local courts and going to Washington, DC, to spar with the "holiest of holies" was never on her early agenda book. With the environment, there was something about the world, Newman later said, about how we are all connected to the universe and how the environment is our responsibility that pushed her, at a young age, in that direction.

"Mine was a hybrid degree, business and other things, you could say," she explained later. "I came out of college with a lot of debt, so I didn't want to go to any kind of grad school, but instead, I opted to pay down my debt."

"Bouncing around" in corporate retail jobs for a while, she "decided to take the LSAT," the Law School Admission Test.

That was 1987.

She entered law school two years later, in 1989, and discovered her passion.

The environmental-law decision she had first desired turned out to be "too statutory and not too exciting."

Newman yearned for the thrill of challenging cases, digging into the research and banging heads in a courtroom with other lawyers and judges. She could envision herself fighting for people's rights.

In law school, when she wrote up a mock oral argument, a professor told her she had a gift for advocacy and argument. "You should think about becoming an appellate lawyer," that same professor advised.

"I had never thought about it," she said. "I had always assumed I'd be in trial court."

During law school, she worked at the Legal Aid Society in Staten Island, New York, its criminal division. It was a "life-changing" experience, she noted.

"I got the criminal-law bug," she said. She saw how people were treated and mistreated and decided to pursue the appellate field, which her professor had recommended.

Finally, after all was said and done, she settled into work at SADO. She had found her calling.

"It was where I wanted to be."

Val Newman has a calm, affecting, soothing tone to her voice. She pauses frequently in between thoughts; and from that, it's clear she thinks about what she says before saying it, something many in the Digital Age have a hard time doing. Likely, this characteristic stems from the amount of time she spends reading through cases that SADO takes on. To appeal a case, one has to know it inside out. One does that by studying every piece of documentation available and also talking to as many of the players involved as one can. In short, appellate lawyers devote days and weeks to reading and taking notes.

Newman knew nothing about Vonlee's case before that coworker pointed it out on the SCOTUS blog. She had not heard the salacious news reports and crass online comments regarding the transsexual who had "murdered" her aunt's husband to get money for a sex change. For Newman, she viewed the case like any other: a defendant wronged by a lawyer and the system, someone who needed guidance and advocacy. It was clear to Newman that Frederick Toca had ruined any chance of Vonlee getting the sentence she deserved. Newman's job wasn't about proving innocence or guilt; it was about righting a wrong.

At home, trial transcripts and other documents scattered around her living room, Newman was looking for the opportunity in Vonlee's case where she could argue to the court that Vonlee had not been given a fair shake by Toca. Most people assume that once a court has stamped its approval of a jury's verdict, it must be just and that the guilty party has been punished properly and it's time to throw away the key and move on.

That was not how she operated—not in those cases where she saw misconduct.

Over the course of twenty years or so, she had worked her way up through the ranks to become one of the go-to appellate lawyers for the state of Michigan on the highest level. She knew her way around the appellate laws better than most and had become somewhat of a high-profile lawyer within that particular field.

When she finished studying Vonlee's case, she saw it as a "no-brainer." There was "deficient performance of counsel" and "prejudice."

No doubt.

But the question remained: could she get at least five Supreme Court justices to agree with her?

"We clearly had deficient performance in Vonlee's case, because we had an attorney who had misadvised a client who didn't understand the law," Newman believed, "and we clearly had prejudice because had [Vonlee] accepted the plea, [she] would have been doing, at the most, eighty-four months, and after trial [she] was serving 185 months on the minimum sentence." (That number included time served and good behavior.)

Every time Newman looked at Vonlee's case, she could only come to one conclusion.

"This was a very tough case factually because there was no record of what Toca actually did in the five days or so he was on the case prior to moving for plea withdrawal. I never thought this case was a hands-down winner."

CHAPTER 90

VALERIE NEWMAN SPOKE TO Vonlee's attorney after realizing Vonlee's case was identical in so many ways to *Lafler* v. *Cooper*—thus, if there was anyone in the country that should be arguing Vonlee's case in the U.S. Supreme Court, it was Val Newman.

The case seemed so simple on paper: bad advice, prejudice, remedy.

And what was that remedy?

"Reoffering the plea bargain," she concluded.

The only wrinkle in it all, as far as Newman could tell, was that Vonlee had agreed to testify against Billie Jean, withdrew that and did not testify. At trial, Billie Jean was found not guilty. So there was no chance of Vonlee ever offering that part of her plea bargain again.

Newman was "not eager to go back to the Supreme Court" and argue a case. "It's an incredible amount of work. In *Lafler* v. *Cooper*, it was my case from day one." Here, she would have to step in at the end of the road, essentially, and take over. She had been with *Lafler* v. *Cooper*, litigating it, for eight years. "To pick up a case at the point where Vonlee's was is an enormous undertaking."

The flip side of it all, however, Newman considered

that if Vonlee's case was "going to be an attack on *Lafler* v. *Cooper*," she definitely wanted to handle it and defend her previous work.

Vonlee was being approached by a lot of different lawyers at the time. There was one particular lawyer who had gone in to see Vonlee and allegedly lied about being part of the team behind *Lafler* v. *Cooper*, and yet this attorney had "zero involvement in that case," said a source. So it appeared that Vonlee was heading back where she'd started: a lawyer promising something he could not deliver.

After "hemming and hawing," or, rather, weighing the pros and cons, Newman met with Vonlee. They sat and talked for a very long time. She took down a lot of information and studied Vonlee, who came across nervous, needy and overwhelmed. This was her final chance. Either she won in the Supreme Court, or she served out the remainder of a twenty-year to forty-year sentence.

At the end of that meeting, Newman said, "Look, you can do whatever you want, obviously, but if you want, my office will represent you."

It was free and Newman was one-for-one in the Supreme Court.

"I saw a clear-cut case of ineffective assistance of counsel and, even worse, maybe malpractice. What Toca did was so despicable, it's hard to describe on every level."

Vonlee did not have to think too hard about what she wanted to do.

CHAPTER 91

ON AUGUST 15, 2012, Newman filed her brief with the U.S. Supreme Court on Vonlee's behalf. This set off a host of filings and responses from the court that went on and on, for months and months. Her argument was detailed. It covered every single beat of Vonlee's case, leaving nothing out. One of the most telling pieces of factual information she presented: *In an affidavit, Ms. Titlow's first attorney, Richard Lustig, stated that "Mr. Toca did not pick up the discovery materials from [Lustig's] office, nor discuss the facts of the case with [Lustig] until January 10, 2002."* This meeting was months after Vonlee had withdrawn her plea-bargaining agreement from the court.

Newman said Toca "recklessly advised [Vonlee] to withdraw a favorable plea and proceed to trial where she faced a possible life without parole."

The Supreme Court argument was set in front of the Supreme Court justices for Tuesday, October 8, 2013, those seemingly stagnant wheels of justice once again moving with the mountain stream.

"At its core," the attorney explained, the argument she presented focused on whether Frederick Toca's performance was "deficient, and if so, did the deficient performance prejudice Vonlee?"

In Newman's and Vonlee's opinions, Toca had failed to investigate Vonlee's case and thus "talked her out of a favorable plea deal and into a trial that was unwinnable."

All for a chance to sell her story to Hollywood!

The battle here for Newman was that the record—all of the previous appeals and Vonlee's original court cases—did not reflect that argument in a carefully detailed manner. This was the reason why she had been so focused on studying the record; she was trying to find that one piece of it she could use to Vonlee's advantage.

What's more, the prosecutor claimed "no deficient performance because," you guessed it, "there was no record as to what Toca did or did not do."

As Newman argued before the justices, the prosecutor was correct, she said, since "a precise factual record does not exist. However, Toca was disbarred due to a myriad of ethical violations so serious that his ethical violations in this case were merely a footnote. . . ."

The other part of it working in Vonlee's favor was that the timing of Toca's involvement was never in dispute. He had not spoken to or obtained the trial counsel's files until well *after* Vonlee withdrew her plea. That alone was effectively enough to seal Vonlee's fate.

"And, perhaps most telling," she went on to argue, "he tried to renegotiate the sentence deal prior to her plea withdrawal, and only when that was unsuccessful did he state that Vonlee would not testify against Billie. And so the prosecution withdrew its deal."

Luckily, for Newman and Vonlee, that final part had all been done on the record.

A decision came in about a month later, on November 5, 2013.

Justice Sonia Sotomayor's written concurrence did a fair job of explaining the justices' collective opinion:

In my view, this case turns on Vonlee Titlow's failure to present enough evidence of what Frederick Toca did or did not do in the handful of days after she hired him and before she withdrew her plea. This had been Val Newman's exact concern from the get-go: not enough record to reflect Vonlee's argument. *As our opinion notes,* Sotomayor added, *she bore the burden of overcoming two presumptions: that Toca performed effectively and that the state court ruled correctly. She failed to carry this burden. We need not say more, and indeed we do not say more. . . . Had respondent made a better factual record—had she actually shown, for example, that Toca failed to educate himself about the case before recommending that she withdraw her plea—then she could well have prevailed.*

Vonlee had lost. All of the justices agreed.

Nine to zip.

"We would have won, had the record been better developed to support the argument," Newman explained later. "Of course, I was not the lawyer until the U.S. Supreme Court, and she had gone through various lawyers throughout the appeal. There could be legitimate reasons why the record below was left undeveloped, but there was nothing I could do about that insurmountable problem by the time I got into the case."

One had to consider if Newman's prior win (*Lafler* v. *Cooper*) in this same house of justices had worked against her. Was that a possibility?

"I don't think the prior case worked against us at all. This was a tough case because of the condition precedent in the plea—Vonlee having to testify against Billie—and that condition being nonexistent as this case wound its way through the appellate courts."

Another issue that hurt Vonlee was Billie Jean's acquittal.

"Most folks assumed criminal agency in Donald's death," Newman concluded. "Despite the medical examiner's testimony at Vonlee's trial, I'm not entirely convinced that Donald died from any criminal activity. It's possible, but to me it is just as likely he died of natural causes. I think that is why Billie was acquitted—cause of death unclear and portraying Vonlee as a nutcase not to be believed."

What's interesting and strikes perhaps at the heart of Vonlee's case in its totality is the fact that the United States Supreme Court was willing to say that Frederick Toca was unethical and that he unequivocally behaved in an unethical manner, but that alone was *not* enough.

Final score: Justice 8, Vonlee 1.

It was over.

Exhausting all of her appeals, Vonlee Nicole Titlow would continue to serve her sentence and be eligible for parole in 2021, the earliest she could possibly be released. The maximum date of her release is 2041. Vonlee would be seventy-four years old if she served her entire sentence.

"I think Vonlee is likely to be paroled at her earliest release date," Valerie Newman concluded. "Even assuming the worst about her actions, she did not kill Don Rogers or do anything that actually contributed to his death. I think Billie would have done what she did with or without Vonlee."

ACKNOWLEDGMENTS

THERE IS NO EPILOGUE to this book because there is no more story to tell. A crime story that began with a death in 2000 ended thirteen years later in 2013 in the U.S. Supreme Court. Vonlee awaits her first parole hearing in 2021 so she can argue to be released. Based on the mishandling of her case by Fred Toca, something tells me it just might happen. But who knows?

I dedicated this book to Cherry, my black Lab. She died while I was working on the book and the loss was more devastating than I could have ever imagined. Funny that an animal could bring so much joy, love and goodness into my life. I understood, in those empty days after Cherry's death, what writers such as Dean Koontz have gone through dealing with a similar loss. I miss Cherry immensely. I want to thank Cherry (wherever she is) for all those years of unconditional love she gave to me and my family.

I received an e-mail one night from a friend, Dave Lane, a producer for a Jupiter Entertainment series on Oxygen, *Snapped*. Dave and I go back a number of years. We look out for each other when it comes to great true-crime stories. If any of my longtime readers have read through to the acknowledgments section of my books, you'll know that I have thanked Jupiter and many of the people at this wonderful company for the stories they've suggested to me.

Under the e-mail subject line "Your next book?" Dave wrote, *I just worked on a [case] that might be of great interest to you. What a story!* He sent me a bullet-pointed list of facts from the Vonlee Nicole Titlow case. I was on the story that night, making calls and sending e-mails the next day. I need to thank Dave Lane, and everyone at Jupiter, for the years of friendship and business.

With special gratitude, I also want to acknowledge Erin Althaus, cameraperson extraordinaire, who I have worked with at Jupiter on many occasions, but have failed to mention in previous acknowledgment pages. I apologize, Erin. I actually thought I had been thanking you, but had confused your name with someone else (sorry again). I know that sounds weird, but, in my defense, there are so many people I come into contact with throughout the course of a year, it's hard to keep track sometimes.

Vonlee Titlow was always available and willing to talk about anything, and I thank her for her time. She is a genuine person, a Southern gal to the core, and I don't feel she participated in this crime the way in which she was convicted and sentenced. Vonlee's crime is not saying anything, not turning Billie Jean in and not testifying against her. Yes, these are serious, felonious acts, but murder? I don't feel she knew there was a murder taking place until it was too late.

Did Billie Jean murder her husband, Don Rogers?

I can only say, in my opinion, I believe Vonlee's narrative of what happened.

Valerie Newman was extremely helpful in understanding this entire case. I could not have written this book without the documents, interviews and e-mail responses she provided. Bill Cataldo was also very helpful, as were many sources that would rather go unnamed.

My fans are the reason I write. I owe all I do to each reader. I put my heart and every bit of passion I have into these books every morning as I begin because my readers deserve it. I wish I could thank each one of you personally.

I want to extend a thank-you to my *Dark Minds* fans: I am honored by your dedication and willingness to watch the series and support it. We managed to make three seasons before a decision was made to end it. I am indebted and grateful to Investigation Discovery for allowing me the opportunity to make the series and profile victims of crime. We have new projects to focus on now, but I want to say that making *Dark Minds* was an experience I will never forget. It was a gift to be able to produce this series.

My publisher, Steve Zacharius, and the entire team at Kensington Publishing Corp.—especially Michaela Hamilton, my editor, Morgan Elwell and Vida Engstrand, from publicity—all of whom deserve my utmost respect and gratitude for the passion each puts into the books I write. These are great people who love what they do. To be part of Kensington's continued success as an independent publisher is an honor. I am lucky. I tell myself this every morning as I awake and go to work. I never take for granted that what I do is a blessing.

I would like to also give my sincere appreciation to everyone at Investigation Discovery and Beyond Productions involved in my work on television, both past and present. I've said this before many times, but it needs repeating. It takes an army of devoted people to produce a television series. Among those I want to personally thank: *Dark Minds* show runner and series producer, Andrew "Fazz" Farrell, and also SVP Production: Content, Geoff "Fitz" Fitzpatrick. Fitz and I have worked closely over the past year together on a lot of television projects and I have learned so much. I cannot thank Fitz and development head Anita Bezjak enough, both of whom have been mentors and great teachers of all things cable TV.

Each of the following, in his or her own way, has taught me everything I know about making quality-grade, great nonfiction television: Alex Barry, Colette "Coco" Sandstedt, John Mavety, Peter Heap, Mark Middis, Toby Prior, Peter Coleman, Derek Ichilcik, Jared "Jars" Transfield, Jo Telfer, Claire Westerman, Milena Gozzo, Geoff Thomas, Cameron Power, Katie Ryerson, Inneke Smit, Pele Hehea, Jeremy Peek, Jeremy Adair, Geri Berman, Nadine Terens, Samantha Hertz, Lale Teoman, Hayden Anderson, Savino (from Onyx Sound Lab in Manchester, Connecticut), David O'Brien, Ra-ey Saleh, Nathan Brand, Rebecca Clare, Anthony Toy, Mark Wheeler, Mandy Chapman, Jenny O'Shea, Jen Longhurst, John Luscombe, Debbie Gottschalk, Eugenie "Jeannie" Vink, Sucheta Sachdev, Sara Kozak, Kevin Bennett, Jane Latman and Henry Schleiff.

For my entertainment lawyer/business manager, Matthew Valentinas, a big thanks for this past year. We've only just begun, my friend!

I would also like to thank Deb Allen, Donna Dudek, Mike Rogers, Maggie Sharbel, Elizabeth Strickland, Jasmine Fox, Katie Harrington and everyone else at Jupiter Entertainment for your willingness to always help me and answer my e-mails.

Mathew, Jordon, Regina and April—thanks.

Special Bonus for True-Crime Fans

Keep reading to enjoy the exciting opening chapters
of the next real-life thriller by
M. William Phelps

DON'T TELL A SOUL

Coming soon from Kensington Publishing Corp.

CHAPTER 1

SHE HAD THAT SOUTHWESTERN charm people adore: a calm disposition, obvious Texas twang in her accent, a generally carefree, relaxed outlook on life, and Christian manner. Since 2002, sixty-eight-year-old Rueon had been married to eighty-three-year-old Gethry Walker, a man who was pretty much set in his ways. Gethry was a gentle spirit—one of those rare men that listened more than he talked, an old-school, church-going Texan who wore suspenders, a dress shirt and slacks, subtle, elegant tie, almost every day. When Gethry did have something to say, in fact, he spoke it at the altar behind a lectern during services at the Greater Love Temple Church in Tyler, Texas. Both Gethry and Rueon were, first and foremost, God-fearing people; they believed in Jesus Christ, redemption of the cross, penances paid for wrongs committed, justice, and—beyond perhaps most anything else—facing demons and coming to terms with who you are as a human being under the guidance, influence, and faith of God.

When Saturday, June 19, 2010, came to pass, and Gethry or Rueon had not heard from Gethry's daughter,

thirty-eight-year-old Cherry Walker, they felt something
was wrong. It was that paternal instinct kicking in.

Where is Cherry?

Still, after thinking about Cherry in a more positive
light, they considered that perhaps she had simply decided not to call. Cherry was entitled to her own life.
Plus, she could be absentminded like that once in a
while. Cherry had suffered from "learning disabilities"
all her life and had just gone off to live on her own. She
was almost thirty-nine, her birthday four months away.
Clinically classified as MR, "mentally retarded," by her
doctors, with all the progress she'd made recently, what
was the big deal with a missed call home once in a while?

That Sunday morning (which also happened to be
Father's Day), as Gethry and Rueon, Cherry's stepmother, got ready for church, Rueon started to wonder
once again why Cherry had not called. She would always
call before church to check in or ask what time the van
was coming to pick her up. But as the morning wore on,
there had still not been any word from Cherry. Almost
two full days now and not a peep.

Totally out of character for Cherry.

Rueon fixed her hair and figured the church van,
which Cherry's brother drove, had picked her up for
services and they'd meet Cherry at Temple Love. She
told Gethry not to fret. It would all be okay. They'd go to
church and run into Cherry there. No worries. Rueon
could kindly scold Cherry and tell her she had forgotten
to call not only the day before, but that morning, and
she was well aware that calling Rueon and Gethry once
a day, if not every other day, was what they expected from
her. They could talk about it, remind Cherry she needed
to take responsibility, be done with it, and enjoy Sunday
service praising Jesus.

Gethry and Rueon looked for Cherry as they walked
into Temple Love, but they did not see her. Cherry had

her favorite seat down in the front row of pews, her name on it. But when Rueon reached the front of the building by the altar, she looked around and Cherry was nowhere to be found.

Rueon sought out Cherry's brother. "Where's your sister?" He had driven the van.

"I thought she was with y'all," he said.

"No, we thought she was coming with you."

Throughout that Sunday service, as anxiety turned more into a genuine concern for Cherry's well-being, Rueon started to call Cherry at her apartment and on Cherry's cell phone.

"We got no response," Rueon said later.

If there was one thing about Cherry that Rueon and Gethry, and anybody close to Cherry knew, the girl did not go anywhere without two things: her money purse and cell phone. These two items were part of her, attached.

For Rueon and Gethry, it was easy to write off any fears or bad feelings by telling themselves, *Cherry probably just went to church with someone else.*

"She sometimes did," Rueon explained later.

When Rueon and Gethry got home, Rueon called Cherry several more times, but there was no response.

"You know," she told Gethry, "I'm going to git her."

It was so unusual—the not knowing. Cherry had struggled, but worked hard, and she'd managed to overcome many difficulties and disabilities to carve out a life for herself with a small studio apartment across town in Tyler, not far from Rueon and Gethry's home. She'd had help from an aide, who came to see her every day, but Cherry was living on her own, doing things for herself. There was no explanation they could think of that would put Cherry in a position of not calling them for this long a period of time. It just did not make sense.

"Call her again," Gethry suggested.

There was no answer.

"Let's go eat, and if we don't hear from her by the time we're done, then we can stop by Cherry's apartment and check in on her," Rueon suggested.

Gethry nodded in agreement.

They ate lunch and still had not heard a word from Cherry. Leaving the restaurant, they stopped back at home to grab the spare key to Cherry's apartment and headed out to West Houston Street in Tyler, the Citadel apartment complex.

Rueon walked in first. She couldn't believe it. The place was in "disarray," which was entirely unlike Cherry, who was a neat freak and was even fixated on cleaning and cleaning supplies in an obsessive-compulsive manner. She'd never, under her own will, leave her apartment with "everything" all over the place. "Her ironing board was up. . . . Her bed was unmade . . . and things were just kind of scatter-y," one source later recalled.

"This is not Cherry, ain't it, Gethry?"

"Sure ain't," he said.

In addition, Cherry would have never walked out of her apartment without taking a bath, changing her clothes—all of which needed to be ironed before she'd wear them—or tidying up. Just wasn't in her DNA. Everything in her apartment had its place, and there was a place for everything. That was how Cherry lived her life.

Structure.

Focus.

Detail.

"This was the first thing I noticed," Rueon later explained. "And you just kind of get a feeling, you know."

A sense. That sinking pit in your gut. A parent's intuition that something, as horrible as it felt to admit, was off.

Rueon looked in Cherry's closet. In her kitchen. All over. She searched for Cherry's cell phone or that specific coin purse Cherry always carried with her. Not finding either gave Rueon a bit of comfort, actually, because there was no chance Cherry would ever leave the house without either of them. With both being gone, there was a bit of relief in knowing that she wasn't whisked away in some sort of home invasion or kidnapping.

Still, walking around the apartment, Rueon couldn't shake the feeling: *Something's wrong.*

Indeed, comb on the vanity counter, mouthwash there by the faucet, spray bottle of tile cleanser on the floor by the shower, where Cherry always left it, the smiling kitty cats on the ironing board apron underneath a pair of socks waiting to be ironed, two cases of Pure Life and Ozark water on the floor by the waste basket can, a roll of paper towels on the kitchen table, Cherry's favorite poster—from the horror film *Shutter*—taped to her wall, her velvety red chair against the wall, stacks and stacks of DVDs, mainly horror or soft-core porn (*Beyond the Busty Stags* and *Night of Perverted Pleasures* and *Experiment in Torture,* among them) around the television, the TV remote sitting on the bed.

Everything in Cherry's life was there waiting for her, but she was missing.

Rueon didn't see it then, but on a calendar on Cherry's wall, two dates in particular stuck out: June 18, the previous Friday (which had passed), and the following Wednesday, June 23 (which had not come to pass). Somebody had written *Babysit* in pen on both days.

Cherry was babysitting? Who would hire her? Who was she babysitting?

This was odd.

One other possibility existed here, Rueon thought as she walked around the apartment on that Sunday afternoon. One of Cherry's closest friends or even her case-worker, Paula Wheeler, a woman who saw Cherry almost every day, had come by and picked her up to go out to eat or shopping. Rueon had been getting on Cherry lately, in a motherly way, "Girl, you know . . . you're [thirty-eight years old] now, and, you know, you need to grow up."

They had been trying to show Cherry what Rueon called "hard love," based partially on the idea that Rueon and Gethry could not be with Cherry forever—she'd need to spread her wings and go off on her own. Was this Cherry doing that very thing: going it alone? Had she taken Rueon's advice? You look at Cherry's collection of DVDs and it was clear she was growing up rather quickly—that is, if she had led a sheltered life Rueon and Gethry had supposed she had while under their roof back at home.

There was another side of Cherry that Rueon and Gethry worried about, however. Cherry might have been thirty-eight; she might have watched soft porn and gruesome horror films, such as *Saw, The Texas Chainsaw Massacre,* and her absolute favorite, *Paranormal Activity,* but she also played with children's toys and could not read or write much more than her name and a few numbers and letters. She was very much a child in an adult's body.

Rueon and Gethry decided to go home and wait (and hope) for Cherry to call. It was early afternoon, Sunday, June 20, 2010. Why grow sick with worry now, they decided. After all, wasn't the entire point of Cherry renting her own apartment and moving out of the house was so she could become a responsible, independent woman?

CHAPTER 2

HE WAS ON HIS way back to work. Such a common, routine task that millions—perhaps billions—of people throughout the world submit to each day. Waking up, heading off to a job, collecting that paycheck on Friday, and enjoying a weekend of rest and relaxation.

On Saturday, June 19, 2010, Bobby Lewis was driving along an area near Smith County Road, known locally as the CR 2191, in Whitehouse. This is a small town north of Houston, east of Dallas, just outside Tyler, directly west of Lake Tyler, a rather massive body of water shaped like a herd of clouds.

Bobby had the radio on. The windows rolled down. That familiar hot, heavy, and wet Texas air was blowing into Bobby's face as he drove. By all accounts, it was a peaceful ride on a lovely day—and should have been nothing more than that.

Somewhere just before three o'clock on that afternoon, however, Bobby's rather predictable life took a turn into the Twilight Zone. He worked at Domino's Pizza in Tyler. He was in Whitehouse this afternoon to pick up a coworker before heading back into the restaurant for more deliveries.

Passing the 15900 block of CR 2191, after pulling into a driveway and turning his car around, thinking he was lost, Bobby saw something off to the side of the road.

What in the hell?

So he pulled over and stopped his vehicle.

Bobby got out. There was a dirt area, "overgrown with weeds," in what was a thickly settled part of town, mostly red clay, some sand, trees and forest on all sides, save for several buildings and a few homes to the southwest, including a driveway in which Bobby had just turned around. It was a semisecluded area, just to the west of that famed Piney Woods section of the state. Whitehouse is small-town America, or very close to it: About seven thousand souls resided there in 2010. The medium household income fell in the neighborhood of about seventy thousand dollars per year, with Texas, overall, coming in at about fifty thousand. So there was some money here in Whitehouse. Most people, eighty-five percent of whom the recent census termed as "white," weren't poor by any means.

From his vehicle, Bobby Lewis saw a black, charred patch of land. After stepping out of his car, curious, he walked closer. It was probably some kids burning up an old mattress or a campfire for a keg party that got a little out of hand and had been left unattended. Maybe even a load of trash some knuckleheaded litterer had tossed out and set on fire. The charred remains spread over a small area of the sandy and red clay ground. The pile had not burned entirely, however, and there was something different about it, the pizza man noticed, that beckoned a closer look.

Bobby Lewis went in for a more personal view.

Getting within about fifteen feet of the debris, Bobby could clearly see that, in fact, it wasn't a pile of trash, an old campfire, or other remnants of furniture or household items that had been lit on fire and abandoned, after all. Bobby Lewis was looking at something entirely different.

Approaching the pile from about three yards away, Bobby did not want to get any closer, he later told police, because it was in that moment when he realized what, in fact, he was looking at.

Holy shit.

A bit of anxiety throbbed as Bobby stepped back, pulled out his cell phone, and, with index finger shaking, dialed 911.

CHAPTER 3

SHE WAS LYING FACEDOWN about fifty feet off the side of CR 2191, where pizza deliveryman Bobby Lewis now stood and waited for police to arrive. As Bobby had approached the pile of charred debris and stood about five yards away, "I already knew what it was," he said later. "So there was no need to go any closer."

It was a dead body (DB)—probably a female, by the look of what little clothing was left and the feminine shape of her body. It was difficult to say for certain because the person was lying on her stomach. Still, the contour appeared to be that of a large female.

The DB had one arm at her side pointed downward, the other pointed up above her head slightly, as though she was raising her hand in class to ask a question. Her legs were spaced apart about a foot, toes pointed into the dirt. She wore black Capri pants (what was left of them from the fire), white sneakers—with black oily stains and (notably) zero dirt on the bottoms, indicating to anyone interested in that sort of forensic-based information that she had not walked to this location on her own, but had been dumped here. (Otherwise, her tennis shoes would have been caked with the same red clay from on the ground, all over the place.)

It was unclear what type of shirt she had on, because it had melted to her terribly charred skin, which had peeled and creased in some sections, spotted in others, burned entirely off in small sections, blistered and gruesome. The shirt, best Bobby could tell from the small pieces still intact, was green with a floral pattern—another indication that the body was female. Even more horrifying: all of her hair was gone; her face, pushed into the ground, appeared to be nearly burned off. Notably, the entire area of her neck was burned. She was unrecognizable. In fact, Bobby did not know from looking at her how old she possibly could be. Best estimate from him was that she was young, maybe late teens to early thirties.

But again, that was an educated guess by a man who had been out delivering pizza and picking up a coworker.

She had no name.

No identification.

No idea where she had come from or who had put her here.

Better yet, why.

The only certainty was that she had not gotten to this place on her own and she was not leaving on her own.

Bobby waited, staring at "the ash all around [the] body," not touching her or touching anything within what was now, it made sense to him, a crime scene.

Two Whitehouse police (sometimes referred to as "peace") officers, Joshua Brunt and David Roberson, arrived on scene to speak with Bobby Lewis at 3:03 P.M. They surveyed the scene, secured it, and unspooled a roll of yellow police tape, tacking the plastic rope up around the immediate area, closing most of it off. Preserving a crime scene as quick as possible might be the most important action any cop can take within this type of investigation.

Outdoor crime scenes pose so many inherent problems from the onset that safeguarding the scene is as important as combing through it with a magnifying glass. There can be no dispute that to have a scene protected from footsteps, passersby, animals, untrained cops, the elements—and anything else that might contaminate the scene and surrounding area—was as imperative this early on as to who was responsible for the crime.

Officer Roberson, per protocol, started a crime scene log, a notebook detailing everything going on at the scene: time, date, action, and personnel. Soon, the entire area, which had otherwise been barren, quiet, and uninhabited except for the neighborhood youngsters and critters, would be teeming with cops and crime scene investigators (CSIs) and detectives and sheriffs and Texas Rangers. All of these law enforcement members would be looking to assist in trying to unravel what had happened here—that is, after the most important task of the moment began: identifying the girl, contacting family members, and beginning to learn who, what, where, when, and how.

Whitehouse police officer Rod Langinias arrived and spoke to Roberson and Brunt, all of whom stood with Bobby Lewis, who was a bit shaken up after being told he had stumbled upon a potential murder scene, and talked about how Bobby had come across the scene. The first suspect in any such case was the person that found the body.

Bobby explained how he had pulled into that driveway, turned his car around, and then—*bam!*—there she was. He said he didn't realize at first what he was looking at, but after getting out and surveying the scene, well, it hit him. She was dead. Someone had lit her body on fire.

No, he had not touched anything, Bobby Lewis told them.

A sergeant arrived, someone with authority who could take control. After talking to Bobby Lewis, Officer Langinias asked his sergeant, "You want me to take some photos until the boys from [CSI] arrive?" Langinias then mentioned that he had spotted some tire tracks in the red clay and skid marks on the road closest to where the body was located. That sort of stuff was important and needed to be documented before it was contaminated or, even worse, destroyed.

"Stay out of the crime scene area and wait for the crime scene people to come," the sergeant ordered.

"Got it," Langinias said.

Langinias and several other officers blocked off the road, so no one could drive down it, toward the scene. There was a rolled-up carpet nearby, some charred ashes just north of the body. In between the victim's legs was a Dairy Fresh Grade A Homogenized half & half creamer cup, one of those tiny plastic things you get with your coffee at McDonald's or, in this case, Dairy Queen, it appeared. The item was used, crumpled up, and just sitting there. It had no age to it, as though it had sat out in the elements for more than, say, a day or more.

Other latent trace was visible right away, mainly those tire tracks and some carpet fibers and other small pieces of what looked to be potentially important evidence. Best thing about red clay was that, for CSIs, it acted as a mold. Footprints and tire tracks had dug into the clay and left solid imprints. There was some sand around the area, too, and they wouldn't get much in the form of molds from that, but the red clay was a bonus. It might not lead to finding out the identity of the woman, but it would certainly help at some point in the investigation when suspects were located and their cars and shoes were looked at.

Ultimately, this was a Smith County Sheriff's Office (SCSO) investigation, with the Tyler Police Department (TPD) and the local Whitehouse Police Department (WPD), along with the Texas Rangers acting assistance. Takes a village, they say. In Texas, everyone understands his or her role when solving crimes: to find and arrest the bad guy. You don't find a lot of hubris and ego and pissing contests going on when crimes as serious as the one they faced here were involved.

Around 4:00 P.M., with the scene secure and now overrun by all sorts of law enforcement personnel, word spread quickly around town that something was going on near CR 2191, just south of Tyler. The local media was alerted, of course. Many would hop into their satellite trucks and little cars with the broadcast banners written in bright blues and reds on the doors and head out to the location to see what could be reported.

SCSO detective Ron Rathbun took a call to head down and find out what he could. Rathbun was one of those old-school, by-the-book guys. He was on scene by 4:55. Pizza man Bobby Lewis was still there, sitting, shaking his head in disbelief, ready and willing to answer any questions he could. Rathbun located him not long after arriving and being briefed about the facts.

"Tyler," Bobby Lewis said after Rathbun asked where he worked. "I was trying to find a coworker out here. I turned around in that driveway"—he pointed—"because I thought I had passed the address I was looking for."

From there, Bobby explained the rest of what he knew.

Meanwhile, Texas Ranger Brent Davis arrived with a Bublcam Sphere 360 and the supplementary software technology needed to employ it, a sophisticated photography unit used to take aerial photos, among other things.

The local district attorney's office had purchased the expensive piece of equipment with more than a quarter million in drug money seized from several recent high-profile busts. The aerial images, once they came back, would give everyone a good indication of where possible evidence was located beyond the range of the naked eye. The camera had the capability to take photos with twenty different lighting levels, giving detectives a much clearer picture of those minuscule pieces of evidence that could be otherwise overlooked by CSIs searching the scene on the ground. No doubt about it, using the Bublcam was a high-tech way to get the upper hand on a case and give it a great shot of adrenaline out of the box.

Detective Rathbun walked down to where the victim was still lying in the same place she had been found. No one had moved her. Beyond a number of interesting factors he noticed immediately while studying the scene, Rathbun was interested in the idea that the victim was facedown, wearing white Ralph Lauren tennis shoes with that familiar polo pony emblem on the sides. The deceased was a black female, whose "pink panties" were showing through her pants only because the Capris she had on were nearly burned all the way off her body. There was a subtle, almost inherent indication within the entire scene—if only by a cop's intuition—that her killer had left a trail directly to his or her doorstep, and that all the SCSO needed to do was put the puzzle pieces together, step back, and take a look at the picture before them. Not that this was going to be an easy crime to solve by any standards—that was a trap inexperienced cops fell into when they went down that road. However, as long as the SCSO took this one step at a time, followed each crumb left behind, this one was going to come together.

There was something on her shoes, Rathbun noticed. He took note after squatting down to have a closer look.

The shoes appeared to be very clean (maybe recently purchased), he wrote in his report of this moment. *I noticed that the bottom soles of the shoes appeared to have a black-colored substance on them.* It was faint, almost like a film. But Rathbun thought she had been, *At one point, walking around on a surface that had black soot. . . .* He immediately leaned toward a "mechanic's shop" which would have "grease, oil, and other materials on the floor."

It was an interesting calculation that opened up specific investigatory possibilities. Considering there was that red clay all over the area around the body, the residue—if it was, in fact, oil—seemed like an important clue to this intelligent, intuitive cop. It said to him, rather clearly, that she had not walked onto the surface where she was lying by herself—someone, probably driving the car whose tire tracks were left nearby, had purposely dumped her here.

Righting himself, Rathbun stared at the woman. She had not been there, he thought, for very long.

Maybe a few hours at most.

Half a day or so.

Between her legs, Rathbun observed a drinking straw, which was contained in a wrapper marked *Chic-fil-A*, left not too far from that plastic, empty, crumpled up Dairy Fresh creamer cup. The creamer cup, especially, Rathbun surmised, had not been on the ground long. He could tell by looking at the way it had just sat there.

After taking a walk around the area and seeing other pieces of garbage, Rathbun was certain these items near the body were fresh—and perhaps left by the killer. The other garbage looked weathered, and appeared to have been part of the landscape for some time.

* * *

Detective James Riggle of the SCSO was on the Loop 323 when he took a call to head over to the Whitehouse crime scene. He arrived near 4:30 P.M. to have a look at the scene himself and to locate Rathbun and other members of the SCSO team convening on the site.

"You're going to be the lead on this," one of the sergeants told Riggle after his arrival. He was then briefed on the entire situation.

Riggle soon found Rathbun after meeting with Brent Davis to verify the Bublcam imagery was in the process of being completed. Banking on the notion that the Chic-fil-A evidence was potentially explosive, the immediate plan was to find any Chic-fil-A locations in Tyler and Whitehouse and get to the surveillance equipment inside the restaurant to have a look before they erased the tape for that day and several preceding it. Restaurants generally never kept copies of surveillance tapes—even when recorded digitally—unless they were robbed or something happened. They'd record over the previous day with the next. Riggle knew the potential was there to see his victim possibly purchasing her last meal—and with any luck, which was something every murder investigation depended on, standing by her side might be a viable suspect or, at the least, someone the SCSO needed to find and speak to immediately.